WOODTURNING
Wizardry

WOODTURNING
Wizardry

David Springett

Foreword by Bill Jones

Guild of Master Craftsman Publications

First published 1993 by
Guild of Master Craftsman Publications Ltd,
166 High Street, Lewes,
East Sussex BN7 1XU

Reprinted 1994, 1998

ISBN 0 946819 38 6

The illustrations on pp.13, 155 and 230 are
from *Manuel du Tourneur*; frontispiece from
Hand or Simple Turning; p.72 from *Turning and
Mechanical Manipulation*.

Designed by Fineline Studios

Printed and bound in Great Britain by
Hillman Printers (Frome) Ltd., Somerset.

Dedication

This book is for Christine, my wife and best friend.

Acknowledgements

I would like to acknowledge the help given to me by many friends, and to give them my thanks:

Ailene Pastilles, for sending me the photographs of the work of François Barreau.

Frank Dutton, for making me various strange metal tools and jigs without question.

Janet Dutton, for allowing me to use the photograph of her fansticks.

Chantal Williams, for translating awkward old French from old French woodturning books.

James McMenemey, for the mathematical formulae and enthusiasm.

Yvonne Fawdrey, for the enormous amount of typing and retyping.

Bill Weprin, for his help with the colour photography.

Liz Inman, for seeing the potential in such a small germ of an idea.

Ian Kearey, for his fine editorial ability.

François Barreau, who I am sorry I did not know.

About the Author

David Springett's interest in woodturning began when he was a woodwork teacher. By reading every one of the few books then available, experimenting, practising and persevering, he slowly improved his skills. Since leaving teaching over 10 years ago, he has earned his living doing what he enjoys most, turning wood.

At the end of a working day, spent turning highly decorated lace bobbins in the traditional English style, he would allow himself the relaxation of experimental turning. From this developed the fascination with the apparently impossible and somewhat improbable in turned wood, which led him to the discoveries shown in this book.

David and his wife Christine live in Rugby, Warwickshire, where they run weekend courses at the British College of Lace.

Contents

Foreword by Bill Jones

For the woodturner who, having had some experience, wishes to extend his range and maybe escape for a while from the run o' the mill woodturning projects that everybody seems to do, and often, sadly, much better than I, David Springett offers real hope and positive inspiration. I have read of many candidates for a 'best turner in the world' award, but how absurd and invidious such an award would be when so many different kinds of turnery exist, each exemplifying different skills.

The projects in this book must be exactly what the poet had in mind when he wrote:

> Some genius has 'wrested from the muse'
> A strange new work that in its novelty
> Arrests the glance and makes us take it up
> And handle it, admiring its quaint charm.

Whoever reads *Woodturning Wizardry* must, of necessity, absorb a wealth of valuable advice on woods, chucks, making tools and accoutrements to mention but a few, and all imparted with such a thoroughness – he seems to forget nothing!

The reader who embarks on the actual projects is sure of unending pleasure for years to come. It is well known that what is attained easily, palls just as easily. Truly the pleasure to be derived from following the very reasonable instructions of Mr Springett will be satisfyingly commensurate with the zeal the reader puts forth.

The book is a genuine original and well worthy of its place on every turner's shelf.

Bill Jones

INTRODUCTION

 T DOES NOT SEEM LONG SINCE I FIRST SAW THAT SET OF PHOTOGRAPHS SHOWING THE WORK OF A LITTLE-KNOWN FRENCH TURNER FROM THE EIGHTEENTH CENTURY. THE PHOTOGRAPHS SHOWED INTERLOCKING SPHERES, CHINESE BALLS, TURNED ITEMS HELD INSIDE SPHERES, AND MANY OTHER PIECES OF TURNED TRICKERY, ALL PRODUCED BY FRANÇOIS BARREAU. I WAS CAPTIVATED BY THEIR COMPLEXITY.

Looking at the photographs and marvelling at the intricacy of the work, I remembered something a friend once said to me, 'If someone else can do it, then so can I',

and that was the spark which fired me into the action which resulted in this book.

I looked long and hard at those photographs, spent time thinking and working out problems. In the following pages are a few solutions, simple solutions I hope, to help produce pieces which at first glance appear quite complex but, if approached with care, are within the capabilities of most woodturners and can be produced in a basically equipped workshop.

Many of the ideas found in this book may seem novel, and I hope they will prompt the turner to consider how many different and varied ways there are in which wood can be held and turned, adding more interest and understanding, and increasing confidence and ability. I hope also that a freedom will be discovered, through making these pieces, which will enable the turner to move in new directions.

There is no magic in turnery which can be bought along with the most up-to-date machinery and tools. Compare what is available to the turner of today to what was available in the seventeenth and eighteenth centuries, and then look at some of the masterpieces produced in those times. On the following pages I intend to show you how to work with basic tools, how to make your own tools, to turn and make your own simple wood chucks, and to think around a problem to produce these pieces of turned trickery, as I call the results.

All the turned pieces shown in this book were turned on a Myford ML8 woodturning lathe using hand-held tools.

Measurements: Cautionary note

Although care has been taken to ensure that the imperial measurements are true and accurate, they are only conversions from metric. Throughout the book instances will be found where a metric measurement has fractionally varying imperial equivalents (or vice versa), usually within ¹⁄₁₆in either way. This is because in each particular case the *closest* imperial equivalent has been given, so that a measurement *fractionally* smaller will be rounded down to the nearest ¹⁄₁₆in, and fractionally greater will be rounded up. For this reason it is recommended, particularly on the smaller projects, that a drawing is made of the work in imperial sizes to ensure that the measurements have not lost anything in the translation. (*See* also the Metric Conversion Table, page 227.)

Also, although the measurements given here are carefully calculated and are accurate, some variation may occur when pieces are hand turned, so care must be taken and adjustment may be necessary as the work progresses.

CHAPTER 1

WOOD

OOD IS WHERE YOU FIND IT, AND MOST FIND IT IN TIMBER YARDS. WOOD FOR TURNERY, FORTUNATELY, DOES NOT NEED TO BE PLANED, SQUARE-EDGED AND CUT TO LENGTH, SO LOOK AROUND. IT IS SURPRISING HOW MUCH GOOD WOOD GOES TO WASTE BURNED, DUMPED OR TURNING INTO CHIPPINGS.

You will find excellent woods in hedgerows being grubbed up, in streets where parks departments remove dead or diseased trees, in tree surgeons' trailers, in friends' gardens – those unwanted overlarge trees waiting and needing to be removed. It is all good quality wood, free and often very unusual.

Always travel with a saw in the car so that when passing roadworks, for instance a rural bypass, where trees are uprooted and heaped for a bonfire, pieces may be rescued.

Let local parks departments and tree surgeons know of your interest in the wood they cut. Get hold of that wood before they feed it into wood-chipping machines. Build up a friendship with these people, and show them your work. Give them a few finished pieces from the wood they have saved for you, and before long you will have more wood than you can manage.

Let friends and family know of your interest in garden trees. I even took out an advert in a local paper: 'Wanted: laburnum trees. Too big for your garden? Trimmed, felled and removed, no disturbance. Free of charge. Need the wood.' Now I have more laburnum, that wonderful English 'exotic', than most timber yards.

If you buy a small electric chainsaw, it will soon pay for itself.

Caring for wood

If you gather or are given wood, most of it will be unseasoned. Seasoning or drying out timber can take time, so start collecting and drying as soon as possible, so that 'free' wood will be available for turnery projects in the future. This wood is only free in that it is not paid for with money. It will be paid for with time and effort if useable pieces, not firewood, are to be produced.

Seasoning
◆ Cut into useable lengths.
◆ Large diameter logs need to be split down the middle to release tension in the log, allowing the halves to dry and shrink more evenly. Of course some woods, such as elm, are almost impossible to split, so this will not work for all timbers.
◆ Paint the end grain surfaces with an agent which seals the surface and slows down the escape of moisture, allowing more even drying. I use PVA glue, and have found it excellent.
◆ Store split logs in a dry, waterproof, well-ventilated and shaded area. Arrange them so that air can circulate around the pieces.
◆ As a simple rule it will take about one year to dry each 25mm (1in) thickness of wood, but this varies. Narrower pieces will dry more quickly, and of course if a piece is partially turned, leaving an allowance for any movement, the drying of that piece will be speeded up.
◆ Try to avoid branchwood if possible. Not only does it sometimes contain an awkward pithy void, but in hardwoods there is a larger growth of wood above the central core of the branch to help support the weight of the branch. This tension wood, when cut, relaxes, and a straight piece will soon bend like a banana.
◆ Turning wet wood is a tremendous experience, and once tried it is hard to go back to the dry-as-dust stuff which comes

packaged from timber yards. Although some of the projects in the following pages do not always lend themselves to wet turning, a little preparatory wet turning which allows the piece to dry more quickly is always possible.

For further information about seasoning timber, *Understanding Wood* by R. Bruce Hoadley (Taunton Press) can be recommended.

Woods used in the projects

Of the 20 woods used in the projects, no more than 6 were bought from a timber yard. Gifts or gathered, I knew most of them as trees.

African Blackwood or 'npinge'. I saw this piece going cheap, a reject block sawn for a clarinet bell. It is as hard as dense plastic, but the finish is perfection; it can grab tools, but usually only blunt ones, and it blunts tools quite quickly. It is raven black in colour.

Applewood A delicious pinky colour. It turns well, but can tear out in places; sharp tools prevent bad tear-outs. This wood can be quite difficult to dry – boards cup and logs crack – so treat it very carefully.

Beech A good, utility turning timber. Cream to pinky brown. I chose to use some beech to show that it is not always necessary to use dense hardwoods.

Boxwood Perfection. It turns well, takes minute detail and finishes extremely well. Using boxwood increases the chance of success in turnery. Pale creamy colour and dense, it is slow to grow and slow to dry. I was given a piece of boxwood as thick as a man's thigh and four feet long. Counting the annual rings, which took a long time as they were so close together, showed that this piece began life when Napoleon fought his first battle in Europe.

Cherry Cream to brown in colour. Some garden varieties are quite dense and turn very well, others can be very stringy and awful to turn. When cherry is good, it's great. It has a rich, deep, dark, burnt smell when cut or turned.

Elm Perfect for chucks and jigs. Brown in colour, with a swirling grain, it is almost impossible to split. With a smell of farmland and farmyards, it turns well, but is a little open-grained.

Hawthorn An English hedgerow timber also called May, for in May-time it has a white snowstorm of blossom, followed in autumn by a harvest of brilliant red berries. Although it is an excellent wood to turn, if I had the choice I would prefer to see the standing tree than turn the wood. Pale salmon pink to brown in colour, when turned thin it has an amber translucency. As good as anything, and better than most woods I have turned.

Laburnum My favourite of all English timbers. In the spring it shows great showering swags of yellow flowers, set against rich green leaves. The wood has a marvellous mixture of colours within – ginger, greeny-yellow and brown – and is great to turn. The tree grows to a good size but often succumbs to fungal attack, so look out for these trees in local gardens as some may need removing.

Lime Used extensively for carving, but a little soft for turning, this is not really a first choice wood but an excellent wood for making the arrows which 'pierce' the bottle and goblet (*see* Chapter 11). It works well and can be crushed quite small when boiled. If you have the opportunity, search out some lime trees on a warm June evening, for the lime blossom smells delicious, leaving a sweet, honeyed scent which hangs in the air.

Mahogany I had the good fortune to be left a few pieces of Cuban mahogany by an old woodcarver. Truly magnificent, truly dense and richly beef-gravy brown. Some mahoganies can be a little 'woolly' to turn, but this Cuban mahogany is strong and firm, taking fine detail work and an excellent surface straight from the tool.

Oak Mid-brown, open-grained, it turns adequately. I used it for one of the sets of slopes which the turned-yew double cones roll 'up' (*see* Chapter 9).

Olivewood Use it wet if you can – it's quite an experience. Quite greasy, too, like teak, it is lovely to turn, and that wild black-brown streaky grain is a wonder.

Pear Pinky-brown in colour. Great for turning, it has hardly any grain pattern. Most English pear trees produce better wood than pears. Dry this one carefully.

Privet Smooth and clean-cutting, with streams and ribbons of shavings pouring off sharp tools, it sands quickly to a silky smooth finish. It is creamy white, with a darker old heart. However, it cracks and splits too easily when drying, so be careful. If you can get any of this garden hedge wood in a reasonable size, grab it – it's wonderful. It compares well to boxwood, and is only a little softer and more gentle.

Indian Rosewood I had a few pieces of this as offcuts, bought from a maker of woodworking tools. Rich and dense, with reds and browns to blacks, it provides a wonderful and sometimes wild grain pattern. It turns very well, but wear a protective mask of some form.

Spindle A sample sent to me many years ago from Westonbirt Arboretum in Gloucestershire worked very well. It is creamy in colour and relatively soft, but finishes well and takes fine detail.

Wild Service A hedgerow timber which is only considered rare because it is not often identified. Dark pink in colour, it turns well but occasionally tears out. There are better woods, so if you can leave it to its 'rare' existence in the hedgerow, fine!

Sycamore A general purpose wood, pale and creamy-white, it turns well but can tear out. Use spindle, privet or hawthorn.

Walnut The pieces I obtained were leftovers from a large felled walnut. The trunk had been taken, but the huge branches were left for firewood; this time I took my chances with branchwood, and it paid off. Lovely dark brown wood which turns very well, it has a distinctive smell when being worked. Get some if you can; you will enjoy it.

Yew I turn some of this occasionally, for the joy of turning and that wonderful smell which lingers in the workshop. A rich pinky-red brown, well patterned, it sometimes has a pale red spreading sunset coloration in parts; this, unfortunately, is rare. A well-known wood amongst turners, with a well-deserved reputation.

So get collecting and drying, beginning the flow of interesting woods into the workshop. Get into production, and start using some of those pieces of wood which are there for the asking.

CHAPTER 2

JIGS AND CHUCKS

Fig 2.1 A general view of chucks.

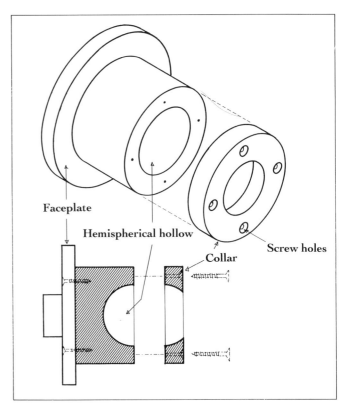

Fig 2.2 Hemispherical chuck and collar.

Faceplate

Hemispherical hollow

Collar

Screw holes

I HAVE TRIED TO MAKE ALL THE JIGS AND CHUCKS, WHICH WILL HOLD THE PARTS WHILE THEY ARE BEING WORKED, SIMPLE, STRAIGHTFORWARD AND EFFECTIVE. I HAVE ALSO TRIED TO ENSURE THAT THEY CAN EASILY BE MADE IN THE AVERAGE WOODWORK SHOP, PREFERABLY ON THE LATHE (*SEE* FIG 2.1).

Only one faceplate is needed – the wooden chucks, once datum points are marked, can be removed and replaced when necessary.

The construction of most of these chucks and jigs is dealt with in the relevant chapters. The following three chucks I felt would most easily be described at the outset. All three are made from elm, a good, tough, relatively light wood which is split-resistant.

Hemispherical chuck

To hold spheres and hemispheres and present part of their surface for re-turning (see Fig 2.2).

◆ From a piece of 50mm (2in) thick elm cut a 110mm (4⅜in) diameter circle.

◆ Screw this piece centrally and securely to a faceplate and turn it to 95mm (3¾in) diameter.

◆ Turn the face flat and true.

◆ Draw a 62mm (2½in) diameter circle on a piece of card – cereal packet is ideal. Mark a centre line across the diameter, then, using scissors, accurately cut out the circle. This card circle will act as a template and help judge when the exact hemispherical shaping is completely turned into the elm block (see Fig 2.3).

◆ With the lathe running mark, in pencil, a circle with a diameter of 62mm (2½in) on the face of the elm block.

◆ Using a 6mm (¼in) gouge, begin turning the hemispherical hollow (see Fig 2.4). Work slowly and carefully, testing regularly with the card template.

◆ Stop when the hollow is exactly hemispherical. The first part is complete.

◆ Prepare three more pieces of elm, each 100mm (4in) wide and long, and planed both sides. The first piece is 6mm (¼in) thick, the

second 12mm (½in) thick and the third 18mm (¾in) thick.

◆ On each of these pieces mark a 100mm (4in) diameter circle. Draw a line across the centre and a further line at 90° to the first.

◆ Set a pencil compass to 40mm (1⁹⁄₁₆in) radius.

◆ Place the point on the centre point of the drawn circle and mark this next circle upon the elm's surface. The points where the circle cuts the two crossing centre lines are the positions for screw holes.

◆ Drill and countersink each piece of elm to accept a No.8 screw precisely at the marked points.

Before work progresses further, draw a 62mm (2½in) diameter circle on paper. Draw a centre line and then three more lines parallel to that line, the first 6mm (¼in) away, the second 12mm (½in) away and the third 18mm (¾in) away. Measure the distance across the circle on each of these lines – the first will be 60mm (2⁷⁄₁₆in), the second 56mm (2¼in) and the third 50mm (2in). These measurements will be used when working the collars – the first measurement relates to the 6mm (¼in) thick collar, etc.

◆ Cut the outer 100mm (4in) diameter circle to produce three elm discs. Each will

Fig 2.3 Using the card template to check that the shaping is correct.

Fig 2.4 Turning the hemispherical hollow.

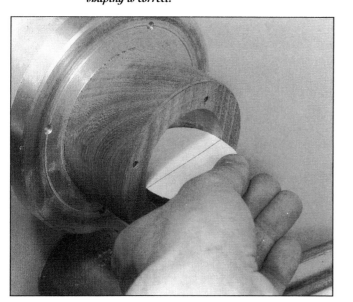

Fig 2.5 The 6mm disc attached. Note the datum line.

Fig 2.6 Turning through the disc and shaping the curved undercut.

in turn be screwed centrally on to the main block and worked in the following manner.

◆ Take the cut disc and screw it centrally to the main block (*see* Fig 2.5).

◆ Turn the outer edge to match that of the block.

◆ Mark in pencil upon its surface a concentric circle whose diameter has been calculated earlier: for the 6mm (¼in) thick disc, the diameter is 60mm (2⁷⁄₁₆in); for the 12mm (½in) thick disc, the diameter is 56mm (2¼in) and for the 18mm (¾in) thick disc, it is 50mm (2in).

◆ Turn on the lathe and turn through the disc, breaking into the hollow beneath (*see* Fig 2.6) and turning exactly to the marked diameter.

◆ Using a round-nose tool and good judgement, turn the underside of the edge without disturbing the exactly turned diameter of the top. Turn underneath so that the cut runs to meet and match that internal joint line.

◆ This collar is turned with an internal curve to match the surface of a 62mm (2½in) diameter sphere and will allow it to be locked firmly in place.

◆ Remove and check the internal shaping of the collar regularly against the template, but *first mark a datum line on the edge of collar and block* so that it can be replaced exactly.

Fig 2.7 The hemispherical chuck holding a part-finished piece.

The hemispherical chuck is complete once the collars have been accurately turned. Have sufficient wood prepared so that if a mistake is made, it can quickly be replaced. Fig 2.7 shows the chuck in use.

Square hole chuck

This chuck, shown in Fig 2.8, is made to hold a wooden cube so that the spiked star may be turned within (*see* Chapter 22).

◆ Cut a 120mm (4¾in) diameter piece from a 55mm (2³⁄₁₆in) thick piece of elm.
◆ Fix this piece centrally upon a faceplate and turn to 110mm (4⅜in) diameter. Face off square and true.
◆ Mark the centre of the piece and draw a centre line across the diameter of the work. Mark a second centre line at 90° to the first.
◆ Measure 27.5mm (1³⁄₃₂in) above and below these lines to the right and left. Join these points to produce a series of lines parallel to the centre lines. A 55mm (2³⁄₁₆in) square can be picked out and lined firmly in.
◆ Mark a position on the turned block and a matching position on the faceplate, then remove the block. These marked positions will help to relocate the block accurately upon the faceplate.
◆ Drill a series of four 25mm (1in) holes inside the boundaries of the marked square (*see* Fig 2.9).
◆ Take the elm block, with the pencil

Fig 2.8 The square hole chuck.

marked square uppermost, to the bandsaw. Cut into the block so that it runs into the square on the diagonal.
◆ Accurately cut to the edges of the square, using the drilled holes to allow the bandsaw blade to turn. Withdraw the blade through the entrance saw cut.
◆ Remove the piece from the bandsaw, and drill a screw hole across at the entrance saw cut so that when a screw is placed in that hole and tightened, the gap will be drawn together (*see* Fig 2.10).

Fig 2.9 Square hole chuck.

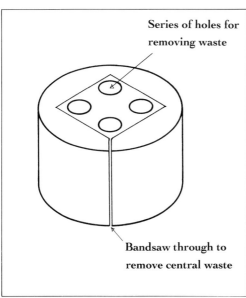

Series of holes for removing waste

Bandsaw through to remove central waste

Fig 2.10 Square hole chuck mounted on faceplate. Note use of screws to close gap.

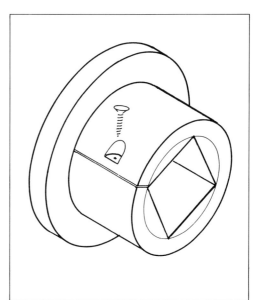

◆ Replace the elm block upon the faceplate, using the marks to accurately relocate.

The square hole chuck is now complete. A few fine wedges may be cut to help hold the wooden cube, later to be turned, in place.

Fig 2.11 Double cone chuck.

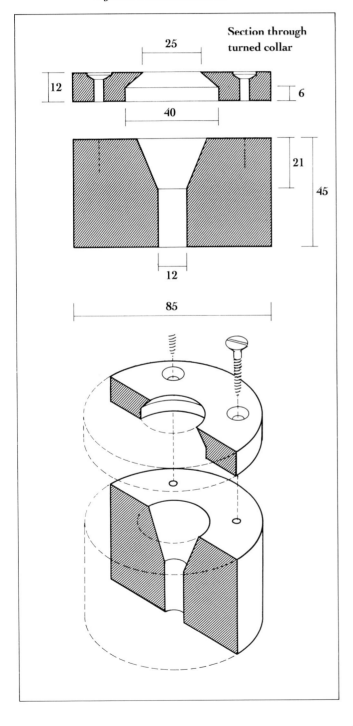

Double cone chuck

This double cone chuck is made in a manner similar to the hemispherical chuck on page 7 (*see* Fig 2.11).

◆ Cut a 100mm (4in) diameter circle from a 45mm (1¾in) thick piece of elm.
◆ Fix this piece centrally upon a faceplate and turn to an 85mm (3⅜in) diameter, facing off the front of this piece flat and true.
◆ Fit a 12mm (½in) drill into a drill chuck held in the tailstock, and mark a point, using white correction fluid on the shank of the drill 21mm (¹³⁄₁₆in) away from the cutting edge.
◆ Drill a central hole to the marked depth into the elm block.
◆ Mark in pencil a 30mm (1¼in) diameter concentric circle on the face of the elm block.
◆ Turn down from the edge of this circle to the base edge of the drilled hole, producing a straight taper.
◆ Bring the 12mm (½in) drill forward and drill through the elm block, completing the hole begun earlier.
◆ Mark in pencil a 65mm (2⁹⁄₁₆in) diameter circle on the face of the block.
◆ Set a pencil compass to 32.5mm (1⁵⁄₃₂in) and 'walk' it around the marked circle. This will produce six equally spaced points. Choose one, miss one, choose one, miss one, choose one, miss one; this will provide three equally spaced points. Use a bradawl to begin a screw hole at these three points.
◆ Take a 12mm (½in) thick piece of planed elm, and mark and cut a 100mm (4in) circle.
◆ Draw a 65mm (2⁹⁄₁₆in) diameter concentric circle upon the elm, and then repeat the above procedure to produce three equally spaced points about that drawn circle. At each of these points drill and countersink to accept a No. 8 screw.
◆ Fit this disc to the elm block, *with the countersunk holes touching the face of the block.*
◆ Screw the disc firmly to the block, using the bradawled holes as location points for the screws.
◆ Turn the outer edge of the disc to match that of the block.
◆ Turn a 40mm (1⁹⁄₁₆in) diameter square edged hollow, exactly 6mm (¼in) deep, into the face of the collar.

Fig 2.12 The inside angle of the collar being turned on the double cone chuck.

Fig 2.13 The internal angle. Note the datum line.

◆ Remove the collar, turn it around so that the countersunk holes now face out, and screw it back on to the elm block. You will now discover how accurately the screw holes were located!

◆ Mark a 25mm (1in) diameter circle in pencil on the face of the collar. Turn a straight-edged hole into the collar at the marked circle, breaking into the hollow beneath.

◆ This 25mm (1in) diameter hole now needs to be joined with a sloping undercut to meet the edge of the 40mm (1⁹⁄₁₆in) diameter hole cut from the other side (*see* Fig 2.12). This undercut slope will fit exactly and hold the sloping sides of the turned double cone firmly, with the lower part seated snugly below (*see* Fig 2.13).

◆ Mark a datum line on the side of the collar and the block so that they may be removed and replaced exactly.

The chuck is now complete, and is shown ready for use in Fig 2.14.

Fig 2.14 The double cone chuck with the part-turned piece ready to be held.

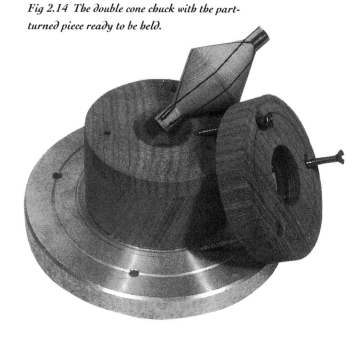

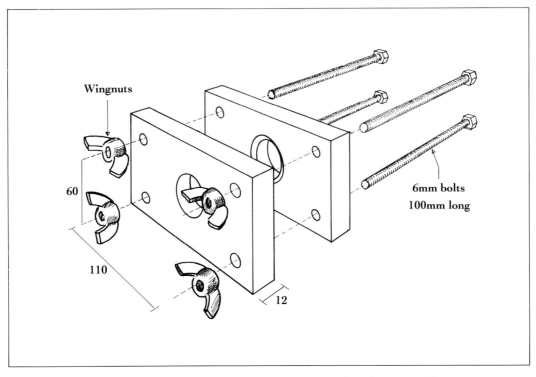

Fig 2.15 Spherical jigsaw cradle parts.

Making the cradle to hold the jigsaw sphere

Fig 2.16
The spherical jigsaw cradle.

The various parts of the cradle are shown in Fig 2.15.

◆ Buy four 100mm (4in) long, 6mm (¼in) bolts with wingnuts to fit.
◆ Cut two pieces of wood, 100mm (4in) long by 60mm (2⅜in) wide by 12mm (½in) thick.
◆ Take one piece and measure at each corner 9mm (⅜in) along and 9mm (⅜in) down.
◆ Tape the two pieces together, and drill a 6mm (¼in) hole at each of these marked points through the two pieces. Now draw diagonals on the face of the wood block.
◆ Drill through both pieces at that central point, using a 25mm (1in) sawtooth drill.
◆ Mark a line across the top of the two pieces of wood before separating them; this will enable them to be repositioned exactly.
◆ Remove the tape, and chamfer the rims of the holes on the inner faces: this will prevent the sharp edges digging into the sphere.
◆ Replace the pieces with the datum line showing they are correctly positioned, then fit the bolts and wingnuts in place, as shown in Fig 2.16.

CHAPTER 3

TOOLMAKING

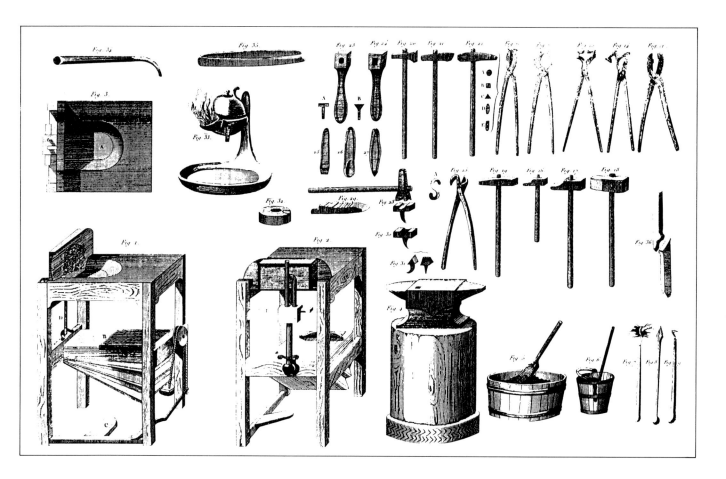

LTHOUGH TO A WOODWORKER WORKING METAL MAY SEEM ALIEN, DIFFICULT AND HARSH, IT IS REALLY VERY EASY. DO NOT WORRY ABOUT SPECIALIST TOOLS EITHER, FOR WHEN LOOKING AROUND ANY GARAGE OR WOODWORK SHOP THE MAJORITY OF TOOLS NEEDED FOR WORKING METAL ARE SITTING THERE WAITING, AND THOSE THAT AREN'T CAN BE BOUGHT QUITE INEXPENSIVELY.

Treat toolmaking as an extension of the workpiece and not as a chore; take pride in producing quality tools, for this skill is one worth acquiring. Just consider the freedom it will give, allowing all those unusual pieces of turnery to be tackled and taking you out of the stream of ordinary woodturners.

Of course, if you are unhappy working metal, encourage a friendship with an engineer, or look in a model engineering magazine for those who, for a price, will make the tool you need.

A simple selection of tools

- Small metal vice
- Electric drill
- Hacksaw
- Files
- Gas torch

- Sharp drills; if you are unable to sharpen the ones you own, buy new
- Tap and tap wrench
- Bench grinder
- Centre punch

This list may appear long, but look around your garage or workshop and you will probably be surprised at how many of these tools you already own.

Metal

If you are unsure of what metal to use, to ask for or to order, simply ask for *high carbon tool steel*. Again, if you do not know where to buy it, see the list of useful addresses, page 226 of this book, or look in a model engineering magazine under 'Materials'.

Do not use old files, as they can be extremely dangerous if not heat-treated correctly, so stick with new metal or new wood chisels.

Making the tools

Many simple tools may be ground directly from inexpensive wood chisels (*see* Fig 3.1), a number of which are described in the chapters. Once these tools have been ground to shape they need to be hardened and tempered (see page 18).

As an example of simple toolmaking, the production of a curved undercutting tool is shown here. The skills described are easily transferred to the making of all the other tools described in this book. The important parts are always the cutting edges and any shoulders of tools which are meant to rub for guidance or support; the remaining parts may be cut as ornately or simply as desired.

Marking out

This needs to be done accurately, but the shiny surface of metal is not easily marked and lines on that surface are difficult to see. Cover the surface of the metal with an agent which can be marked. Metalworkers use engineers' blue; use it if you can get it, otherwise use typists' white correction fluid.

- Paint the surface of the metal with engineers' blue or correction fluid.
- Mark out the dimensions shown in Fig 3.2 on that surface accurately, using either a sharp metal pointer or a pencil on correction

Fig 3.1 A selection of tools.

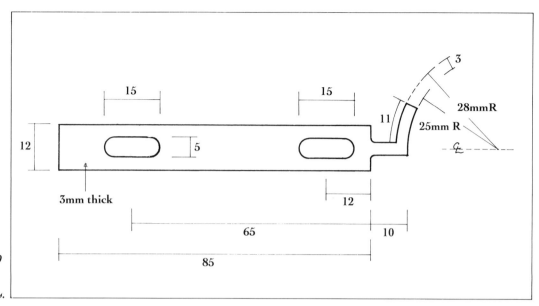

Fig 3.2 Curved undercutting tool dimensions.

fluid, as shown in Fig 3.3.

◆ If a compass is used, mark the centre point with a centre punch; this will create an indent into which the compass point will seat without slipping.

◆ Mark the centres of all holes to be drilled using a centre punch – *see* Fig 3.4. This gives a non-slip start for the drill.

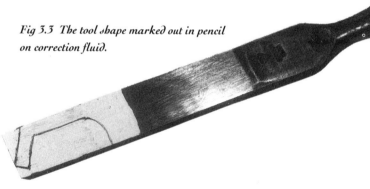

Fig 3.3 The tool shape marked out in pencil on correction fluid.

Fig 3.4 Marking out the centres of holes to be drilled, using a centre punch.

Cutting

◆ Always remember that the saw is mightier than the file, so cut as close to the line with the hacksaw as your skill allows – *see* Fig 3.5. Choose the best quality high carbon hacksaw blade you can, as it will pay for itself.

◆ Where a curved line needs to be cut, use a series of holes drilled close to that curve as a starter. This is called chaindrilling (*see* Fig 3.6). It removes waste metal quickly, begins

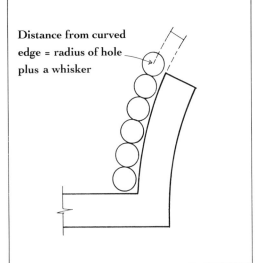

Distance from curved edge = radius of hole plus a whisker

Fig 3.7
Chaindrilling.

Fig 3.8 *Cut through the chain of holes, then file the curve to shape.*

Fig 3.9 The area to be ground presented to the grindstone. (The hands are positioned to allow the work to be seen.)

Fig 3.10 Grinding the tool.

the curved shaping and makes sawing easy, as it can be done in small stages. Measure half the diameter of the drill away from the curved edge (plus a hair's breadth) then centre punch each position before drilling (*see* Fig 3.7). Once this chain of holes has been sawn through and the waste removed,

file down to the curved edge (*see* Fig 3.8). In some cases the bench grinder may be used to remove some of the waste metal (*see* Fig 3.9), but be cautious: if you do use the bench grinder, make sure that the work is supported firmly upon the rest in front of the rotating grinding wheel. Wear goggles, and have a container of water close by for quenching, as shown in Fig 3.10.

Cutting out internal slots

Use a series of drilled holes inside the marked slot (chaindrilling), and cut through each of these holes into the next, using an abrafile (a circular section file-cum-saw blade) held in a hacksaw (*see* Fig 3.11). File out the central section starting with needle files to open the hole, then use larger files, when they fit.

Filing

To complete any filed surface so that it looks really smooth and clean, drawfile it. Hold the file at 90° across the surface and place the thumbs on the nearest edge and the fingers on the opposite edge, with one hand on either side, as shown in Fig 3.12; just draw the file back and forth, and a fine finish will be the result.

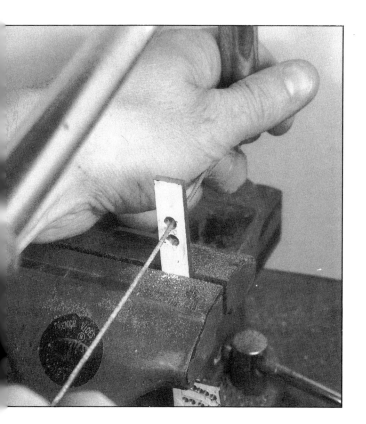

Fig 3.11 Use an abrafile held in a hacksaw to cut internal lines.

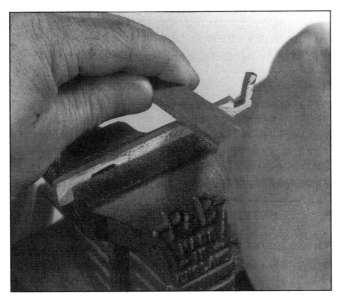

Fig 3.12 File edges clean.

Drilling and tapping a hole

Occasionally a hole will need to accept a threaded screw. One quick method is to superglue a matching nut on to the underside of the hole, but if the underside needs to be flush, then the hole will have to have a screw thread cut into it.

◆　Choose a threaded screw of a known thread size.
◆　Purchase a tap (which cuts the thread) matching the size of the chosen thread, from a hardware store. Also buy a tap holder and the correct size drill for this tap; the hardware store should advise which drill will be the correct tapping drill size.
◆　Hold the workpiece in the vice, and drill the tapping hole in the marked place.
◆　Place the tap, now held in the holder, in the hole. Make quite sure that the tap is held vertically at 90° to the workpiece – *see* Fig 3.13.
◆　Pressing down lightly, turn the tap holder half a turn clockwise and then a quarter of a turn back, repeating the operation. This quarter-turn back releases the waste metal, allowing the tap to cut more freely.
◆　Continue the motion until the hole is fully threaded, then carefully unscrew the tap from the hole and test the screw in the hole. If it is too tight, use the tap again.

Hardening and tempering

These processes change the internal structure of the metal, improving its hardness. Hardening makes the metal very hard and brittle, and tempering brings the metal down to the exact degree of hardness required.

If you can get the tools professionally hardened and tempered, fine; if not, the instructions below will help.

As a gas torch will be used, it is safest to work in an area away from flammable material. Avoid any area with shavings or wood dust, paints or finishes, and make sure the area is protected with fire bricks, asbestos type insulation or metal sheeting; always have an extinguisher, water and/or sand on hand.

Heat the prepared tool using a gas torch, holding the metal tool in pliers and wearing a pair of leather gloves (gardening gloves are acceptable). Have ready a container of water for quenching the hot tool, and wear goggles.

Hardening

Heat the tool to cherry red, making sure that the cutting part is a good colour, and then, without hesitation, quench it in cold water, swishing the tool around in the water to assist cooling.

Clean the top surface of the tool so that it is bright and shiny.

Tempering

When the metal is slowly heated oxide colours will appear upon the surface. As the heat increases they will move and change, starting at straw, then bronze, purple, blue and pale blue. These oxide colours are very helpful, for they indicate the temperature of the metal and the degree of hardness. The early colours indicate a harder, more brittle state than the later colours.

Heat the metal some way away from the edge to be tempered, heating evenly, gently and slowly. A straw colour will appear; continue the gentle heat, and the colour band will widen and begin to move along the metal away from the flame as the heat conducts along the tool. Bronze will be linked to the straw, followed by purple, then blue. Keep the bands as wide as possible with gentle heat, and encourage them towards the

Fig 3.13 Using the tap and tap wrench to cut a thread inside a hole.

Fig 3.14 Harden and temper the tool with a blowtorch. The faint shadow of the oxide colours can be seen on the (now cool) tool.

cutting edge. A blue colour on the cutting edge is that which is required, so keep on gently working that wide blue band towards the edge. Have a pot of water ready for when the blue band touches that edge, and quench immediately, again swishing the tool in the water until fully cool.

The tool may be left with the temper colours (*see* Fig 3.14), or cleaned up bright. Sharpen as you would any other tool, but do not overheat when sharpening, or the temper will be lost.

If the temper is lost by overheating whilst sharpening or in use, or if the correct temper colour is missed, begin the process over again. Start with the hardening, and then temper. So don't worry: hardening and tempering is a simple process and may be repeated as necessary.

Toolmaking not only gives more freedom to the woodturner, but also gives an added respect for the tools of the trade.

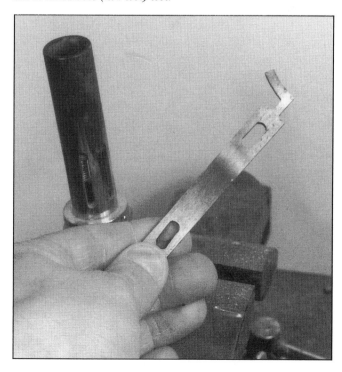

CHAPTER 4

MATHEMATICS

HIS CHAPTER FEATURES A SELECTION OF USEFUL AND SIMPLE MATHEMATICAL FORMULAE WHICH ARE EASILY FORGOTTEN AND DIFFICULT TO FIND WHEN NEEDED.

π = 3.142

The area of a circle – πr^2 – where r equals the radius of the circle.

The circumference of a circle – πD – where D equals the diameter of the circle.

The volume of a sphere – $\frac{4}{3} \pi r^3$ – where r equals the radius of the sphere.

The surface area of a sphere – $4 \pi r^2$ – where r equals the radius of the sphere.

Volume of a cone – $\frac{1}{3} \pi r^2 h$ – where r equals the radius of the cone base and h equals the vertical height of the cone.

To find 12 equally spaced points upon the surface of a sphere, the following information will be needed:

Using the ratio figure 0.526 x diameter of the sphere equals the vertex separation.

Take the sphere diameter as 62mm (2½in).

0.526 x 62mm = 32.612mm

(0.526 x 2½in = 1.315in)

Set the compass to 32.6mm (1⅜in) and use this to mark off the 12 equally spaced points as described in Chapter 5; and to find 6 equally spaced points upon the surface of a sphere, also refer to Chapter 5.

MARKING POINTS ON SPHERES

ARKING 12 EQUALLY SPACED PRIMARY AND 20 CON-STELATION POINTS ON A 62MM (2½IN) DIAMETER SPHERE

A   To discover the start points (top and bottom) of a 62mm (2½in) diameter sphere made from two hemispheres.

When each hemisphere is turned, its top centre position cannot be exactly located. To accurately position these start points, use the joint line as a point from which to begin.

◆   Set a pencil compass to 44.5mm (1¾in) radius and place the compass on any part of the joint line. Draw a circle about this point.

◆   Place the compass on any other point on the joint line, preferably on the opposite side, and mark a circle about this point.

◆   Where the circles intersect will be the top and bottom points of the sphere – the first two primary points. Erase all pencil marks except for the top and bottom points.

B   Marking primary points of a 62mm (2½in) diameter sphere

◆   Set a pencil compass to 32.5mm (1⁵⁄₁₆in) radius (*see* Chapter 4).

Fig 5.1 The 12 primary points marked on the sphere.

◆ Place the compass on the top point of the sphere and mark a circle about that point, and then place the compass on the bottom point of the sphere and mark a circle about that point.

◆ Place the compass point at any point on *one* of the circles; draw a circle about that point.

◆ Now choose any point where the circles intersect to place the compass, and draw new circles.

When all possible points have been used, it will be noted that there are (including top and bottom points) 12 intersections – these are the primary points – *see* Fig 5.1.

C   Marking primary points on a plain sphere 62mm (2½in) diameter

◆ Choose one point closest to the top; set a pencil compass to 32.5mm (1⁵⁄₁₆in) radius, placing the point on the chosen position. Draw a circle about this point.

◆ Place the compass at any position upon this circle and draw another circle. Where the circles intersect, place the compass point and draw circles.

◆ When all possible points have been used, it will be noted that there are 12 intersections. These are the primary points.

D   Marking constellation points for a 62mm (2½in) diameter sphere

Constellation points are a series of 20 points equidistant from each other and their nearest primary points.

◆ Set the compass to 20mm (¹³⁄₁₆in) radius.

◆ Place the compass point in turn on each of the primary points and draw a circle.

◆ Carefully mark a dot where these circles intersect. These are the constellation points.

E   Marking out the 6 main points on a 62mm (2½in) diameter sphere

This is a practical approach to calculating the positions for 6 equidistant points upon a spherical surface.

◆ Take a pencil compass and set to the radius – in this case 31mm (1¼in). Draw a circle of that size on paper.

◆ Draw a line horizontally across the circle passing through the centre. Where the line cuts the circle on one side mark the letter A, on the other side B.

◆ Extend the compass to around 50mm (2in) radius (this measurement is not vitally important – it just has to be larger than the radius of the circle).

◆ Place the compass point on A and strike an arc above the centre line.

◆ Place the compass point on B and strike an arc above the centre line.

◆ Join with a pencil line the point where the two arcs intersect and the centre of the circle. Where this line cuts the circle, on one side mark the letter C and on the other mark D.

◆ Set the compass point on A and extend the pencil to touch point C. Measure this distance – 44mm (1¾in) – which we will now call the main radius.

◆ Take the 62mm (2½in) diameter wooden sphere, placing the compass point on one end grain end of the sphere. Mark this position clearly with a letter E for end grain.

Fig 5.2 The six main points marked on the sphere's surface.

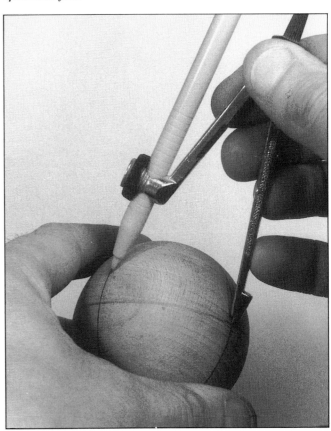

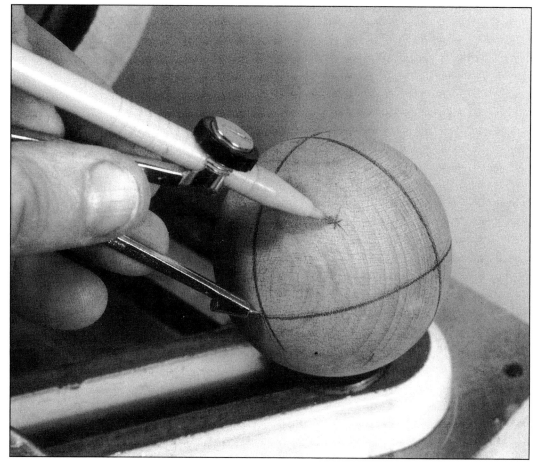

Fig 5.3 The clearance point marked on the sphere equidistant from the three surrounding main points (six in all).

◆ Strike an arc around the sphere.
◆ Take the compass point, and place it upon any point on the newly marked circle. Strike a second arc around the sphere (*see* Fig 5.2).
◆ Place the compass point where these two circles intersect, and strike a third arc around the sphere.
◆ 6 points will be marked where these three circles intersect; they will be set at an equal distance from one another.
◆ At the point opposite the first marked with an E mark a second E; this will be the other end grain position.

F   Marking 8 clearance points
This exercise again takes a purely practical approach and works on the sphere.

◆ Select three 'main' points, which form the boundary for one quadrant of the sphere.
◆ Place the compass point on any one of these three points. Extend the compass until it is close to what is judged as the central point between the three main points of that quadrant. Strike an arc.
◆ Move the compass to the second of the main points and strike an arc, then move to the third and strike an arc.
◆ It can now be judged exactly where the central point will fall, for the three arcs, if not meeting exactly, will help target the central position. Readjust the compass until the precise centre is discovered. In this case the measurement is 28mm (1⅛in).
◆ With the compass set to this measurement, place the compass on each of the main points, striking small arcs and marking clearly the 8 clearance hole positions – *see* Fig 5.3.

CHAPTER 6

TURNING SPHERES

HINKING ABOUT TURNING SPHERES IS FAR MORE WORRYING THAN ACTUALLY MAK-ING THEM, SO LET'S BEGIN.

Turning by hand

◆ The sphere described below is 62mm (2½in) in diameter. To produce this, first cut a block 120mm (4¾in) long by 75mm (3in) square. Draw diagonal lines upon its ends and then plane off the corners of the block before it is set centrally between centres, using the diagonals as a guide.

◆ Turn down the block to a precise 62mm (2½in) diameter cylinder. A centre line is drawn in pencil 60mm (2⅜in) from the tailstock end, and two lines drawn, one on either side, 31mm (1¼in) away (*see* Fig 6.1). On the outer edges of these two lines turn down, using a parting tool, to 25mm (1in) diameter, cleaning back on the one side towards the headstock and on the other towards the tailstock, using a gouge (*see* Fig 6.2). This leaves a centrally placed cylinder

62mm (2½in) diameter, 62mm (2½in) wide, with a pencilled centre line, as shown being measured in Fig 6.3.

◆ Now mark and cut two templates from card – cereal packet will do. Draw a 62mm (2½in) diameter circle on the card. Draw a centre line through, then a line parallel 12.5mm (½in) above it. A further centre line is drawn 90° to the first. Cut along the line drawn parallel to the diameter, then follow the inside of the circle until it reaches that same line on the other side. Again, follow that line with the scissors; this will produce a template which will fit on to the part finished sphere, touching the dowels either side. The second template is cut as a quarter circle, hollow cut like the first.

◆ Begin turning the central block, using a 9mm (⅜in) gouge. Turn away the edges, checking with the template as a guide. Remember to work slowly and carefully, for too much cut away cannot be replaced. The main bulk to be turned away is at a point 45° away from the centre of the sphere and

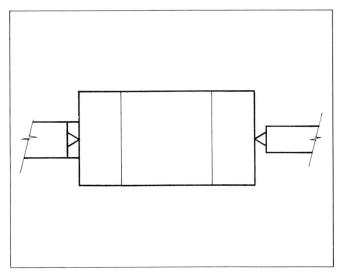

Fig 6.1 Turn block 'round' between centres.

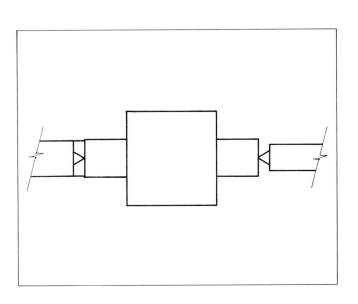

Fig 6.2 Turn spigots on either end.

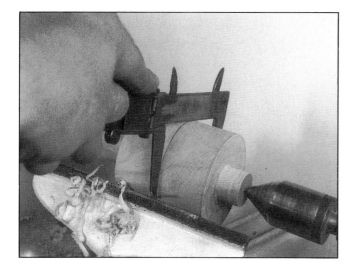

Fig 6.3 The block is turned accurately to 62mm diameter and 62mm wide.

central axis of rotation (*see* Fig 6.4). The top and sides need the least amount turning away, so cut steadily on those portions. Test regularly with the template (*see* Fig 6.5), and do not cut any wood from the pencilled centre line.

◆ Turning these spheres is a matter of care and particular judgement. The more spheres that are turned, the easier they become.

◆ When the sphere's surface matches that of the template, stop. Remove the toolrest and sand the work smooth. The dowels at either end are now sawn, leaving a 6mm (¼in) stub at either end (*see* Fig 6.6). Set this piece aside while two supporting pieces are turned.

◆ Turn a block 85mm (3⅜in) diameter, 50mm (2in) thick on a faceplate, and turn a 35mm (1⅜in) diameter hole 18mm (¾in) deep into the face. Chamfer the edge of the hole with a good 45° cut. Turn the outer edge away, sloping back towards the faceplate but not disturbing the turned chamfer. This

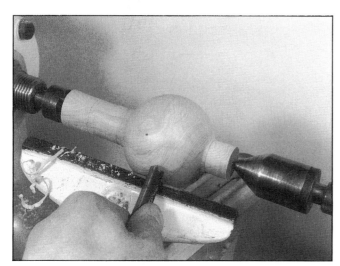

Fig 6.4 The sphere is hand-turned with gouge and skew.

Fig 6.5 A template is used to check the shape.

Fig 6.6 The spigots are sawn close to the sphere, leaving a short stub.

Fig 6.7
Spigots turned
off to produce
a true sphere.

chamfered hollow will support the part turned sphere.

◆ Turn a 30mm (1³⁄₁₆in) diameter cup about 18mm (¾in) long, with a central hollow at one end into which the revolving centre will fit, and a curved hollow at the other, to match the curvature of the 62mm (2½in) sphere.

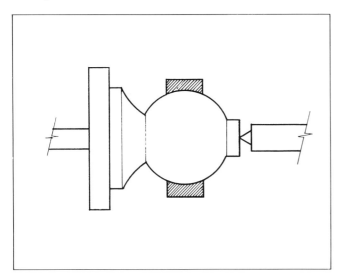

◆ With the faceplate still held at the headstock and a revolving centre fitting into the tailstock, place the part turned sphere into the chamfered hollow on the faceplate – *see* Fig 6.7.

◆ Make sure that the two small stubs are positioned so that when the turned cup is brought up, supported by the revolving centre, and pushed against the other side of the part turned sphere, they are in the central exposed portion, allowing them to be turned away. Ideally they should be at 90° to the axis of rotation. Bring the toolrest across and rotate the work by hand to make sure that nothing catches. When the lathe is switched on, the two stubs will show as 'ghost' images, and the curved spherical surface will appear solid (*see* Fig 6.8). Cautiously bring the gouge into contact with the 'ghost', and turn each away so that the outer surface of the sphere is untouched. If the 'sphere' has not been turned true, there will be a ghosting of the untrue area, allowing that to be turned away, thus producing a truly spherical shape. This completes the first sphere.

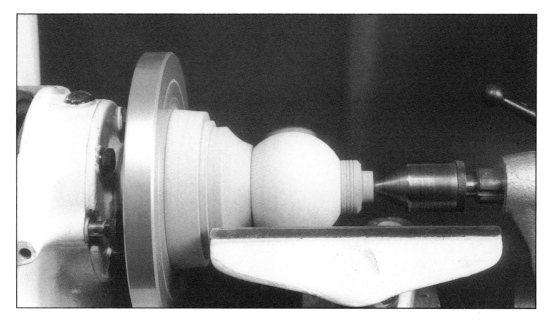

Fig 6.8 The sphere held between turned block and end cap, with the pure surface seen below ghost images of the two short stubs.

Turning a sphere using a spherical jig

The jig I first used was engineer-made, but for those not fortunate enough to know an engineer, I will describe how a simple but effective jig may be made from wood. An exploded view of this jig is shown in Fig 6.9, and Fig 6.10 also shows the chuck and spheres.

The position on your lathe which holds the toolrest must be able to be adapted to accept the central pivot hole of the wooden jig: this position must be directly below the central axis of the lathe.

Preparation

1   Buy or acquire a square metal turning tool about 9mm (⅜in) square, and grind one end of this tool 60° back, with a round fingernail shaping upon its end.

2   Buy a piece of 9mm (⅜in) plywood (or size to match the tool) of a size to cut three pieces sufficiently large to make a jig which will fit your lathe. The size will depend upon the centre height of the lathe, and precise details can be worked out after looking at the drawings.

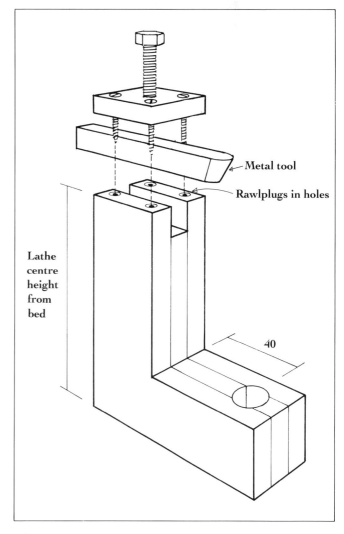

Fig 6.9 Exploded view of wooden sphere-cutting jig.

Fig 6.10
Wood spherical
jig, chuck and
sphere.

3 Have ready a small nut and bolt, four screws and four Rawlplugs.

As all lathes are of different sizes, the important dimensions are given here. The top of the tool will have to be set at centre height. The distance from the drilled pivot hole to the point where the tool protrudes must be about 40mm (1⁹⁄₁₆in).

◆ Cut three L-shaped pieces from the ply: the centre piece is 9mm (⅜in), i.e. the thickness of the metal turning tool, shorter than the two outer pieces. Glue and cramp these together.

◆ Mark and drill the centre pivot hole to the size of the fitting which holds the toolrest upon your lathe, and cut a cap piece from the ply to sit on top and bridge the tool slot.

◆ Drill a hole centrally into this cap piece to allow the small bolt to slip through. The underside is drilled or cut out to accept the nut, so that it can be set flush with the surface. The nut may then be glued in place using epoxy resin; do not let the glue enter the screw thread.

◆ Mark and drill four positions, two on either side, on the top of the cap piece. These holes need to be large enough for the screws.

◆ Place the cap on top of the jig so that it covers the tool slot and is flush with the edges. Mark through the holes on to the top edges of the jig on either side of the tool slot.

◆ Drill holes at these points sufficient to take the Rawlplugs; these plugs will firmly hold the screws, where the bare plywood edge would allow the screws to eventually break out.

◆ Fit the tool in the slot, fit the cap in place (once the epoxy glue has set) and screw down. Now fit the bolt into the nut on the underside and lock the tool firmly in position.

Using the jig
◆ Turn the block between centres as shown earlier, with dowels at either end and a centre line. Before removing the toolrest, turn off the corners of the block, leaving sufficient to cut the sphere.

◆ Remove the toolrest, replacing it with the jig (*see* Fig 6.11). The tool must initially be set right back into the block.

◆ Set the jig so that the top of the tool is at centre height and the front middle tip of the tool and the pivot point of the jig are exactly in line with the centre line around the block (*see* Fig 6.12).

Fig 6.11 *The wooden spherical jig in action.*

Fig 6.12 *The metal spherical jig centred.*

Fig 6.13 *The corners of the 62mm wide piece are
cut first.*

◆ Swing the jig to the right. Bring the tool
out so that it touches the turned off corner of
the block. Lock the tool down firmly, bring
the jig back to the central position and turn
on the lathe.

◆ Slowly swing the jig to the right, cutting
a small amount from the surface of the block.
Swing to the left, then return to centre, as
shown in Fig 6.13. Turn off the lathe, and
adjust the tool so that it cuts a fraction more.

◆ Repeat the cutting process, swinging
right, swinging left and back to centre,
adjusting and cutting. Each cut must be
slight – *see* Fig 6.14.

◆ The final cut is made so close to the
drawn centre line that it almost touches. Do
not cut any wood from the centre line.

◆ Once the final cut is made, turn off the
lathe, remove the jig and sand up the part
turned sphere. Cut the stubs at either end,
leaving 6mm (¼in) as before.

◆ Complete the turning of the sphere held
between the faceplate hollow and the
tailstock cup, again turning away those ghost
images of the stubs until a true sphere
remains.

Fig 6.14 *The spherical surface is fully cut down
to the spigots.*

CHAPTER 7

SAFETY

THE PROJECTS DESCRIBED IN THE FOLLOWING CHAPTERS ARE FOR ENJOYMENT AND PLEASURE; IF SIMPLE COMMON SENSE RULES ARE FOLLOWED, THAT PLEASURE SHOULD BE LASTING.

◆ Always wear eye protection when turning or grinding metal.

◆ Keep loose clothing away from the lathe when working.

◆ If you use a three- or four-jaw metal chuck, be aware of those spinning jaws. Before the chuck is used on the lathe, remove the jaws and grind back the sharp external edges. If the jaws hit the hand whilst turning it may cause a bruise, but with the sharp edges removed it will prevent a serious cut. In addition, if the ends of the jaws are painted white, it makes them more visible when the lathe is operating.

◆ Make absolutely sure that any screws used in wooden chucks are fully tightened before turning on the lathe.

◆ It is good practice to revolve the work by hand to ensure that nothing catches, before turning the lathe on.

◆ Have the lathe and lathe area well lit, and if a deep cut is being made, arrange the light fitting so that it may be moved to illuminate the cut being worked.

◆ Do not overextend the tool for deep cuts; try to reposition the toolrest for maximum support.

◆ Keep all tools sharp.

◆ A few precautions are necessary if laminated parts are being turned: plane off the edges of the work before turning; initial cuts should be light; if possible, secure the block ends with tape or cable ties for added safety.

◆ Safety is often thought of in terms of protecting fingers or eyes. Consider your lungs, and protect them from the fine dusts produced when turning. There are some excellent masks available; the better types filter the air and blow clean cool air across the face behind a protective visor.

Be sensible, take simple precautions, don't try to shortcut them. Enjoy turning in safety.

CHAPTER 8

WHISTLING TOP

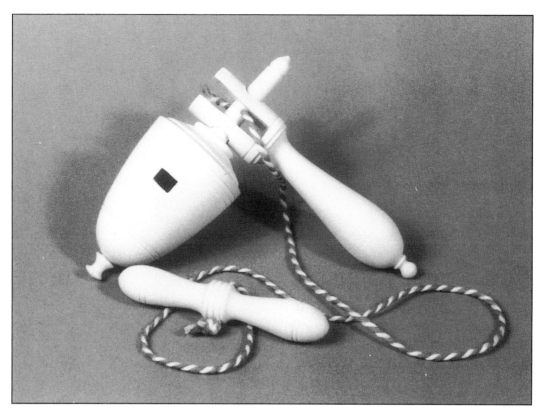

Fig 8.1 The whistling top.

I BOUGHT A SMALL, EXTREMELY DELICATE IVORY TOP FROM AN ANTIQUE SHOP. IT HAD THE CLASSICAL LINES OF A REGENCY STYLE URN, WITH BANDS OF BLACK SET AROUND AGAINST THE CREAM OF THE IVORY. A SMALL WINDOW CUT INTO THE HOLLOW BODY CAUSED A SHRILL WHISTLE WHEN IT WAS SPINNING AT SPEED. I AM SURE THIS WAS NO CHILDRENS' TOY; MAYBE AN ADULT SET IT IN MOTION FOR A CHILD TO WATCH AND BE THRILLED BY THE TRILL OF ITS WHISTLE, BUT IT WAS MORE LIKELY AN ADULT TOY FOR USE ON THE DRAWING ROOM TABLE.

For a piece so fine as this, a close-grained wood is an advantage. This top gave me the opportunity to use a length of spindle that had been in the workshop for some years, and I was delighted to have another use for such a gentle and pleasing wood. It fitted the bill ideally, for not only did it turn excellently but it also had a creamy yellow colour, very close to ivory (*see* Fig 8.1).

Preparation

◆ The dimensions of the top are given in Fig 8.2.
◆ Cut three pieces of wood, one 75mm (3in) long by 40mm (1⅝in) square, the second 75mm (3in) long by 12mm (½in) square, and a further piece 40mm (1½in) long by 12mm (½in) square.
◆ You will need a three- or four-jaw chuck.

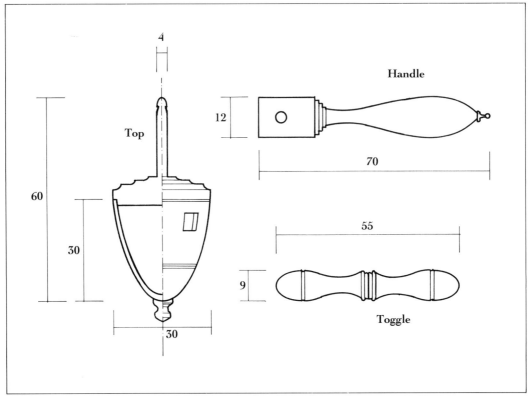

Fig 8.2
Handle, toggle
and part
section of
whistling top.

◆ Have ready a 3mm (⅛in) and a 1.5mm (¹⁄₁₆in) drill.

◆ You will need a tagua nut or other small piece of vegetable ivory, a small piece of bone or a good hard piece of wood from which the spinning point may be turned.

◆ A 3mm (⅛in) round-nose tool is necessary.

◆ Make up two card templates (a cereal box will do) for the inner and outer profiles,

Fig 8.3
Templates for
whistling top.

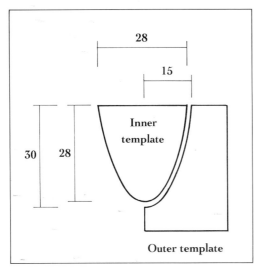

as shown in Fig 8.3.

◆ A selection of needle files would be helpful when cleaning out the whistle hole.

◆ Make up a small wood V-block sufficient to hold a 12mm (½in) diameter part. This will be used whilst cutting part of the handle on the bandsaw.

◆ The lathe speed for the larger parts is 1250 rpm, and for the smaller parts 1500 – 1750 rpm.

Turning the body

◆ Turn a piece of the chosen wood 75mm (3in) long by 40mm (1⅝in) square, between centres to round.

◆ Part off cleanly a 35mm (1⅜in) length, setting aside the remaining part.

◆ Remove the driving dog from the headstock, fitting a three- or four-jaw chuck in its place.

◆ Hold the 35mm (1⅜in) length in the chuck, with the parted face showing to front. Face off clean and square.

◆ Remove the part, measure 30mm (1³⁄₁₆in) from the faced off end and mark that position in pencil. Replace it in the chuck, with the turned end inside the chuck

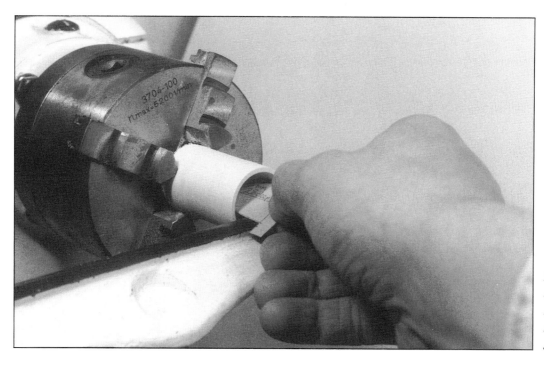

Fig 8.4 The card template used to check the internal shape.

jaws. Turn off cleanly to the 30mm (1³/₁₆in) mark.

◆ Fit the 3mm (⅛in) drill in the drill chuck, fitted in the tailstock. Turn on the lathe and drill through the piece held at the headstock.

◆ Mark in pencil a 28mm (1⅛in) diameter circle on the face of the work.

◆ Mark a point on the blade of the round-nose tool, using white correction fluid, 28mm (1⅛in) from its tip.

◆ Bring the toolrest across the face of the work, setting it so that the round-nose tool cuts at centre height.

◆ Begin cutting out the internal shape of the top, using the round-nose tool. The 28mm (1⅛in) diameter pencil line marks the maximum width that should be cut. The marked point on the tool is the maximum depth that should be cut. Use the card template to test the internal shaping (*see* Fig 8.4). Take particular care to turn exactly to this internal shape, for a matching template will be the only guide when shaping the outer surface.

◆ Take light cuts using the round-nose tool, beginning close to the centre and working into the drilled hole, gradually cutting wider and deeper.

◆ When satisfied that the internal shape is correct, turn off the lathe and remove the part from the chuck, setting it to one side.

◆ Take a turned scrap (by scrap I mean a piece other than those being used on this project) of wood, fix it in the chuck and turn a 28mm (1⅛in) diameter step on its outer face. Test the hollow part on the step, making sure that it is a good fit (*see* Fig 8.5).

◆ Bring up the tailstock holding a revolving centre, and tighten the centre into the drilled hole, firmly trapping the hollow

Fig 8.5 *The hollow body of the top is fitted to the turned step on the 'scrap' in the chuck.*

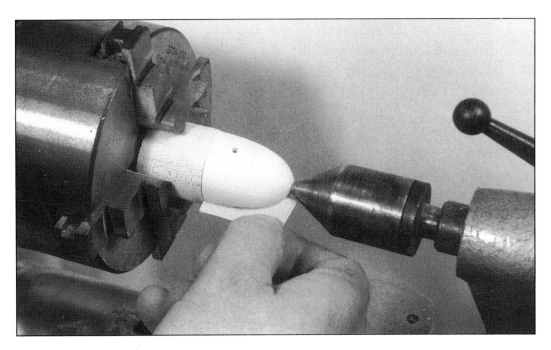

Fig 8.6 The outer shape is checked against the template. A small pilot hole has been drilled as a starting point for the whistle hole.

Fig 8.7 Internal shaping of the whistle hole.

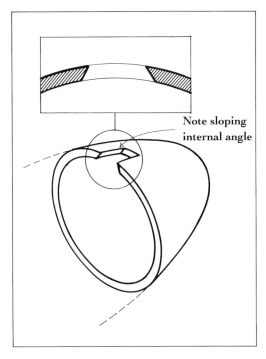

Note sloping internal angle

part between the part held in the chuck and the tailstock.

◆ Bring the toolrest across the work, setting it so that the turning gouge is cutting at centre height. Begin careful shaping of the base of the top, again using a card template as a guide (*see* Fig 8.6). Raise the toolrest when the skew chisel is brought into operation to produce that final clean cut. When the shape conforms to the template, the wall thickness should be 2mm (³⁄₃₂in).

◆ A pilot hole may be drilled for the whistle hole before the outer shaping is complete. This will help to give an idea of the wall thickness as work proceeds. The pilot hole 2mm (³⁄₃₂in) may be drilled at any point on a line measured 9mm (³⁄₈in) from the joint line towards the revolving centre.

◆ Mark out the whistle hole (around the pilot), a rectangular shape 3mm (¹⁄₈in) by 6mm (¹⁄₄in), the longest measurement parallel with the joint line.

◆ Open up the whistle hole, using a variety of needle files and keeping the edges of the hole crisp and square.

◆ The two 3mm (¹⁄₈in) sides need to be sloped internally so that a sharp edge is made (*see* Fig 8.7); this helps to produce the whistle when the top is spun.

To test the whistle, with the lathe stationary, blow across the hole as you would a flute. Slightly adjust the opening if you feel it would improve the sound. Generally the sharper the edge, the better the whistle.

◆ Move the tailstock back and remove the whistle body, replacing the scrap piece in the

Fig 8.8 The top's body fixed to the prepared part so the spindle may be turned.

chuck with the 40mm (1⅝in) piece.

◆ Turn a small 28mm (1⅛in) shoulder to accept the whistle body.

◆ Holding the 40mm (1⅝in) piece with the majority of its length outside the chuck and the whistle body fixed on the shoulder and tightly held by the tailstock, begin turning the upper part of the spinning top (*see* Figs 8.8 and 8.9).

◆ Measure 9mm (⅜in) from the joint line towards the headstock; at that point turn down to 4mm (³⁄₁₆in) diameter, again towards the headstock for a length of 25mm (1in).

◆ Turn the two parts so that they flow together as one across the joint.

◆ From that joint measure 2mm (³⁄₃₂in) towards the headstock, and using a skew chisel, carefully turn a fine slope down to meet the smaller diameter, cutting two steps into the slope for added interest.

◆ Mark a pencil datum line across the joint. Separate the pieces, apply glue, then fix back together, allowing the pressure of the tailstock to clamp the joint. Use the pencil datum to ensure the parts fit back together exactly as they came apart.

◆ Using the top corner of a square end tool, mark two fine grooves around the body close to the tailstock, as shown in Fig 8.10. Next mark three more grooves, one on the joint line and one either side; this not only adds decoration to the body but also disguises the joint.

◆ Complete the end of the spindle closest to the chuck, turning a small collar and a decoratively turned 'topknot' on the last 6mm (¼in). Apply the finish you feel most comfortable using before parting off. Lay this part to one side.

As most of the wood has been turned from the inside of this piece and much of the wood has been turned from the outside of the spindle, it should be as light as a feather.

Fig 8.9 The body removed to show the step joint and the thin walls of the body.

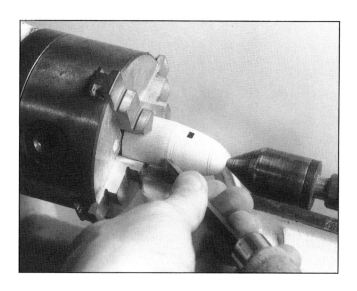

Fig 8.10 Lines are cut into the top's body after the whistle hole has been shaped.

Turning the handle and toggle

Both parts are turned between centres, but as they are quite small in diameter a finer driving dog is needed so that they are not split. Remember also to increase the lathe speed.

Handle

◆ Turn a piece 75mm (3in) long by 12mm (½in) square to round, removing as little waste wood as possible.

◆ Shape the handle as in Fig 8.2, using gouge and skew. Arrange the part so that the turned finial is at the tailstock and the main bulk at the headstock.

◆ Measure 70mm (2¾in) from the tailstock, and at that point cut the beginning of a parting groove.

◆ Mark grooves using the corner of the parting tool at the positions marked on Fig 8.2, paying particular attention to the groove 20mm (¾in) away from the parting groove. This line marks the position where the slot, cut later, will stop.

◆ Sand and polish the piece, then part off.

◆ From the parted end measure 9mm (⅜in), marking a point. At this point drill a 5mm (⁷⁄₃₂in) hole cleanly through, making sure that it is drilled centrally. If the work is placed upon a clean scrap of wood before drilling, the exit drill hole will not break out and damage the surrounding area.

◆ With the drilled hole set horizontally, mark a line from the parted end to the groove on top of the piece. Make sure that this line is parallel to the sides of that turned portion. Mark, in pencil, two further lines on either side of this line, each 3mm (⅛in) away and parallel to the first marked line. These outer lines will be the guide for the bandsaw when cutting the slots.

◆ Place the handle in the prepared wood V-block with the drilled hole horizontally. The marked lines should be on top and the squared-off end facing the bandsaw blade.

◆ Carefully cut down to the groove on the inside (waste side) of these two lines. The saw will cut into the wood V-block as well, but this ensures that the work is fully supported throughout (see Fig 8.11).

◆ Either remove the centre waste with further bandsaw cuts or take the work from the V-block, removing the waste by cutting

Fig 8.11 The handle is supported upon a V-block while the slot is cut.

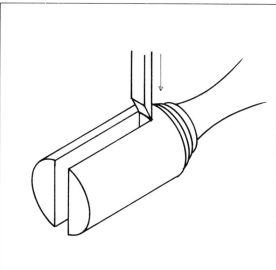

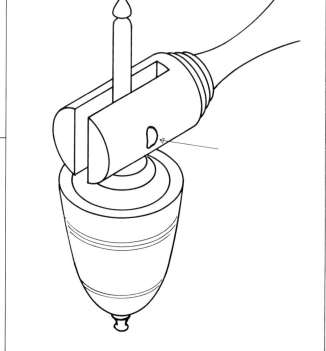

Fig 8.12 *Wood chisel used to square up inside shoulder of slot.*

Fig 8.13 *Position of the cord hole in the top's spindle.*

out with a coping saw and cleaning up the inside shoulder using a small chisel, as shown in Fig 8.12.

◆ To judge exactly where on the top spindle the hole to take the cord must be drilled, place the handle drilled hole over the spindle (*see* Fig 8.13). Push the handle down to meet the turned shoulder where the spindle joins the top. The pull-string hole must be marked centrally on the spindle halfway between the two bandsawed faces of the gap in the handle. Drill a 1.5mm (¹⁄₁₆in) hole at this point.

Toggle

◆ This is a straightforward piece of spindle turning between centres. Turn the remaining piece 40mm (1½in) long by 12mm (½in) square to the shape shown in Fig 8.2. Polish and part off. At the centre point of the toggle drill a 1.5mm (¹⁄₁₆in) hole; this will take the fixed end of the pull-string.

I felt that the point upon which the top spun would need to be a little harder than the spindle used for the main body to take the wear of the, hopefully, high speed spin. The material for the point should also be of a similar colour, to blend in with, and almost be a part of, the whole top. Tagua nut (vegetable ivory) seemed an excellent choice: hard and white, and a good excuse to try it out. Tagua nut does have one failing: it often has a crack or void through its centre, and

some pieces are worse than others. Only by cutting into the nut can the size of the split be judged and the piece arranged so that it can be worked around.

Turning the spinning point

◆ Prepare a small, flat and true wood faceplate.

◆ Cut the top section from a tagua nut to produce a flat surface. Either sand flat using glasspaper laid on a completely flat surface, or place the cut face against a sanding disc.

◆ Draw in pencil a series of concentric circles on the wood faceplate; these will help centre the oddly-shaped tagua nut.

◆ Place the nut on the faceplate, judging where best it would fit, and squeeze a moderate amount of superglue on the flat surface of the nut and press it into position. Do this quickly, at the same time bringing the revolving centre in the tailstock to press it firmly into place (*see* Fig 8.14). Although superglue is fast acting, give it a minute or two, particularly if you have applied a generous squeeze.

◆ Have the medium 6mm (¼in) and small 3mm (⅛in) round-nose tools ready, also the 3mm (⅛in) square end tool and a smaller skew chisel. I have found these tools most effective when turning tagua, which has the texture and turning properties of very hard plastic. Long looping shavings will run off these tools, particularly if they are kept extremely sharp (*see* Fig 8.15).

◆ Round the eccentrically shaped nut using the medium round-nose tool and taking very light cuts.

◆ When the nut is rounded, remove the tailstock, continuing to turn the part using the smaller round-nose tool. Bring the workpiece down to 4mm (⁵⁄₃₂in) diameter.

If the nut has presented a crack or void in an awkward place, then all that can be done is to replace it with a fresh piece.

◆ Remove the tailstock and then dome over the end face, turning out any mark left by the tailstock centre. This surface will be the one upon which the top spins.

◆ From that turned end measure 4mm (⁵⁄₃₂in), and turn down to 3mm (⅛in) diameter towards the faceplate.

◆ Using both the skew and the smaller round-nose tool, shape the part between the turned down diameter and the domed end.

◆ When satisfied with the shaping, clean up thoroughly, parting off a total of 10mm (⅜in), 6mm (¼in) of which is the thin turned diameter which fits in the base hole of the spinning top.

◆ Take the turned tagua nut end and glue it into the hole with a PVA glue.

I experimented with various shapes for the spinning point: the best was the same as I

Fig 8.14 The base of the tagua nut fixed to the faceplate and held by the tailstock while the glue sets.

Fig 8.15 The turned tagua nut endpiece and the small tools used to work the nut.

had seen on an old bone dice spinner, a dome-shaped end. It seemed to support the top, not allowing it to topple, yet only had a small area in contact with the surface upon which it was spinning. This of course reduced the friction and helped the top to spin much longer.

To use the top, just string it up: knot a 30cm (12in) piece of cord at one end and lace it through the hole in the toggle. The other end just slips through the hole in the shank with, of course, the handle just being in place. Wind the cord slowly on to the spindle, not too much. Hold the handle in the left hand with the top's spinning point on the table top or floor. Pull the toggle, held in the right hand, and when the cord comes free and the top is spinning, lift the handle, and the top will spin away, whistling like the wind through the trees.

CHAPTER 9

CONE AND SLOPE

Fig 9.1 The double cone about to roll 'up' the slope.

I N A SCIENCE LESSON AT SCHOOL, THE TEACHER TOOK TWO FUNNELS AND TAPED THEM TOGETHER AT THEIR WIDEST ENDS. HE THEN FOLDED A PIECE OF CARD IN HALF AND MADE AN ANGLED CUT SO THAT WHEN THE CARD WAS OPENED TO A WIDE V SHAPE THE HIGHEST POINTS WERE AT ITS OPEN END. HE PLACED THE JOINED FUNNELS AT THE LOWEST PART OF THE CARD RAMP AND ASTONISHED US ALL WHEN THE JOINED CONES ROLLED *UP* THE RAMP. HE NEVER EXPLAINED WHY; HE JUST LEFT US GUESSING, LIKE A GOOD MAGICIAN, BUT NOT NECESSARILY LIKE A GOOD SCIENCE TEACHER.

Years later I remembered the trick, and have here decided to turn the double cone and make two open V-shaped ramps from wood. The cone can now run up one ramp, drop on to the next and continue its run upwards (*see* Fig 9.1).

I must say that I became quite excited at the thought of these double cones rolling *up* slopes, finding it quite difficult to sleep one night for I was certain that I had discovered perpetual motion; just arrange the ramps in a circle, and the double cones will travel forever!

Sorry to disillusion you, but the double cone only *appears* to travel upwards – it does, of course, roll downwards. If you look at the centre line of the cone, it does move downwards as it rolls along the upward sloping ramp.

To make the cone look more interesting and to show movement, it is turned from laminated wood.

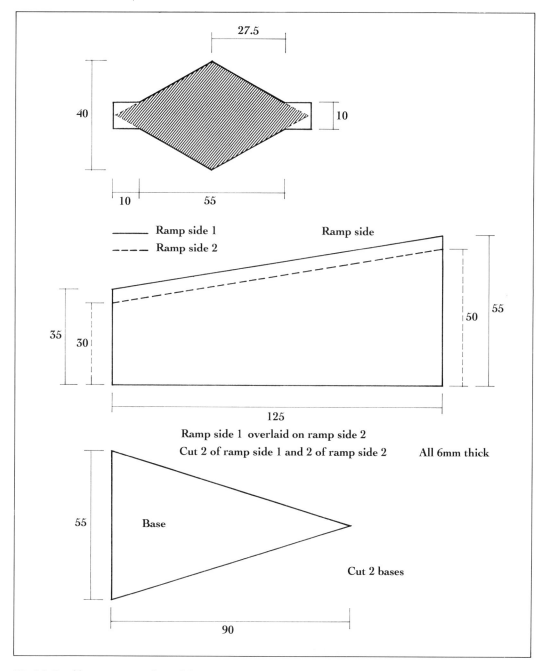

27.5

40

10

10

55

—————— Ramp side 1
– – – – – Ramp side 2

Ramp side

35

30

50

55

125

Ramp side 1 overlaid on ramp side 2
Cut 2 of ramp side 1 and 2 of ramp side 2

All 6mm thick

55

Base

Cut 2 bases

90

Fig 9.2 Double cone, ramp sides and base.

A second ramp adds interest, and third and fourth ramps may be added, but each ramp's starting point must always be slightly lower than the starting point of the one before.

Preparation

◆ Refer to Fig 9.2 for the dimensions for all parts.

◆ Cut a 150mm (6in) length 50mm (2in) square of a good quality close-grained wood; yew is my choice here, as it turns so well and smells so good.

◆ Before slicing the wood to take the veneer laminate, drill and countersink screw holes at the extreme ends of the wood, making sure a fine pilot hole runs through to the other side. These screw holes will help realign the wood when the veneer is in place,

Fig 9.3 *Cutting the wood on the bandsaw. Note the marked triangle.*

keeping the grain pattern running true.
◆ Set the bandsaw to cut a 12mm (½in) slice.
◆ Lay the square section piece of yew on the bandsaw table, with the screw holes on the side. On the top face mark a triangle in dark pencil or black felt pen; this will ensure that the cut parts can be easily realigned.

◆ Run the wood through the bandsaw, cutting a 12mm (½in) slice from one edge, keeping the triangle mark on top – *see* Fig 9.3. Turn the wood so that the opposite edge can be run through the bandsaw to cut a 12mm (½in) slice.
◆ Cut two dark pieces of veneer 150mm (6in) by 60mm (2⅜in). Fit the three parts of the cut yew back together, gluing the veneer between the slices and allowing it to show on both edges. Make sure the triangle is lined up, then fit the screws in place and tighten down, as shown in Fig 9.4.

The screws ensure that the wood grain is held in alignment. Make the grain pattern match exactly, thus preventing any slippage.

◆ Clamp the whole firmly, making sure there are no gaps, then leave to dry.
◆ When the glue has dried, clean off excess veneer and glue from the face.
◆ Turn the wood so that the veneer layers are horizontal, and mark a triangle on the top surface.
◆ Remove the screws, and then drill and countersink screw holes as before on the extreme ends, this time on the sides into which the veneer bands are inlaid.
◆ Run the wood through the bandsaw as before, taking a 12mm (½in) slice from either edge.

Fig 9.4 *The first sliced side is cramped together with leaves of veneer glued between the cuts.*

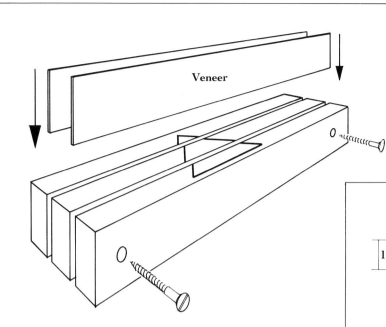

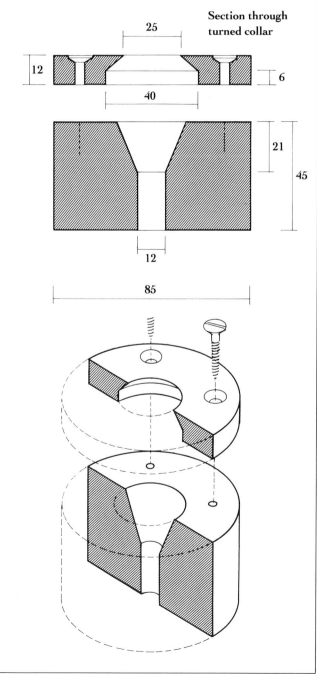

Section through turned collar

◆ Cut two more slices of dark veneer the same size as previously cut.

◆ Glue the veneers, align the triangle, fix the screws and tighten, clamp firmly and leave to dry (*see* Fig 9.5).

◆ When dry, remove the screws and clean off excess veneer and glue. Finally, trim off the screw holes at either end.

◆ Have the double cone chuck described in Chapter 2 ready. The measurements are given in Fig 9.6.

◆ Lathe speed should be around 1000 rpm.

Beginning the work

As this part is being turned from a laminated section, be cautious: it may be sensible to plane down the corners of the piece to prevent any sudden jarring, which may occur if the part is turned from square. The jarring may, in exceptional circumstances, cause the laminations to break apart and fly from the lathe. You may wish to wrap each end with plastic cable ties as added security.

◆ Before planing the corners, remember to draw or cut the diagonals to find the exact centres at either end.

◆ Set the workpiece between centres. It is preferable to fit the dog across the diagonal to avoid splitting the work.

◆ Turn down to 40mm (1⅝in) diameter.

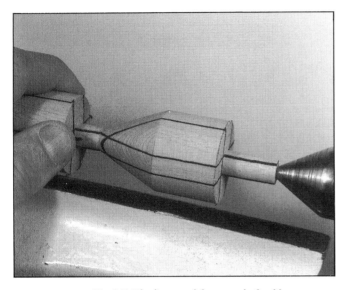

Fig 9.7 The first angled cut on the double cone.

◆ From the centre line turn down to point X on one side and point X1 on the other (*see* Fig 9.8). This surface must be flat, true and straight. Clean up and glasspaper lightly if necessary.

It will now be noticed that the veneers which have been laminated between the cut surfaces are a little more interesting, following the shape of the slope and beginning to curve. Save the waste ends which will soon be cut off, and try turning them with hollows and beads; it is very intriguing to see the way in which the laminated lines change shape and curvature. Maybe you might like to try various other forms of laminating and turning when making other double cones. The possibilities are endless, and the results often surprising.

◆ Measure 50mm (2in) along the turned piece from the tailstock end, and mark this point as a centre line around the work.
◆ From this centre line measure 27.5mm (1¹⁄₁₆in) at either side, marking these points X and X1.
◆ From the centre line measure 37.5mm (1½in) at either side, marking these points Y and Y1.
◆ Between points X and Y, X1 and Y1, turn down to exactly 1cm (¹³⁄₃₂in) diameter (*see* Fig 9.7).

◆ Cut off the end pieces on the waste side of Y and Y1. Do not cut directly on the line, otherwise the points to be turned of the double cone will be sliced off.
◆ Remove the driving dog from the headstock, and replace it with the double cone chuck.
◆ Fit the prepared piece into the chuck, and tighten the collar down evenly.
◆ Bring the toolrest across the workpiece, and revolve the chuck by hand to make sure nothing catches.

Fig 9.8 The second slope turned down on the double cone.

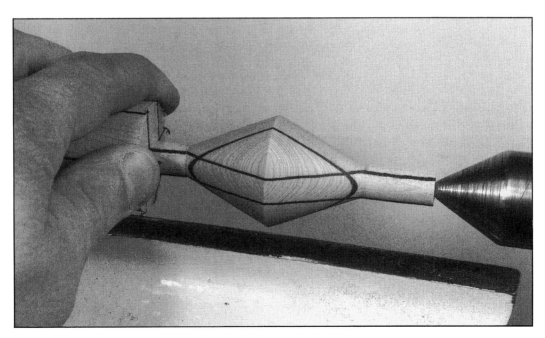

Fig 9.9 The double cone about to be replaced in the chuck so that the end dowel can be turned to a point.

Fig 9.10 The gouge is ready to turn the end of the double cone to a point.

◆   Turn on the lathe and look to see if the work is revolving on centre. If it is, fine, if not, hold a pencil up to the stub end of the workpiece and touch against it lightly. Where the pencil touches is a high point, so undo the screws on the chuck collar and gently tap the pencil-marked high point to bring the work back on centre. Tighten the collar and try again. If it is not on centre this time, repeat the pencil marking and reset the work until it runs on centre.

If the double cone shape happens to be slightly loose in the chuck, this can be easily rectified. Take a small piece of double-sided tape 18mm (¾in) long, sticking one side to the back of a piece of medium glasspaper. Cut this into three equal pieces. Peel off the backing and stick these pieces of glasspaper to the inside of the chuck, spacing equally. This not only takes up some of the space, but also helps grip the double cone.

   Turning the ends of these double cones in the chuck (*see* Figs 9.9, 9.10, 9.11 and 9.12) is such a release, turning fine shapes to a point, open-ended, free of any tailstock and certain that the piece is firmly held – somehow it is unlike turning lids, knobs or bowl bases; this time you end up with a fully turned piece, with no signs of how it was held.

Fig 9.11 The point cut.

Ramps

◆ *See* Fig 9.13 for the various stages of the ramps.

◆ Prepare a piece of wood 75cm (2ft 6in) long by 60mm (2½in) wide by 6mm (¼in) thick, and plane it all round. This will be sufficient for two ramps.

◆ Cut two sides 125mm (4⅞in) long from the prepared piece. Each side has one end 55mm (2⅛in) high, tapering down to 37mm (1⁷⁄₁₆in). Mark the base line, the one which has not been cut to a taper, with a cross X.

◆ Cut two more sides for the smaller ramp 125mm (4⅞in) long by 48mm (1⅞in) high at one end, tapering down to 32mm (1¼in) at the other end. Again mark the base line with a cross X.

◆ Cut two triangles, base size 55mm (2⅜in), height – base to apex – 90mm (3½in); the length of side will then be 95mm (3¾in).

◆ Along the base of each tapered side (marked X) drill a series of fine holes to take veneer pins 3mm (⅛in) up from the bottom edge.

◆ Carefully glue and pin the sides to the triangular base. The low ends fit on the point of the triangular base so that the highest part of the ramp is at its open end.

For the double cone to run easily up the ramp it must be always be set level. Now you

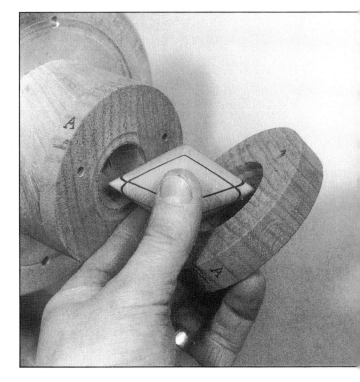

Fig 9.12 The finished double cone is removed.

might like to make a number of ramps, set them in a circle, and see if *you* can create perpetual motion.

Fig 9.13 The parts of the ramp on the left, the part-finished ramp on the right, and a completed ramp at the middle back.

CHAPTER 10

MAGIC TRICK

EVER BEEN TAKEN IN BY A MAGICIAN? IT'S GREAT TRYING TO WORK OUT HOW A TRICK HAS BEEN DONE, AND HALF THE FUN IS NEVER BEING TOLD, KNOWING THAT THE ANSWER MUST BE SO SIMPLE.

This magic disappearing ball trick is a simple idea and as old as the hills, but is still effective.

When showing the trick, lift the top with the right hand to show the ball sitting in place inside (*see* Fig 10.1). The left hand holds the base and the secret middle section together. Replace the lid, making incantations, secret words, and signs (*see* Fig 10.2). Now readjust your grip so that the right hand lifts the top as before plus the secret middle section, leaving behind the base, this time with an empty hollow (*see* Fig 10.3); the ridge and groove surface on the spherical top hides the joints.

Preparation

◆ The dimensions of the magic trick are shown in Fig 10.4.
◆ Cut a 125mm (5in) by 40mm (1⅝in) square piece of wood, preferably a very plain piece without any grain or distinct markings; I used boxwood.
◆ Place between centres and turn to round – be careful to centre as closely as possible so that it will remain as near to 40mm (1⅝in) diameter as possible.
◆ A 6mm (¼in) parting tool will be required.
◆ Have ready a 3mm (⅛in) round-nose tool.
◆ A three- or four-jaw or other suitable chuck is needed.
◆ A selection of standard turning tools will be used.
◆ Lathe speed 1250 rpm.

Fig 10.1 Abra...

Fig 10.2 ...ca...

Fig 10.3 ...dabra!

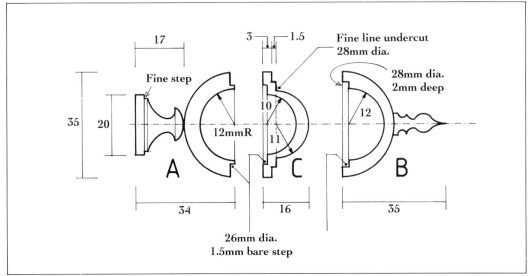

*Fig 10.4
Section through
magic
disappearing
ball.*

For such a fine and small piece of turnery, although the metric measurements have been translated into imperial, it will not always be totally accurate. If you are working in imperial measurements it would be sensible to make a careful measured drawing before you begin.

Starting work

◆   Hold the prepared turned 125mm (5in) by 40mm (1⅝in) diameter piece in the chuck fitted to the headstock. Bring the revolving centre up to support the tail end.

◆   From the tailstock end measure 35mm (1⅜in), and mark a pencil line around the work.

◆   From the marked line measure 4mm (³⁄₁₆in) – this will provide an area sufficient for parting off. Again mark a pencil line.

◆   From this line measure 16mm (⅝in), marking a pencil line.

◆   Now measure a further 4mm (³⁄₁₆in), once more marking a pencil line; this area is an allowance for parting off.

◆   Finally, from that line measure 34mm (1⅜in) and mark a pencil line. This position is the base of the foot.

◆   Draw a line along the length of the wood to act as a datum to help when fitting the parts together for their final turning (*see* Fig 10.5).

◆   Disregarding the 4mm (³⁄₁₆in) parting areas, there will be three distinct sections: mark the section nearest the headstock A, the part nearest the tailstock B and the centre section C.

◆   Carefully part off between Sections B

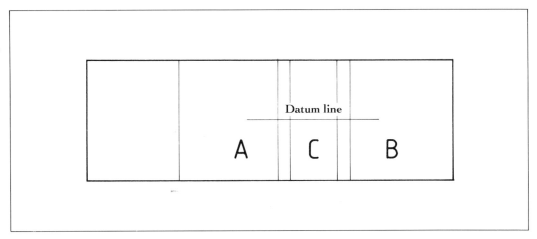

*Fig 10.5
Datum line
marked across
pre-turned
cylinder.*

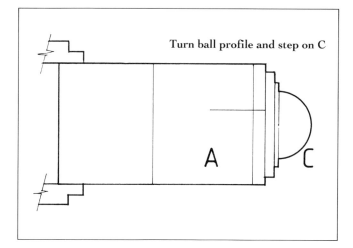

Turn ball profile and step on C

A C

Fig 10.6 B parted off.

and C, and place B safely to one side (*see* Fig 10.6).

◆ Bring the toolrest across the face of the work.

It is now time to profile the false 'ball' and a step on the face of C, as shown in Fig 10.6. The step will fit into a recess which will be cut into B. Mark and cut out from card (a cereal packet is ideal) an 11mm (⅞₆in) radius quarter circle to act as a template.

◆ **Cutting the step**. From the parting line touching C, measure 3mm (⅛in) away from the headstock, and at that point turn down to 28mm (1⅛in) diameter. A further 1.5mm (¹⁄₁₆in) away, turn down to 22mm (⅞in) diameter.

◆ **Turning the false ball**. It takes a combination of judgement, careful checking and the use of the card template to ensure that the false ball looks truly spherical and as if it were a ball sitting in a hollow. To encourage this deception, create a fine line undercut with the tip/edge of the parting tool at the point where the curve of the ball meets the face of the work (*see* Fig 10.7). The work should come straight from the tool, for glasspapering can cause joints and steps to be rounded over, making for a sloppy fit.

◆ Once satisfied that the 'ball' and step are cut exactly, part off between A and C, placing C carefully to one side.

◆ Face off A squarely, removing as little material as possible (*see* Fig 10.8). Use the tailstock revolving centre to support the end

of the work, and also mark the centre to relocate it exactly when it is replaced in the chuck.

It is essential that all shoulders, steps and faces are turned flat, true and square. This will ensure that joints will fit well, and the joint lines will become 'invisible'.

◆ Remove A from the chuck and replace with B. The parted-off face should now be showing to the front.

◆ Bring the toolrest across the face of the work and begin turning the inside profile.

◆ Using a parting tool, cut a 28mm (1⅛in) diameter step 2mm (³⁄₃₂in) deep. It is better to leave it a little undersize to be opened out later, rather than risk cutting it too large at the start.

◆ Draw a 12mm (½in) radius circle on a piece of card, and cut around carefully to make a template.

◆ Mark, using white correction fluid, a point 14mm (⁹⁄₁₆in) from the tip of the 3mm (⅛in) round-nose tool. This will act as a

Fig 10.7 Turning the 'ball', which is then parted from the cylinder.

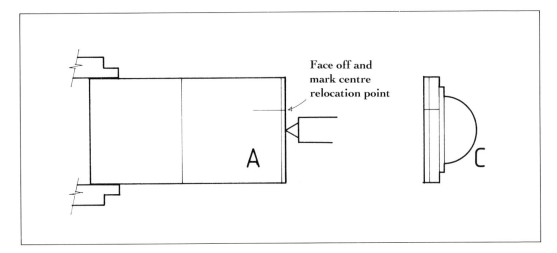

Face off and
mark centre
relocation point

Fig 10.8 C parted off.

depth guide when cutting the internal
hemispherical shaping.

◆ Using the 3mm (⅛in) round-nose tool,
and the template as a guide, carefully turn
out the 12mm (½in) radius hemispherical
cavity, as shown in Fig 10.9. Remove the
toolrest occasionally and check if C fits,
adjusting where necessary (*see* Fig 10.10).

When C fits into B perfectly, it is time to join
the two together so that the inside of C may
be turned to shape. To do this cut a piece of

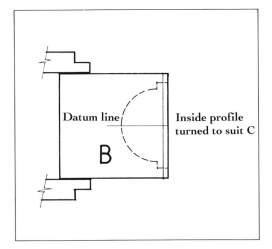

Datum line

Inside profile
turned to suit C

Fig 10.9 B held in chuck.

*Fig 10.10 The
ball is fitted
into the top
portion.*

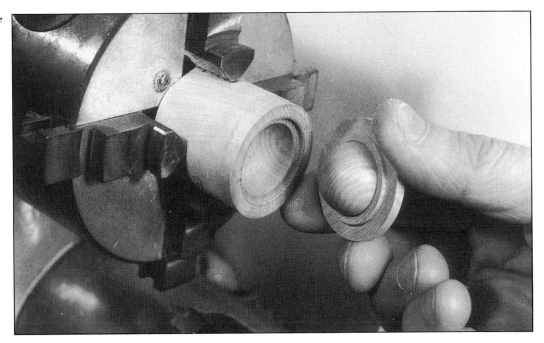

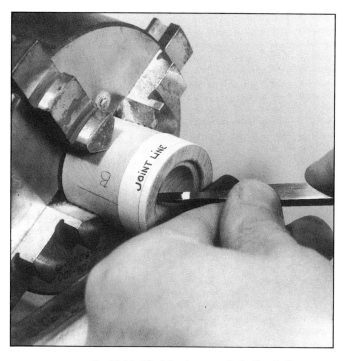

Fig 10.11 The joint between the ball and the top portion is fixed with paper and glue.

paper about 9mm (⅜in) wide, wrap it around the work and trim off, allowing a slight overlap. Push B and C **firmly** together so that the joint shows no gap at all; make sure the horizontal pencil datum line is aligned. Apply glue to one side of the paper and wrap it glue side down so that it straddles the joint. Make sure that the paper stays flat against the work and glues down well on to the wood. Leave until fully dry. This paper glued strip should ensure that B and C turn as one piece, but always be careful when turning into C to take light cuts.

♦ Begin on the internal profile of C, having carefully faced off the work (*see* Fig 10.11).
♦ The distance between the joint line (still visible through the paper) and the face of the work should be 3mm (⅛in).
♦ Turn an internal 26mm (1in) diameter step 1.5mm (¹⁄₁₆in) deep on the face of C.
♦ Cut a 10mm (⅜in) radius card template.
♦ Remove the white depth mark from the round-nose tool, replacing it with another, this time 11.5mm (½in) away from the tip; this will act as a depth guide when cutting

the hemispherical hollow into C.
♦ Carefully cut the 10mm (⅜in) radius hollow into C (*see* Fig 10.12), checking the shape with the card template and the depth against the mark on the tool. Take light cuts.
♦ When satisfied that the step and hemispherical hollow are correct, remove B and C (now firmly joined) from the lathe.
♦ Replace A in the lathe, bringing up the tailstock holding the revolving centre so that the point of the centre locates in the dimple made earlier in its faced-off end. Tighten the chuck, making sure the piece runs on-centre.
♦ Remove the tailstock and centre, bringing the toolrest across the face of the work.
♦ Carefully cut a 26mm (1in) diameter step 1.5mm (¹⁄₁₆in) deep (*see* Fig 10.13). Remove the toolrest and check the fit against the face of C.

It is essential that the joints between B and C and A and C are comfortable fits – not too sloppy and not too tight. It will make the trick far more convincing if the joint does not fall apart or, at the other extreme, does not have to be prised apart.

♦ When the joint is exact, begin the hemispherical hollowing of A.
♦ Mark on the round-nose tool a point 12mm (½in) from its tip, having first removed the previous mark, and again using white correction fluid.
♦ Cut a 12mm (½in) radius card template as a guide, and carefully begin cutting out

Fig 10.12 Inside of C turned to shape.

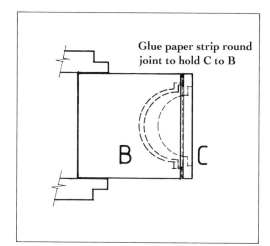

Glue paper strip round joint to hold C to B

B C

Fig 10.13 *The hollow in the base is turned.*

Fig 10.14 *A relocated in the chuck.*

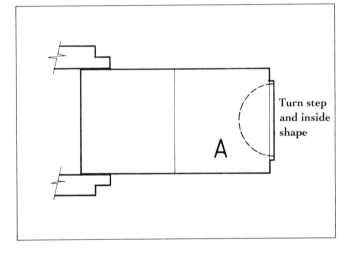

Turn step and inside shape

A

the hemispherical hollow with the round-nose tool (*see* Fig 10.14).

◆ When the hollowing has been completed satisfactorily, remove the toolrest, fit C (plus B) in place, lining up the pencil datum line. Bring up the tailstock with revolving centre in place, and tighten against the work.

◆ Bring the toolrest parallel to the work.

At this point a degree of measurement, plus a degree of judgement, comes into play. Occasionally it may be found that although a curve is cut exactly, it can look slightly 'wrong'. Make adjustments where necessary, but bear in mind the internal hollows (*see* Fig 10.15 for the external shape).

◆ Turn the workpiece to an exact 35mm (1⅜in) diameter, cleaning off the paper bandage.

◆ From the joint line between C and A, measure 17mm (⅝in) towards the **headstock**, marking a pencil line.

◆ From the joint line between C and A, measure 18mm (⅝in) towards the **tailstock**, marking a pencil line. These two lines mark the extremes of the circular profile of the piece.

◆ Using judgement, eye, gouge, skew chisel, and card template if you wish, turn a clean rounded shape, leaving a 7mm (⁵⁄₁₆in) diameter part at the tailstock limit of the spherical shape and a 12mm (½in) diameter part at the headstock limit.

◆ Using the corner of the parting tool, cut a groove into each of the joint lines and then

Fig 10.15 *External shape of the magic trick.*

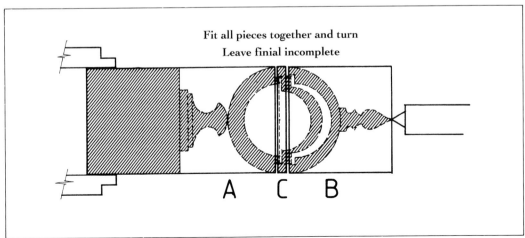

Fit all pieces together and turn
Leave finial incomplete

A   C   B

one between them. This is now the guide for the distance between the rest of the grooves which will be cut upon the spherical surface of the work. These grooves disguise the joint lines, and also act as a decorative finish.

◆ Complete the profile of the part towards the headstock, undercutting the 12mm (½in) diameter section where it meets the spherical shape. A smaller skew can cut a good fine line here.

◆ Shape the stem using a small gouge, remembering to cut down from either end to meet towards its middle, making the shaping as fluent and graceful as possible. On the edge of the foot (20mm or ¾in diameter), cut a fine step to add that little detail which ends the shaping crisply.

◆ Polish the work and part off under the foot.

◆ To complete the underside of the foot, turn a jam-chuck – a small step in a piece of wood which will accept the step in the top of A. The joint needs to be tight enough to hold but not split the work. Bring up the tailstock, holding the revolving centre to give a little support while the base of the foot is turned off. Slightly hollow the underside of the foot so that it will stand well. The final centre pip where the tailstock touched can either be carefully turned out with light cuts or cleaned off with a gouge and then polished.

◆ To turn the top finial, again make a good fitting jam-chuck with a step to fit B (*see* Fig 10.16). Bring up the tailstock and revolving centre for support.

◆ Turn the top finial to shape with a small

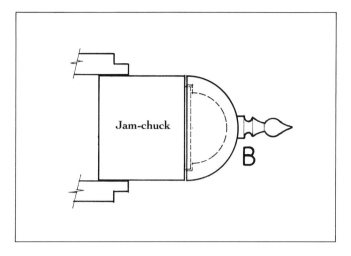

Fig 10.16 Turn a jam-chuck, fit B, and turn the finial.

gouge, the final details being turned with the 3mm (⅛in) round-nose tool and skew. For the fine cove shaping beneath the onion-shaped top, use the nose tool, taking gentle cuts. Slice down either side to make clean sharp edges, using the skew chisel. Again using the skew, *slightly* undercut where the top finial meets the main body of the work. This undercut highlights the crispness and difference between the body and joining finial.

◆ Remove the tailstock and centre to complete the final point, polishing to finish.

The trick is now ready (*see* Fig 10.17), so find some unsuspecting child or gullible adult and work your magic.

Fig 10.17 All three parts of the trick exposed.

CHAPTER 11

BOTTLE, GOBLET AND ARROW

WHEN TRAVELLING IN AMERICA, I VISITED A RURAL MUSEUM IN WHICH, AMONG OTHER PIONEERING TREASURES AND ARTEFACTS, STOOD A GLASS BOTTLE WITH A WOODEN ARROW PIERCING IT (*SEE* FIG 11.1). A CARD BENEATH IT STATED THAT THE ARROW WAS ALL OF ONE PIECE, AS WAS THE BOTTLE. THE CARVED POINT AND FLIGHT OF THE ARROW WERE OBVIOUSLY TOO LARGE TO GO THROUGH THE DRILLED HOLE IN THE BOTTLE, AND THERE WAS NO EXPLANATION ON THE CARD.

This piece of trickery did not leave my mind. Every now and then it popped up, and I would experiment, forget about it for a little while, then back it would come again.

It appeared to me that the wooden arrowhead needed to be soaked or boiled to make it pliable. The problem was that, although pliable, it might well be helped through one hole in the bottle by being squeezed, but by the time it reached the second hole on the other side of the bottle, it would expand. It would then be impossible to get close to the now-enclosed head to apply any pressure to help it through.

The breakthrough came, like most things, by accident. I had just boiled the shaped block which was to be the arrowhead, and began crushing it in the vice to soften it further. For some reason I had to leave the work suddenly and do some other job. The crushed arrowhead remained in the vice over the whole weekend. When I returned to the workshop, remembering the experiment, I thought that it would be ruined. On taking it from the vice, the arrowhead was truly squashed, had dried squashed and remained squashed. I cut back the sides sufficiently for it to get through the holes in the bottle's side, and pushed it all the way through. Then I was stuck – how to expand the crushed head? I dunked it in a cup of boiling water, and it expanded to its original size; all that remained was to carve the arrowhead to shape.

I have found a variety of woods which have worked well for arrows – ash, beech and sycamore. The wood should not be too dense. Lime proved to be ideal for turning, carving and compressing.

Fig 11.1 Bottles and goblet with arrows through them.

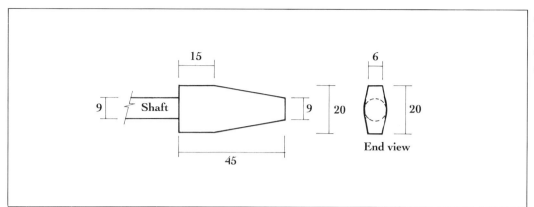

Fig 11.2
Initial shaping
of the
arrowhead.

Preparation

◆ Cut a piece of lime or ash 24cm (9½in) long by 25mm (1in) square.
◆ Mark diagonals on either end to locate the centres.
◆ Lathe speed 1500 rpm.

Turning the basic block for the arrow

◆ The arrowhead dimensions can be seen in Fig 11.2.
◆ Place the piece between centres.
◆ Measure 60mm (2⅜in) from the tailstock end, and mark a line square around at this point.
◆ Measure 40mm (1⅝in) from the headstock into the work, marking a line square around.
◆ Beginning at the tailstock, use a skew chisel to start the cut into the work (*see* Fig 11.3). This will cut a clean line into the square stock, enabling the central portion to be turned without splitting out the end parts.
◆ Make a similar cut at the line marked close to the headstock.
◆ Take a small 9mm (⅜in) gouge and gently turn the central square section to round. Take gentle cuts, as this will avoid large pieces splintering off. Turn this gradually down to 9mm (⅜in) diameter, as shown in Fig 11.4.

It is easiest if the diameter is reduced closest to the tailstock first and then gradually worked towards the headstock. This will reduce the amount of vibration when turning this thinner section. Also make sure that this 140mm (5½in) centre section is turned down through all its length to fractionally below 9mm (⅜in), so that it will easily slip through the hole drilled in the bottle.

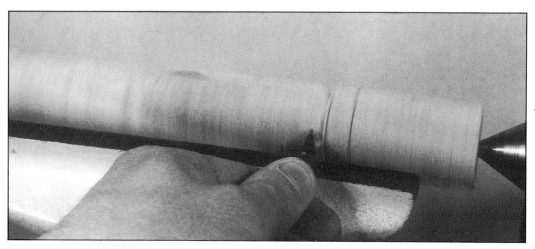

Fig 11.3
Using a small
skew chisel to
cut into the
block at the
flight end.

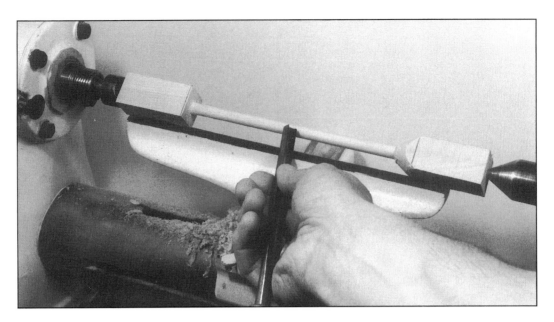
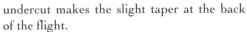

Fig 11.4 The stem of the arrow being turned with blocks left either end from which the point and flights are carved.

◆ Turn a small part close to the revolving centre down to 9mm (⅜in) diameter at the tailstock end. Undercut slightly: this will produce the round section at the end where the arrow is 'nocked', providing a continuation of the shaft (*see* Fig 11.5). The

Fig 11.5 The end of the arrow is turned so that the shaft is seen at the end of the flight.

undercut makes the slight taper at the back of the flight.

◆ Using the skew chisel, make an angled cut at the 60mm (2⅜in) line away from the tailstock. This makes the starting taper of the flight.

◆ The block may now be removed from the lathe. Cut the 'flights' into what was the tailstock end, on the diagonal measuring 3mm (⅛in) thickness. Using the turned section of the shaft and the shaft itself as a guide for depth, cut down the 'flight' sides with a fine saw (*see* Fig 11.6). Carefully remove the waste wood between the flights (*see* Fig 11.7), shaping the base to match the curve of the shaft to make it appear that the flight is fixed to the shaft. Clean up using fine glasspaper to remove any toolmarks.

◆ The 'nock' or notch can now be cut into the end of the shaft. Two angled cuts with the fine saw will effectively remove the waste and produce the required groove.

◆ Cut the square section at the arrowhead end so that it is 9mm (⅜in) thick lining up with the shaft, but still 25mm (1in) wide (*see* Fig 11.8). Now adjust the width from 25mm to 20mm (¾in), taking the wood evenly from both sides.

◆ Measure 30mm (1³⁄₁₆in) along the arrowhead, marking all round in pencil.

Fig 11.6 Sawing a diagonal path to produce the flight.

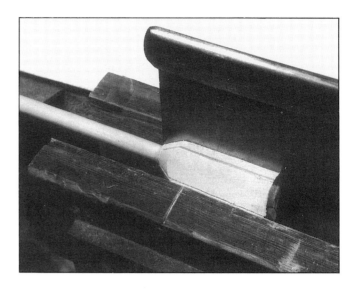

Mark the centre line at the end of the head, then measure 4.5mm (³⁄₁₆in) above and below. Join this point to the 30mm (1³⁄₁₆in) point along the head on top, and do the same for the part below. This begins to show the tapering of the point, and when the waste wood is sawn away it will begin to look more like an arrow.

◆ Gently carve a taper off the bulk of the wood above and below the centre line, cutting evenly from both sides (*see* Fig 11.9). Removing this waste will allow the head to be crushed more easily.

Turning the rings

To make the bottle trick appear more interesting I have added a few loose rings; these are turned of the same type of wood used for the arrow.

The size of the ring relates to the opening in the neck of the bottle which has been used. The bottle opening here is 18mm (¹¹⁄₁₆in), so I turned the outside of the ring 20mm (³⁄₄in). If the annual rings running through the turned ring are held so that they are vertical, the ring can be gently squeezed across its width and pushed down into the neck and into the bottle, never to come out again. It may be necessary to turn a few extra rings to allow for practice and breakage.

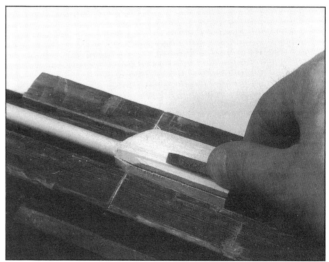

Fig 11.7 Cutting the waste wood away between the arrow's flights.

◆ Turn a piece of lime 20mm (³⁄₄in) diameter between centres.
◆ Turn down with a narrow parting tool to 9mm (³⁄₈in) diameter either side of a 3mm (¹⁄₈in) piece. Round over the top on either side with a skew chisel, using a sweeping, rolling action (*see* Fig 11.10). Widen the area either side of the ring sufficiently to bring the tool into play; I use a specially ground cobblers awl which can be used left or right. Undercut each side, maintaining the curved shaping of the top at its underside, so that when the ring is cut it will have the shape of a ring doughnut, with a full, if small, circular section (*see* Fig 11.11). If the 9mm (³⁄₈in)

Fig 11.8 Bandsawing the point to thickness.

diameter surface which the parting tool cuts remains untouched, the hole through the centre will be sufficiently large to fit over the centre of the arrow. Make four to six of these rings, enough for accidental breakage.

◆ Take each ring in turn, and squeeze and fit it into the bottle. Stop when three rings have been successfully pushed into the bottle.

The bottle was drilled by the local glass-cutter. A 10mm (⅞in) hole was drilled 100mm (4in) up from the base through one side, lined up with the other side, and then drilled from the opposite side to meet. I understand that the holes were drilled using a masonry drill held in a hand drill, with a reservoir of paraffin, held within a small

Fig 11.10 Turning the loose rings.

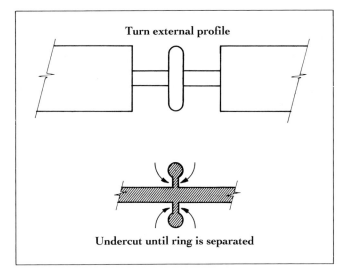

Turn external profile

Undercut until ring is separated

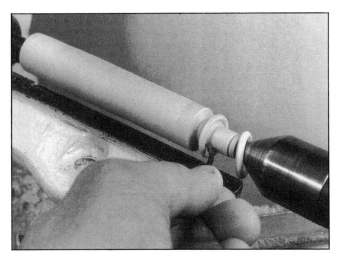

Fig 11.11 Undercutting the loose ring.

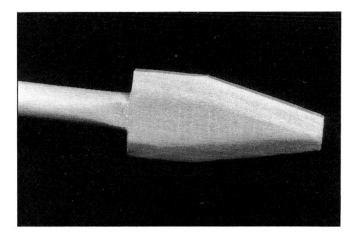

Fig 11.9 Shaping the arrowhead.

putty dam around the drill site, as a lubricant.

◆ Before the arrow is ready to be threaded through the holes in the bottle, take a dowel and push it through the bottle holes, stringing two of the loose rings on to it in preparation (*see* Fig 11.12). Leave the third ring lying in the bottom of the bottle so that when the arrow is fully through, holding the other two rings, you can ask your victim to tip out the loose ring, only for them to find it is too large to come out, thus increasing the puzzle.

Fitting the arrow through the bottle

◆ Boil the arrowhead in water for 10 minutes in a clean saucepan, as shown in Fig 11.13.
◆ Have a vice open to the right size ready and waiting, with the jaws lined with polythene: this prevents iron staining from metal vices and general muck and glue stains from wood vices.
◆ Take the saucepan and arrow to the vice.
◆ Place the arrow in the vice, with the head horizontal.
◆ Crush the head firmly, taking care to make sure that the edges are fully crushed and not just folded over (*see* Fig 11.14).

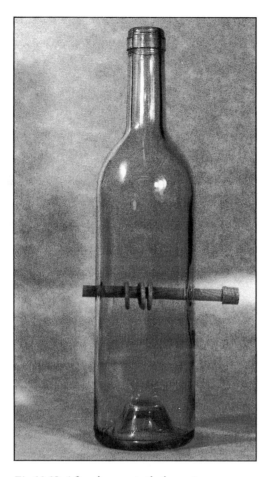

Fig 11.12 *A dowel supports the loose rings.*

Fig 11.13 *Boil the arrowhead for 10 minutes.*

Fig 11.14 *Crush the boiled arrowhead in a vice.*
Polythene prevents rust marks affecting the
arrowhead.

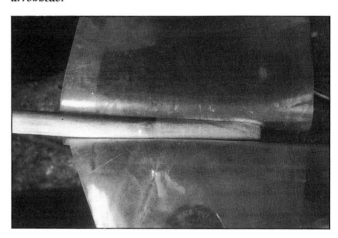

◆ Leave the arrow in the vice for at least two full days, and longer if possible.

◆ Remove the arrow only when you are sure it is fully dry and at a time when you are ready to fit it into the bottle straightaway.

◆ The arrowhead, although crushed and dried, will expand slightly and continue to do so for a short while, so work quickly and efficiently.

◆ Try the crushed head in the hole. If it fits, push it through, pushing the supporting dowel ahead (*see* Fig 11.15). String the loose rings over the head, and push the head through the other hole.

◆ If the head does not fit immediately, shape the outside very slightly with a chisel; every 1mm (⅛in) cut off will expand into 3mm (⅛in), and this will be lost from the finished piece. When the arrowhead has been carved to fit, push it through, threading the loose rings from the supporting dowel as described above.

◆ When the arrowhead is outside the bottle, take a cup of boiling water, dip the arrowhead in; before your eyes the head will expand to its original size. No damage will have been done by crushing, so when it is fully dry carve to shape.

The arrow through the bottle is a good trick, for it is known that glass is solid and cannot easily be twisted, bent or stretched, and the arrow can be proven to be of one piece. The arrow through the wood goblet has more challenge for the woodturner, as it is a fully turned piece.

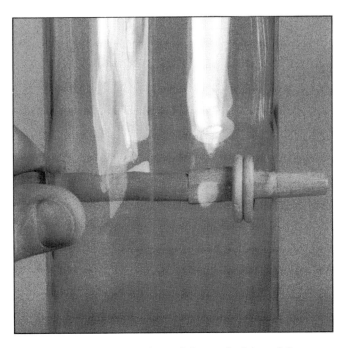

Fig 11.15 The crushed arrowhead is pushed through the hole in the bottle, and the loose rings are threaded on.

Preparing the goblet

◆ Take a piece of elm 18cm (7¼in) long by 100mm (4in) square.

◆ Mark the diagonals on either end to locate the centres.

◆ Plane off the corners before placing between centres.

◆ Lathe speed 1000 rpm.

Turning the goblet

◆ Turn the block to 90mm (3½in) diameter.

◆ Turn a 25mm (1in) spigot 20mm (¾in) long at the headstock end.

◆ Remove the piece from the lathe, replacing the driving dog with a faceplate holding a 100mm (4in) diameter, 25mm (1in) thick piece of wood.

◆ Drill or turn a 25mm (1in) diameter hole 22mm (⅞in) deep in the centre of this piece.

◆ Apply glue to the turned spigot and surrounding face of the turned elm piece.

◆ Fit the spigot into the hole in the wood faceplate, and bring up the tailstock holding a revolving centre (*see* Fig 11.16). Tighten

the centre on to the end of the elm piece to apply pressure while the glue sets and also to keep the piece on centre.

◆ Leave the work overnight until the glue is set firm.

◆ Begin by re-turning the outside of the elm piece so that any eccentricity can be removed.

◆ Withdraw the tailstock, bringing the toolrest across the end face of the work.

◆ Turn the hollow 'cup' of the goblet, using a gouge to take sweeping cuts down and into the work (*see* Fig 11.17). Cut to 40mm (1⅝in) deep, producing an almost hemispherical hollow (*see* Fig 11.18) and leaving a 3mm (⅛in) outer rim.

◆ Clean the inside of the hollow before moving on.

◆ Remove the piece from the lathe and then turn a shaped plug to fit inside the hollow as a support while the external shaping is done.

◆ Replace the faceplate and goblet blank, fitting the plug into the hollow and bringing up the revolving centre in the tailstock for support (*see* Fig 11.19).

Fig 11.16 The turned spigot is glued into the prepared hole in the faceplate.

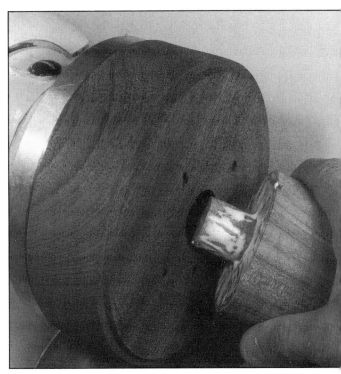

◆ As the inner depth of the goblet is 40mm (1⅟₁₆in), the outer curve follows, curving in 45mm (1¾in) away from the rim (*see* Fig 11.20). Turn a 20mm (¾in) collar here as a junction between the bowl of the goblet and the stem.

◆ Sweep the gouge down and away from the collar, turning the stem to a slim 9mm (⅜in) diameter (*see* Fig 11.21).

◆ Measure 135mm (5¼in) from the rim, and at that point turn down with a parting tool to begin the base of the goblet.

◆ From this marked point begin to turn the foot down towards the stem with fluent cuts of the gouge.

Always view the goblet by turning the head sideways: the work always looks much lighter horizontally. When it is viewed as it would to stand, the true proportions show, and what appeared to be quite fine can look heavy. Now is the time to make adjustments.

◆ Make sure the foot has a good fluent shape, that the stem flows well and is sufficiently fine before the final clean-up and parting off.

◆ Part off at the position already started,

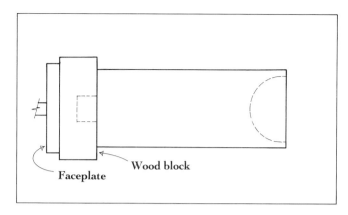

Fig 11.17 Turn the internal hollow of the goblet.

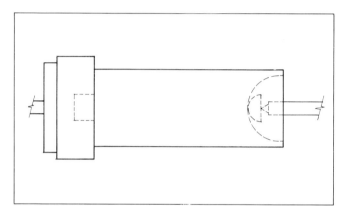

Fig 11.19 Support the internal hollow with a shaped plug and revolving centre.

Fig 11.18 The goblet is hollowed out.

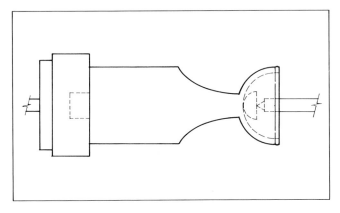

Fig 11.20 Begin the external shaping to match the internal hollow.

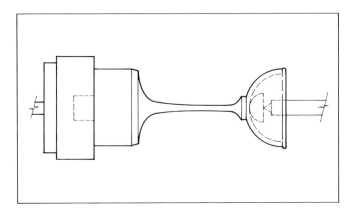

Fig 11.21 Begin turning the stem.

Fig 11.22 Part off to finish undercutting the foot.

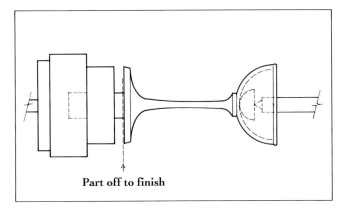

Part off to finish

Fig 11.23 The goblet is supported by the revolving centre (with a wooden block between it and the workpiece) while being parted off.

135mm (5¼in) from the rim (*see* Fig 11.22). Widen the cuts away from the foot so that the parting tool will not be gripped; remember to angle the cut, slightly undercutting the foot so that it will stand steadily when fully parted (*see* Fig 11.23).

◆ Part off down to the final pip, which may be cleaned off with a small chisel or gouge.

Drilling the hole in the goblet

Before the goblet is given its final finish, mark the positions for the 10mm (⅞in)

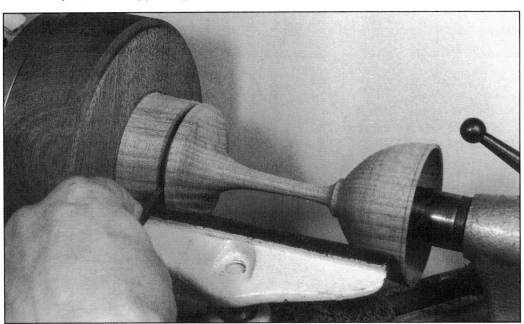

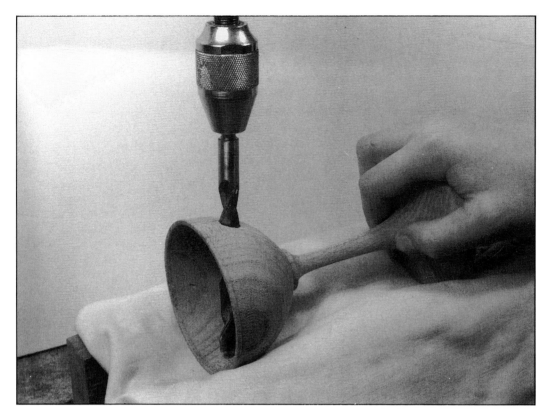

Fig 11.24 The goblet is carefully drilled by hand.

drilled holes. Mark these holes on the sides with the least attractive grain.

♦ Measure 20mm (¾in) down from the rim on an imaginary vertical line.

♦ Fit a spur-pointed 10mm (⅞in) drill in a hand drill.

♦ Open a wood vice to about 60mm (2⅜in), and cover with a cloth. This will act as a cradle for the goblet when drilling.

♦ Place the goblet in the cradle, with one drill mark uppermost.

♦ Support the goblet with one hand, while holding the drill bit on centre.

♦ Turn the hand drill (at this point your head will come into play, supporting the top handle of the drill – of course, help from a friend would make the job much easier) slowly and easily, drilling vertically to the face. Drill lightly through the goblet side.

♦ Take particular care when breaking through: progress very slowly, and ensure a clean cut.

♦ Push the drill through to the opposite side of the goblet lining so that it is parallel to the top rim, and then begin drilling through the other side (*see* Fig 11.24).

♦ Stop when the spur point beings to show through on the outer surface of the goblet. Remove the drill, turn the work around and complete the drilling from the other side to give a good clean cut.

♦ Clean up the two holes, and then polish the goblet: I've come to like matt polyurethane varnish.

♦ Turn four loose rings from the same wood as the arrow, as described earlier.

♦ Fit the four rings on a supporting dowel, two inside the bowl and the other two one on either side of the bowl.

♦ Turn and carve the arrow as before. Boil the arrowhead, compress and leave to set.

♦ When the head is compressed and dry, bring it to the goblet and use it to push the supporting dowel through the holes and in its turn threading through the loose rings.

♦ When all the loose rings are in place the arrowhead can be submerged in a cup of boiling water. Hold back the closest loose ring whilst the head expands.

♦ When the head is dry, carve to a convincing shape.

CHAPTER 12

TUNBRIDGE YO-YO

Y O-YOS, I UNDER-
STAND, ARE
DERIVED FROM A
KOREAN WEAPON.
I HAVE NOT BEEN
ABLE TO VERIFY
THIS, BUT THE
PRINCIPLE SEEMS QUITE SOUND: A
HEAVY MISSILE ABLE TO BE AIMED
AT THE HEAD OR OTHER VULNERA-
BLE PARTS, RETURNING WHEN ITS
LETHAL JOB IS DONE.

This yo-yo, with its Tunbridge stickware
inset, is for pleasure only, both in the making
and using (*see* Fig 12.1). The stickware, first
developed in Tunbridge Wells in the late
eighteenth century (*see* Fig 12.2), is a
challenge in itself and very satisfying when
complete. It is made up of a variety of sticks,
all short-grained so that the long grain will
be shown on its exposed end face, some
triangular in section, others diamonds and

yet others square. They are cut at angles of
30°, 60°, 45° and 90°. For the long tall
triangles, eight of which make an octagonal
centre, 67.5° is the angle used for cutting.
The sticks are fixed together with the
geometric pattern running their length like
letters through a stick of rock. Take slice
after slice, and each will match the other: a
very early form of mass production.

To cut these triangular and diamond
section parts I have had a small circular saw
with tilting table made (note that in the
photographs the riving knife and guard have
been removed so that the process can be seen
clearly). The table can be accurately set to
cut the angles described above (*see* Fig 12.3).
If you have a bandsaw or circular saw, then
tilt the table to the correct angle. If the table
is fixed, make up a series of angled wooden
blocks (false tables) to hold the work while
cutting.

Tony Archer, the most talented and

Fig 12.1 The yo-yo and the stickware block.

Fig 12.2 *Some antique pieces of Tunbridge stickware: tape measure, pin wheel, pricker and old stickware block.*

Fig 12.3 *The saw set up to cut the diamond section pieces. Note that the guard has been removed to show the process.*

expert bone turner I have met, told me of a repair he had been asked to make on an antique piece of Tunbridge stickware, which was a yo-yo. It was quite rare and valuable, so he took his time carefully cutting, matching and fitting the pieces that were missing. It was a perfect match, so he told me, but when completed he could not resist trying it out. With the first spin the centrifugal force threw it into hundreds of bits, leaving him with an almighty puzzle, as the repaired pieces were the only ones to stay put. A job which should have taken a few days took three weeks to complete.

This yo-yo, newly made and fixed together with fresh glue, should not give way under use. I have given one I produced a lot of hard work, and it is still in good order. The preparation for this project is far longer than the actual production.

The stickware block

I will describe here the woods I used, but others of a similar colour may be substituted.

◆   For the centre star prepare two pieces planed all round, one of mahogany, the other

of cherry, each 45cm (18in) long by 100mm (4in) wide by 6mm (¼in) thick.
◆   Set the saw to cut at 45°.
◆   Take one slice off the 100mm end of one of the pieces. Measure the length of the cut; it should be around 8mm (⅜in), but be exact. Using this measurement, set the fence that distance away from the base of the saw – where it shows through the saw table.

Fig 12.4 Eight diamond section sticks are fixed together to form the centre of the block.

◆ Push the wood through the blade again, supporting it squarely with a mitre-guide, and this will produce a diamond section short-grained stick 100mm (4in) long. Each of the sides of the diamond will be the same size.

◆ Cut a total of six mahogany and six cherry pieces, which allows two of each for spares.

◆ Gluing the star together, work just in pairs: take one cherry and one mahogany piece. Run PVA glue down one side grain edge of the cherry piece. Push the side grain edge of the mahogany piece so that the two form a V shape, and then rub the joint together until the glue stiffens and holds. Make sure the edges of both pieces line up, and take care handling these parts, as they are short-grained and quite delicate.

◆ Hold the pieces together in an elastic band while working on the next three sets.

◆ Now take two pairs, remove the elastic bands and fit them together so that they form half the star pattern and the wood colours alternate. Glue the parts together, making sure the flat side is truly flat. Rub the joint until the glue stiffens and grips.

◆ When the two halves of the star are glued, spread glue on to the two flat sides and join together. Make sure that the colours alternate and that the centre of the star is perfectly matched. Take four elastic bands and tightly wrap them around the star shape, being careful to avoid slippage and always re-adjusting if there has been any (*see* Fig 12.4).

The eight square sections can be prepared while the centre star is drying. If you use

Fig 12.5 The black-and-white laminated veneers are cut.

solid wood for these parts, remember to cut short grain. Here I have used a chequerboard pattern for half the number of squares, and turu for the remainder; this is a wood from a form of palm growing in Guyana and was last used to any great extent in Victorian times as a novelty wood, often in Tunbridge stickware pieces. Turning turu has been likened to turning a bundle of straw – but the finished effect is far better.

◆ To produce the chequerboard pattern, cut 16 sheets of sycamore veneer and 16 sheets of black dyed sycamore veneer, all 150mm (6in) long by 100mm (4in) wide.

◆ Glue the sheets together, two light, two dark, into a stack; the double thickness makes the squares more clearly visible when cut. Clamp the stack firmly between two boards to keep it completely flat, remembering to place some polythene sheeting between the stack and the boards to prevent the whole gluing into one solid mass.

◆ Allow the glue to set overnight, and then take 1mm (¹⁄₂₄in) slices from the block across the width (*see* Fig 12.5); 32 slices are needed to produce four sticks (the exact size of cut relates to the thickness of one light band in the stack).

◆ Take one slice and flip it over, then stack the next on top; flip the next, stack the next, repeating until eight layers are made. The chequerboard pattern will be seen when the end is viewed, and any misplaced pieces can be readjusted. Glue the layers together, align exactly, and clamp firmly. Make four sticks in this manner.

◆ Leave the sticks to glue firmly before returning to the star centre. The elastic band clamp should be removed and the inner channels cleaned of any excess glue, leaving a good clean 90° angled corner at each of the eight intersections.

Both the turu squares and the chequer squares must fit exactly into these angled channels, so, remembering the exact measurements of the side of the diamond shape, cut the square sections so that their sides match the diamond's sides. Take care to leave, where possible, full edge sections when cutting the chequered block. The turu, unlike the other woods mentioned, should be cut long-grained, as it is the end grain which is the most interesting.

◆ Glue the turu and chequer squares alternately into place in the angled channels,

Fig 12.6 The chequerboard and turu squares fitted in place, with an outer rim of diamond section parts.

running the joints again until the glue stiffens and grips. Line up the ends of the squares with the ends of the star pattern, and then use elastic bands to clamp the whole together.

◆ For the eight outer diamonds I used walnut sapwood, a creamy yellow colour, preparing it to the same dimensions as the first pieces and cutting the diamond section pieces to exactly the same size.

◆ When the squares have firmly set in place, the elastic bands can be removed. The glue in the outer channels should be cleaned out before gluing the eight diamond sections into place, with elastic bands again hold them firmly in place (*see* Fig 12.6).

It will be noticed that the 'stick' now has an octagonal shape. It may look a little untidy and one or two joints may not appear to fit accurately, but when the piece is completed and a section trimmed off, it is always surprising to see how well the whole piece fits together and how accurately the joints fit.

The outer rim of triangles can now be cut and fitted.

◆ Set the saw to cut accurately at 67.5°.
◆ Take one slice from the remainder of the cherry and mahogany from which the diamond sections were cut, and flip the piece over, sliding it so that the saw lines up to trim a triangular section to the full thickness of the wood from the end of the piece. Set the fence to repeat the cut, and cut triangular sections of short-grained pieces, flipping the piece to cut another. Repeat the operation until 24 triangles of each wood are cut, with a few extras allowed for, in case of breakage.

◆ When the glue has set on the 'stick', remove the elastic bands and clean up the outer surface.

◆ Begin applying the triangular section sticks alternately to the outer edge; one cherry, one mahogany. Start at one corner of the octagonal shape, with the first triangular piece base down. The next piece will fit apex down, and so on. Glue all the jointing parts.

◆ Stop when two edges of the octagonal block have been covered. Line every triangular block up square, pushing the joints together firmly and then keeping in place with elastic bands. Allow the glue to grip (PVA will need half an hour) before moving on to the next two edges.

◆ Slowly work round section by section, gluing, cramping and stopping, until all sides have been covered. Finally clamp the block with elastic bands, setting it aside for the glue to dry thoroughly (*see* Fig 12.7).

Fig 12.7 The outer triangles glued in place and firmly held with elastic bands.

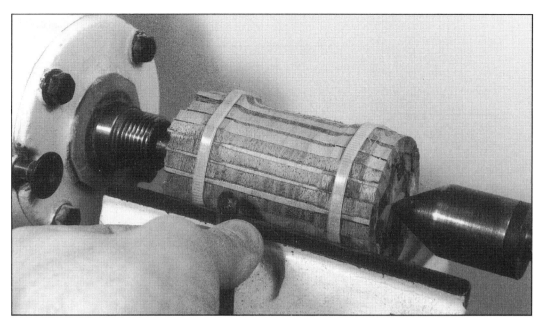

Fig 12.8 The stickware block, bound for safety, is turned.

For this stickware block to fit into the yo-yo wood surround, it must be circular in section, not octagonal, so turn it round between centres. Be careful to make the driving dog grip the work and not split it. Also, and most importantly, make sure that the driving dog and revolving centre are exactly on centre. Do not proceed until the block is central.

◆ Be cautious when turning, for if there is a sudden grab or knock there is always the possibility that it may fly apart. So, using cable ties, bind the work firmly, and with the lathe running at 1000 rpm, turn a centre portion round (*see* Fig 12.8). Move the ties to the turned section, tighten them, and then turn the remaining section round and parallel-sided. Measure the diameter of the work: this piece is 52mm (2¹⁄₁₆in) diameter.

◆ The final operation for the stickware is to cut slices from its end: the first slice should remove the waste only, to reveal the clean finished section. Cut at least two sections 6mm (¼in) thick, one for each side of the yo-yo.

Preparing the yo-yo

◆ A cross section view is shown in Fig 12.9.

◆ Lathe speed 1250 rpm.

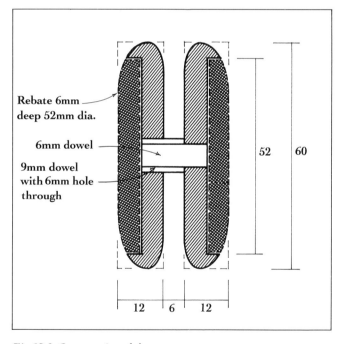

Rebate 6mm deep 52mm dia.

6mm dowel

9mm dowel with 6mm hole through

52 60

12 6 12

Fig 12.9 Cross-section of the yo-yo.

◆ Cut from a piece of English walnut, 150mm (6in) long by 75mm (3in) wide and 12mm (½in) thick, two discs each 75mm (3in) diameter.

◆ Drill a 9mm (⅜in) hole 6mm (¼in) deep at the centre of each disc.

◆ Turn up two 9mm (⅜in) diameter dowels, each 12mm (½in) long. The first has a 6mm (¼in) hole drilled 9mm (⅜in) deep into one end, and the other has a 6mm (¼in)

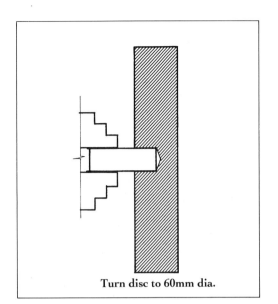

Turn disc to 60mm dia.

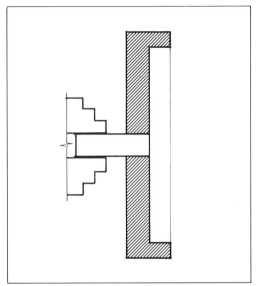

*Fig 12.11
Turn a 52mm
diameter
hollow 6mm
deep into the
face of the disc.*

diameter spigot 6mm (¼in) long, turned at one end.

◆ Glue the dowels into the drilled holes in the walnut discs, leaving the drilled hole in one and the turned spigot on the other, facing out.

Beginning the work

◆ Hold the dowel end of one face of the yo-yo disc in a three- or four-jaw chuck. Bring up the tailstock holding a revolving centre, and use it to support the face of the walnut disc. Carefully turn the outer diameter of the disc, taking light cuts so that any twisting forces put upon the central dowel are not too great. Turn the outer diameter to exactly 60mm (2⅜in), as shown in Fig 12.10.

◆ With the revolving centre still supporting the face of the walnut disc, begin to cut a 52mm (2¹⁄₁₆in) diameter rebate 6mm (¼in) deep (*see* Figs 12.11 and 12.12). Cut

Fig 12.12 The face of the walnut disc is turned out to accept the stickware section.

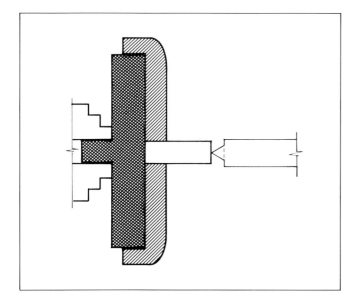

Fig 12.13 Work held on a jam-chuck.

Fig 12.14 The inner edge and face are turned before the stickware section is glued in.

Fig 12.15 The stickware disc is ready to be glued in. Note the jam-chuck.

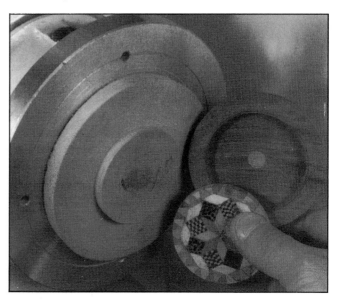

this accurately, as it has to accept the stickware disc with no visible gap.

◆ Remove the tailstock to complete the excavation of the rebate. Test the stickware disc, and fit it accurately. Repeat the process for the second walnut disc.

◆ Before the stickware parts are glued in place, turn a jam-chuck 52mm (2¹⁄₁₆in) diameter, on to which will fit the walnut disc.

◆ Bring the tailstock with revolving centre up to support the dowel end so that the internal face of the yo-yo may be turned to shape (*see* Fig 12.13). A slight angle near the outer edge will ensure that the string will slip between the two internal faces evenly (*see* Fig 12.14).

Take great care with these two walnut parts; they must match exactly, and must be balanced, otherwise the finished yo-yo will not spin evenly. Whatever is turned off one part must be turned off the other.

◆ Clean and polish the internal faces.

◆ Reverse the pieces in the lathe, again holding the dowel in the chuck. Glue the stickware section in place, pressing home with the revolving centre (*see* Fig 12.15).

◆ When the glue has set, lightly turn the stickware face to a nice gentle curve, turning into the walnut surround (*see* Fig 12.16). Be aware of the possibility of a heavy cut

twisting the dowel off. Again, shape both halves exactly the same.

◆ When the two halves are complete, fit them together to check that they match. Remove, apply glue, then push them together and lightly clamp, making certain that the two internal faces are parallel. Do not put too much glue on to the dowels, as it is difficult cleaning off the squeeze-out down between the two halves of the yo-yo.

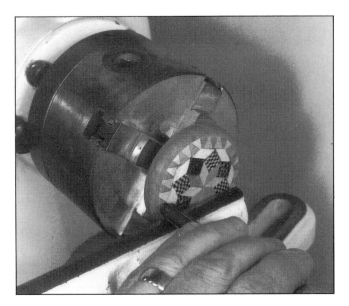

Fig 12.16 The outer face is turned to shape.

Glossy shining pieces are attractive to children, so I finished this piece with gloss polyurethane. It is a hard-wearing finish, and the piece will hopefully get plenty of hard wear. String it up and try it out.

Stickware designs are almost endless, as shown in Fig 12.17. This piece has used only 45°, 67.5° and 90°, working on an octagonal shaping. 60° and 30° cuts produce hexagonal pieces. If you are really keen to see part of the huge range and the imaginative variation that the early craftsmen produced, a visit to the museum at Tunbridge Wells or the Pinto collection in the Birmingham City Museum and Art Gallery will be worthwhile.

I am certain that not all the variations have yet been worked out. Experiment: there is so much to be discovered, and so many new ideas just waiting.

Fig 12.17 Some further uses of stickware.

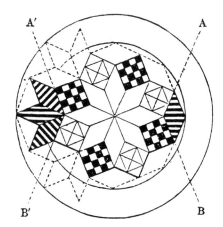

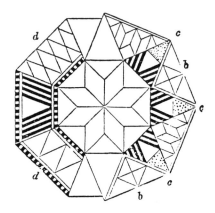

CHAPTER 13

STACKING CONE BOXES

ITH THESE STACK-ING BOXES I WANTED TO PRO-DUCE SOMETHING A LITTLE DIFFER-ENT AND MORE INTERESTING WITH WHICH TO EXPERIMENT. RUSSIAN DOLLS, JAPANESE DOLLS AND OTHER STACKING BOXES HAVE LITTLE OR NO FUNCTION: THEY ARE JUST PLEASANT TO LOOK AT. SO I DECIDED TO MAKE A SET OF CONE-SHAPED BOXES (*SEE* FIG 13.1).

Each box has laminations for decoration. The largest has two veneer lines which cross.

The second is made from a series of offset rings, twisting and slowly going from light to dark. The third has a rainbow of veneers. The fourth is plain yew and the fifth olive-wood, both woods attractive in themselves.

The preparation of these boxes takes a little time, and the turning is slow, but it all adds to the satisfaction when the work is completed. I would hope that the thinking and organisation needed, the viewing of the lamination as it is turned, the use of unusual chucks, will all add to a valuable experience.

The larger cone blanks are prepared first, working down to the smaller, but the smaller cones are turned first, working up to the larger. A cross section of the cone boxes is shown in Fig 13.2.

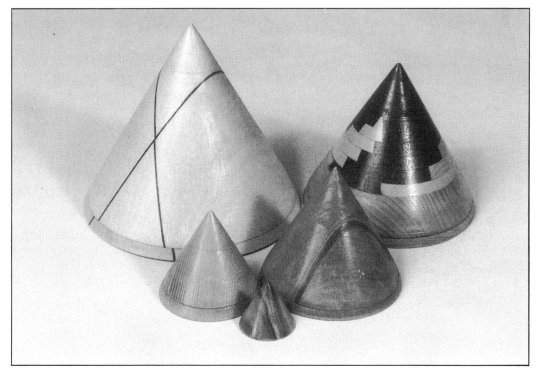

Fig 13.1 The set of stacking cone boxes.

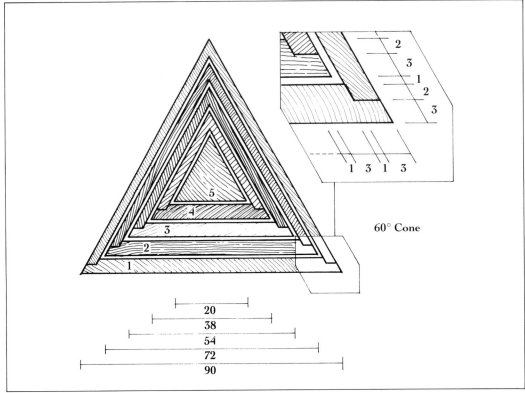

60° Cone

20
38
54
72
90

Fig 13.2 Cross section of the stacking cone boxes.

Preparation for cone 1

◆ The cone is made from sycamore, with two laminated padauk veneer lines.

◆ Cut a 150mm (6in) length of 100mm (4in) square of sycamore.

◆ Cut two pieces of padauk veneer (or any other dark veneer) 170mm (6¾in) long by 100mm (4in) wide.

◆ Working on the side face of the block, measure along one edge 10mm (⅜in) from the end. Mark the point in pencil. From the same starting point measure 125mm (4⅞in) along the same edge, and from that point draw a line square to the side on the face, measuring in 65mm (2½in). Mark that point with a pencil. Join up the first and last points with a pencil line, continuing it until it runs off the edge.

◆ The angled pencil line is a guide for a bandsaw cut. Place the wood on the bandsaw and cut it.

◆ Having made the saw cut, carefully glue one angled face, applying a piece of the pre-cut padauk veneer to that surface. Apply glue to the top surface of the veneer, fitting the cut half of the sycamore back in place. Clamp the whole together, lining up the edges and sides so that the block is exactly as it was before the saw cut, with the veneer filling the area of the saw cut. Take care to ensure that the joint does not slip.

Fig 13.3 Dark veneers glued in the sycamore block.

◆ Once the glue has set, mark an angled line, using the above measurements on the side opposite that used before, which will make the newly sawn line bisect the previous saw cut.

◆ Carefully glue the second piece of padauk veneer between the two cut sycamore pieces, being very careful to align the parts (*see* Fig 13.3). It is essential that all the pieces are perfectly aligned, so the point where the veneers cross will have no 'step' in it.

◆ When the glue has set, put the part to one side.

Preparation for cone 2

Cone 2 is the most complex of all five boxes, but very rewarding when complete. It is made from old dark, dense, Cuban mahogany that had been waiting in the workshop for years just for this day, and some brand-new yew, which hadn't.

◆ Cut a piece of yew 110mm (4⅜in) long by 80mm (3⅛in) wide by 43mm (1¾in) thick.

◆ Cut a further piece of yew 90mm (3½in) diameter and 30mm (1¼in) thick.

◆ Cut two pieces of mahogany or other dark coloured wood 120mm (4¾in) long by 80mm (3⅛in) wide by 20mm (¾in) thick.

Fig 13.4 The Cuban mahogany glued firmly in place around the central yew block.

◆ Measure 15mm (⅝in) up from the base on one edge of the larger piece of yew. Join this point to the opposite top corner (110mm or 4⅜in up) across the 43mm (1¾in) face.

◆ Using a bandsaw, cut along the marked line, taking care to cut a true and straight line. If the line is uneven, clean it up with a plane, as it is very important that these joints are perfect and that the glue bonding is as good as possible.

◆ Glue one of the mahogany pieces to the

Fig 13.5 Turn this glued block with extreme care.

angled cut, clamping firmly and leaving to dry (*see* Fig 13.4). It is better to have the majority of the mahogany piece towards the thick end of the yew.

◆ When the glue has set, measure 15mm (⅝in) along the opposite edge to that measured before. Draw a vertical centre line up the middle of the yew, measuring 62mm (2½in) upwards. Joint the two points with a straight line, continuing through the glued mahogany piece.

◆ Cut the angled pencil line with a bandsaw, again taking care to cut a perfectly straight line and adjusting if required.

◆ Glue the second piece firmly in position.

The next stage needs particular care, for this very eccentric part is to be turned in the lathe (*see* Fig 13.5). For safety, ensure that all corners are deeply planed off so that there will be a minimum of bumps whilst turning, which could break weak joints apart. Make sure that safety goggles or glasses are worn (as they should be at all times). Turn with considerable care, taking light, gentle cuts. The lathe should be running at low speed 500 rpm to begin with. If you are at all uncertain of turning a piece like this, then laminate as for cones 1 or 3.

◆ Hold the yew at the headstock and the mahogany at the tailstock, and turn the piece between centres to 80mm (3⅛in) maximum diameter, cautiously turning the rest to a slight taper until rounded. The partial conical shape will be seen to have two dark outer sides and a light wedge of yew inside.

◆ Turn a 9mm (⅜in) diameter spigot 9mm long at the tailstock end.

◆ Turn just the yew part to a 25mm (1in) diameter spigot at the headstock end.

◆ Turn six grooves from the large diameter at the headstock, leaving six ridges. Measure 5mm (¼in), then a groove a little wider than the parting tool you are using. Measure another 5mm (¼in) ridge followed by a groove, continuing in this way to the tailstock (*see* Fig 13.6). The groove is not deep at this stage.

◆ Reverse the piece in the lathe, exchanging the driving dog for a three- or four-jaw chuck. Hold the 9mm (⅜in) spigot in the chuck, bringing the revolving centre up to locate the centre point at the tailstock while tightening the jaws. This should ensure concentricity.

Fig 13.6 Having turned the laminated block to a cone shape, part off the parts needed.

◆ Remove the revolving centre and replace it with a drill chuck.

◆ Take a 12mm (½in) sawtooth drill, and mark a point 65mm (2⅝in) from its cutting tip on its shank.

◆ Drill to the marked point.

◆ Remove the drill and chuck, and replace them with the revolving centre. Fit the revolving centre into the drilled hole for support.

◆ Part off the 25mm (1in) diameter yew spigot.

◆ Bring up the revolving centre into the hole, and face off the end. Part off the disc, cleaning up the inner face at the same time. Repeat until all discs are cut and the conical top remains with the end faced off (*see* Fig 13.7).

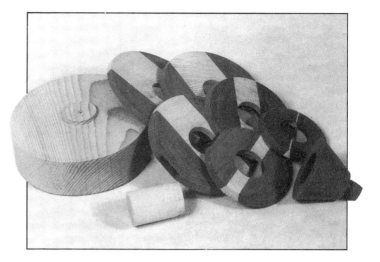

Fig 13.7 The parts ready for reassembly.

It is important that each of the parted off discs have flat and square faces top and bottom, so that when they are rejoined they go together precisely.

◆ Turn the 90mm (3½in) diameter piece of yew between centres, so that at the tailstock end a 3mm (⅛in) long, 12mm (½in) diameter stub spigot is turned. Also turn up from

'scrap' a 12mm (½in) diameter, 35mm (1⅜in) long dowel, which will be used to fix all the parts together whilst gluing.

◆ Place the yew base on the work bench, applying glue to the area around the spigot and on the spigot itself. Lay the largest ring over the spigot, and press down firmly. Glue the top surface of the ring and inside the hole, pushing the turned dowel into the hole.

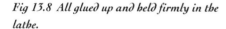

Fig 13.8 All glued up and held firmly in the lathe.

Fig 13.9 A series of veneers ready to be glued between the two blocks.

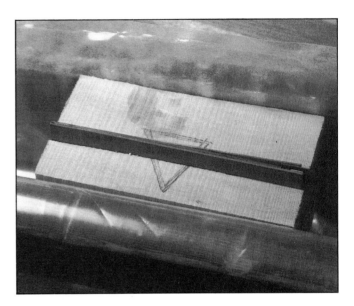

Fig 13.10 The 'rainbow' veneers glued and cramped in place.

Bring the next largest ring, slip it over the dowel and press down firmly, having rotated it so the pattern has shifted halfway over the pattern beneath. Continue gluing each disc in place, rotating each slightly so that the whole pattern has a twist in it. Finally glue on the mahogany top.

◆ Fit the piece back in the lathe, with the yew part held on the driving dog at the headstock and the revolving centre tightened on to the mahogany end, clamping the parts together whilst the glue dries (*see* Fig 13.8).

Preparation for cones 3, 4 and 5

◆ Cut a piece of wood (in this case wild service) 100mm (4in) long by 60mm (2⅜in) square.

◆ Cut four pieces of various dyed veneers each 100mm (4in) long by 60mm (2⅜in) wide. The colours I chose were deep red, blue, orange and pale green. More veneers may be used if wanted, but less makes the pattern a little thin.

◆ Take a 20mm (¾in) slice from one edge of the wood for the full length of the prepared block. Mark a pencil line across the block before the cut is made, to act as a datum when gluing back together (*see* Fig 13.9).

◆ Before the strips of veneer are glued together into the block, make sure that clamps are open and ready to take the glued part and that the parts are set out so that they can be correctly positioned as the gluing progresses.

◆ Apply PVA glue to one side of the wood and place a piece of veneer upon that surface. Glue the top part of that veneer, spreading evenly, then apply the next veneer. Continue until all the veneers are in place and the final piece of wood has been glued on top.

◆ Check that the datum mark is lined up, then clamp up firmly. If clamping up in a wood vice, place polythene sheeting over the jaws to prevent the whole mass sticking together (*see* Fig 13.10). The preparation for cone 3 is now complete.

◆ Cones 4 and 5 are plain wood – for cone 4 cut a piece of yew 75mm (3in) long by 50mm (2in) square. For cone 5 cut a piece of olive wood with a nice bold grain, 50mm (2in) long by 30mm (1¼in) square.

◆ A simple wood hub chuck should be made to internally shape the cones. Begin with a block 80mm (3⅛in) long by 110mm (4⅜in) square. Fix the block centrally on to a faceplate and turn as close to 110mm (4⅜in) diameter as possible. As each cone needs to be supported, an internal conical shape to suit each size will be turned. The conical part will be held in the matching conical hollow with double-sided tape.

◆ To shape the final deep point of both the hub chuck and the inside of the conical boxes, a simple tool is ground from a 9mm (⅜in) wide wood chisel. To ensure that the marking out is visible, cover the surface of the chisel with white correction fluid, and then mark upon that surface in pencil (*see* Fig 13.11). With the tool facing away and the flat side uppermost, measure 15mm (⅝in) from the cutting edge down along the left-hand side. Join that point with the top right-hand corner of the chisel's cutting edge. Grind away the angled part to the left of the line, leaving a pointed tool which will exactly fit the internal shaping of the cone point (*see* Figs 13.12 and 13.13). Be careful to cool the tool regularly while grinding.

◆ Note that part of the angled edge of the tool has been ground back so that only a small part will make cutting contact with the work. This will help to avoid the tool being 'snatched' by the revolving work. The remaining angled end to the point is undercut, grinding to a cutting edge.

Turning cone 5

◆ Simply turn this cone between centres from the prepared piece.

◆ Place the wood between centres. Turn to an exact 20mm (¾in) diameter.

◆ Turn a 15mm (⅝in) long 9mm (⅜in) diameter spigot at the tailstock end.

◆ From that shoulder measure 17mm (¹¹⁄₁₆in), parting off from that point (*see* Fig 13.14).

◆ Remove the driving dog from the headstock, replacing it with a three- or four-jaw chuck.

◆ Hold the turned spigot in the chuck.

◆ Turn down from the shoulder closest to the spigot, so that the work tapers from the 20mm (¾in) diameter to a point at the end, 17mm (¹¹⁄₁₆in) away (*see* Fig 13.15), cutting cleanly and accurately.

Using the hub chuck

◆ To clean the base of the olivewood cone, mark a 15mm (⅝in) diameter circle on the face of the hub chuck (mark in pencil with the lathe on).

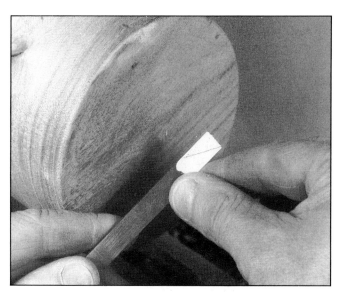

Fig 13.11 Mark out the special tool.

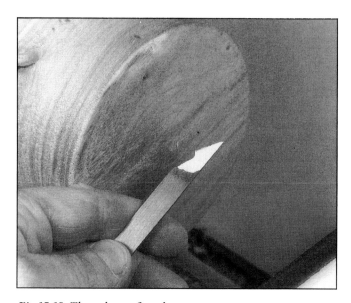

Fig 13.12 The tool ground to shape.

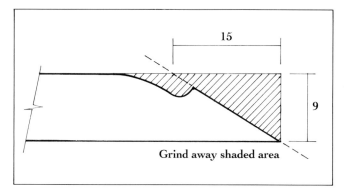

Fig 13.13 Make special tool from a 9mm wide wood chisel.

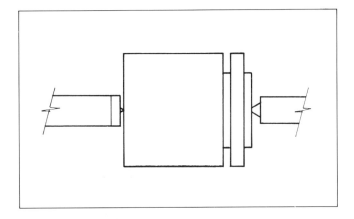

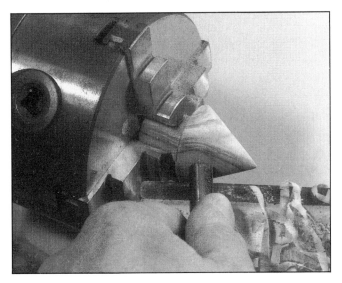

Fig 13.15 *The olivewood cone being turned.*

Fig 13.14 Turn and part off base.

◆ Measure 13mm (½in) from the tip of the point tool, marking this position upon its surface.

◆ Using this tool, make small cuts beginning at the centre, and open out the conical shaping until the 13mm (½in) depth and the 15mm (⅝in) diameter are reached (*see* Fig 13.16).

◆ The resulting conical hole will be a good fit for the olivewood cone. Adjust if necessary. It will be noticed that the cone does not fit to its full depth; this is to enable it to be pulled free once the base has been turned.

◆ Fix pieces of double-sided tape equally spaced around the conical surface.

◆ Using the revolving centre in the tailstock, push the cone into the matching hole. The centre not only pushes the tape up firmly, but ensures that the cone will be centrally located and the base will run true.

◆ Leaving the revolving centre in place, begin turning the base flat and true, undercutting the spigot. Complete by turning off the spigot, withdrawing the tailstock and centre, and bringing the toolrest across the

Fig 13.16 The special ground tool is used to cut the final pointed hollow for the olivewood cone in the hub chuck.

Fig 13.17 The base part is turned on the yew block.

work. Then finish the base fully and flatly.

◆ Pull the end of the cone firmly to remove it from the hub chuck. When the amount of pull needed to remove the cone from the chuck is experienced, more confidence will be given to the ability of the chuck to hold the work firmly.

◆ Remove all tape from the cone surface and the chuck.

Turning cone 4

◆ The yew cone is not solid like the olive wood cone, but is a hollow box to accept the smaller cone.

◆ Take the prepared piece of yew, place between centres and accurately turn to 38mm (1½in) diameter.

◆ Measure 5mm (¼in) from the tailstock end, and at that point turn down to exactly 23mm (¹⁵⁄₁₆in) for twice the width of the parting tool that is being used.

◆ Again measuring from the tailstock end, mark a position 2mm (³⁄₆₄in) in and turn a step accurately to 23mm (¹⁵⁄₁₆in).

◆ Part off, leaving a 2mm (³⁄₆₄in) step 23mm (¹⁵⁄₁₆in) diameter at either side (*see* Fig 13.17). Lay this piece to one side.

◆ Accurately relocate the centre using the revolving centre.

◆ Remove the revolving centre and replace it with a drill chuck holding a 9mm (³⁄₈in) drill. Mark along the drill a distance of 9mm (³⁄₈in) from the cutting edge.

◆ Drill into the yew to the marked depth (*see* Fig 13.18).

◆ Remove the part from the lathe, gluing a 50mm (2in) long 9mm (³⁄₈in) dowel into the

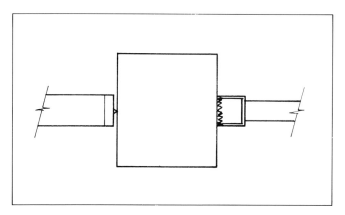

Fig 13.18 Drill hole to accept holding dowel.

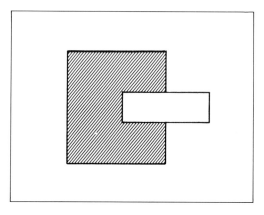

Fig 13.19 Dowel glued in place.

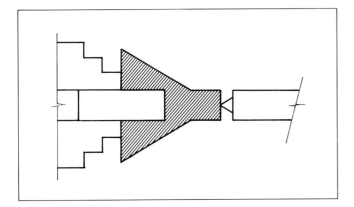

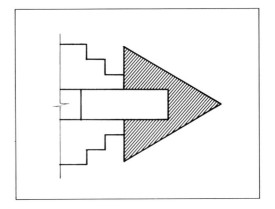

Fig 13.20 *Piece reversed and dowel hold in chuck.*

Fig 13.21 *Remove tailstock and turn the cone to a point.*

drilled hole (*see* Fig 13.19).

♦ Set aside until fully dry.

♦ Remove the driving dog from the headstock, replacing it with a three- or four-jaw chuck.

♦ Remove drill and chuck, and replace them with a revolving centre.

♦ Hold the yew piece in the three-jaw chuck, with it gripping the glued dowel. Leave a little gap between the shoulder of the work and the chuck jaws. Bring up the tailstock to support the end of the work. Now turn the whole part down to 34mm (1⁵⁄₁₆) diameter; this small diameter is necessary to allow for the slope cut on the side of the cone.

♦ Measure 21mm (¾in) from the shoulder closest to the headstock towards the tailstock. At that point turn down to 9mm (⅜in) diameter, again towards the tailstock.

♦ Turn from the shoulder at the headstock down to the 9mm (⅜in) diameter, producing a perfectly straight sloping cut (*see* Fig 13.20).

♦ Part off the piece so that, measuring from the shoulder at the headstock end, it is exactly 29mm (1¼in) long. Withdraw the tailstock.

♦ Continue turning the 9mm (⅜in) area until the full cone shape is produced (*see* Fig 13.21).

♦ Remove the part from the lathe. Remove

Fig 13.22
Drill an initial hole for the yew cone in the hub chuck.

Fig 13.23 The yew cone is fitted into the prepared hollow in the hub chuck and held by double-sided tape.

the chuck, replacing it with the wood hub chuck.

Preparing the hub chuck to accept cone 4

◆ Drill a hole 9mm (⅜in) diameter 15mm (⅝in) deep into the hub chuck (*see* Fig 13.22).

◆ Mark in pencil on the face of the chuck a 26mm (1in) diameter circle.

◆ Carefully join the outer circle edge to the base of the drill hole with a straight angled cut. This will produce the start of a conical hole. Complete the inner point of the hole following the angled side using the prepared angled tool. This will also be useful practice for cutting the interior of the cone box.

◆ Test the yew cone in the shape, making adjustments where necessary.

Turning the inside of cone 4

◆ Cut the dowel from the base of the cone.

◆ Fix double-sided tape evenly around the surface of the cone.

◆ Press the cone evenly into the hub chuck, bringing up the tailstock to add pressure (*see* Fig 13.23).

◆ Remove the tailstock, bringing the toolrest across the base of the cone.

◆ Lightly face off the cone, then cut a 23mm (¹⁵⁄₁₆in) diameter, 2mm (³⁄₃₂in) deep internal step into the base (*see* Fig 13.24). Test the piece parted from the end into the hollow, adjusting for a good fit.

◆ Fit the parted piece on to the cone, with what was the inner face facing towards the tailstock. Turn the face of this part, but do not disturb the turned step. Support using the revolving centre if necessary (*see* Fig 13.25).

◆ Reverse the parted piece with the now cleanly turned face inside, so that the true

Fig 13.24 The joint line is cut into the base of the yew cone before it is hollowed out.

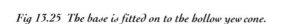

Fig 13.25 The base is fitted on to the hollow yew cone.

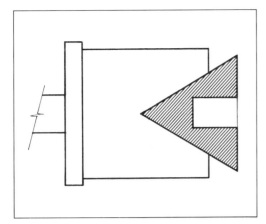

Fig 13.26 Section through the hub chuck holding the cone with starting hole drilled.

Fig 13.27 Section through the hub chuck showing internal shaping of cone complete.

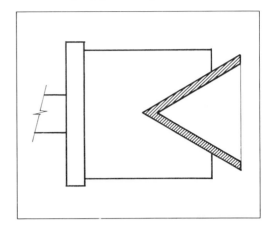

base can be fully cleaned off. Turn the true base completely flat, again supporting with the revolving centre if needed, removing the temporary step, which was used only for support while the inside face was turned.

◆ Remove the base, withdraw the tailstock and replace the centre with a drill chuck holding a 9mm (⅜in) drill.

◆ Drill a 9mm (⅜in) hole to a depth of 14mm (⅝in) – *see* Fig 13.26. Withdraw the tailstock and drill, bringing the toolrest back across the base of the yew cone.

◆ Taking light, fine cuts, using a small gouge or round-nose tool and the specially prepared angled tool, join up the step edge to the base of the drilled hole. This will provide the correct angle to be followed to complete

the internal cut down to an internal point (*see* Fig 13.27). The angled tool is particularly useful here.

◆ Test cone 5 inside the cone, fitting the base. If it does not fit, make adjustments to the internal shaping until it does.

◆ With cone 5 set to one side, replace the base, supporting it with the revolving centre.

◆ To complete the cone 4 box, bring the toolrest to the side of the work, turning the base so that it flows into the angled sides

Fig 13.28 Starting to turn the rainbow cone.

*Fig 13.29
The rainbow
cone turned
to shape.*

maintaining the slope of the cone protruding from the hub chuck.

◆ Turn off the lathe, and carefully and gently pull the cone shell from the hub chuck. Remove the tape from the chuck and the surface of the cone.

◆ The first cone box is now complete.

The remaining three boxes are turned in exactly the same manner, but the measurements are of course different.

Box 3

◆ Turn to 55mm (2³⁄₁₆in) diameter at the tailstock end.

◆ Turn a 2mm (³⁄₃₂in) step, 42mm (1¹¹⁄₁₆in) diameter at the tailstock end. A section 3mm (⅛in) wide is left full diameter, then a 2mm (³⁄₃₂in) step, again 42mm (1¹¹⁄₁₆in) diameter.

◆ Part off the shaped end, leaving both steps intact.

◆ Drill the end 9mm (⅜in) diameter, 12mm (½in) deep, then glue and fit a dowel as before.

◆ Hold the dowel in the chuck, supporting the other end with a revolving centre.

◆ From the shoulder at the headstock end measure 26mm (1in) towards the tailstock, and at that point turn down to 20mm (¾in) diameter. Turn the headstock end to precisely 50mm (2in) diameter. With a straight tapered cut, join the 50mm (2in) diameter to the 20mm (¾in) diameter (*see* Fig 13.28).

◆ Part off at 45mm (1¾in), measured from the shoulder at the headstock.

◆ Turn the remaining end at the tailstock so that it continues the angled sides of the cone, finishing in a point (*see* Fig 13.29).

Preparing the hub chuck for box 3

◆ Drill a 20mm (¾in) hole 20mm (¾in) deep into the hub chuck.

◆ Mark in pencil on the face of the chuck a 44mm (1¾in) diameter circle. Join this line to the edge of the 20mm (¾in) hole, cutting down to produce the correct internal slope. Complete the shaping, using the sides as a guide for the prepared angled tool.

Hollowing the interior of cone 3

◆ Cut the dowel flush to the cone face.

◆ Place small pieces of evenly spaced double-sided tape on the cone's sloping surface.

◆ Push the cone into the hollow, pressing home using the tailstock revolving centre.

◆ Turn a 2mm (³⁄₃₂in) 42mm (1¹¹⁄₁₆in)

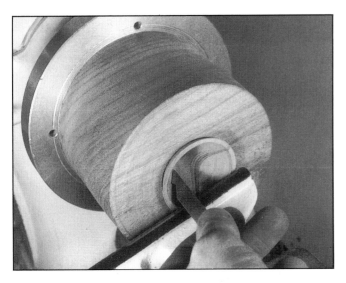

Fig 13.30 The inside of the rainbow cone is hollowed in the hub chuck.

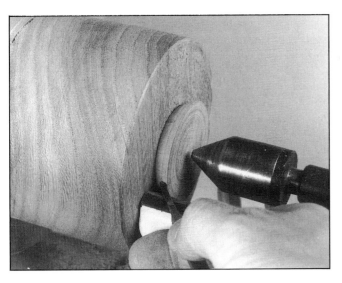

Fig 13.31 The edge of the base is turned to flow into the shaping of the side of the rainbow cone box.

diameter internal step into the base of the cone, fit the base and turn as before. Remove the base when finished.

◆ Drill into the cone with a 15mm (⅝in) drill, to a depth of 25mm (1in).

◆ Join the turned step to the base of the drilled hole, cutting down to produce the correct internal angle. Complete the shaping using the sides as a guide for the prepared angled tool (*see* Fig 13.30). Try the yew box inside to make sure that it fits, adjusting where necessary.

◆ Fit the base and turn the edge to make

the angled side continuous (*see* Fig 13.31).

◆ Remove from the chuck, cleaning off all double-sided tape.

Box 2

◆ Turn the prepared block, with the mahogany end held at the headstock, between centres to 72mm (2⅞in) diameter.

◆ Turn a 2mm (³⁄₃₂in) step at the tailstock, 58mm (2⁵⁄₁₆in) diameter, followed by 3mm (⅛in) full-size, then another step as before. Part off, leaving both steps complete.

◆ Remove the revolving centre and replace it with a drill chuck holding a 15mm (⅝in) drill. Drill to a depth of 15mm (⅝in). Glue in a dowel with its end protruding.

◆ Turn the piece around in the lathe, exchanging the driving dog for a three- or four-jaw chuck. Hold the dowel in the chuck, supporting the other end with a revolving centre.

◆ Measure 45mm (1¾in) from the shoulder at the tailstock, and at that point turn down to 15mm (⅝in) diameter. Turn down to 68mm (2¹¹⁄₁₆in) diameter at the headstock. Join with a sloping line the 15mm (⅝in) part at the tailstock to the major diameter at the headstock.

◆ Measure 60mm (2⁷⁄₁₆in) from the headstock, parting off at that point.

◆ Turn the end of the cone to a point flowing in with the angle of the side.

◆ Remove the chuck, replacing it with the wooden hub chuck.

Hub chuck for box 2

◆ Drill 20mm (¾in) diameter to a depth of 32mm (1⁵⁄₁₆in).

◆ Mark a 50mm (2in) diameter circle in pencil on the outer face.

◆ Join the 50mm (2in) circle to the base of the hole with a straight tapered cut.

◆ Complete the pointed end of the hole, following the angled sides and using the angled tool.

Turning the inside of cone 2

◆ Trim the dowel level with the base of the cone.

Fig 13.32 Double-sided tape fixed to the outside of the laminated cone box.

◆ Fix the cone in place, using double-sided tape (*see* Fig 13.32).

◆ Turn a 2mm (³⁄₃₂in) internal step, 58mm (2⁵⁄₁₆in) diameter.

◆ Fit and turn the base as before, and remove the base.

◆ Drill a 20mm (³⁄₄in) hole, 35mm (1³⁄₈in) deep.

◆ Join the stepped cut to the base of the hole with a straight angled cut. Continue the hole to an internal point with the angled tool, following the angle of the sides.

◆ Fit the base, turning it as before so that its side follows the angle of the side of the cone.

◆ Fit cone 3, adjusting hole shape if necessary.

◆ Remove from the chuck, taking off the double-sided tape from the cone and chuck.

Box 1

◆ Turn between centres to 90mm (3½in) diameter, with the part where the veneers come through the end of the wood at the tailstock.

◆ Turn a 2mm (³⁄₃₂in) step, 76mm (3in) diameter, 3mm (⅛in) full diameter, and another 2mm (³⁄₃₂) step, 76mm (3in) diameter at the tailstock end as before.

◆ Part off, leaving both steps complete (*see* Fig 13.33).

◆ Replace the revolving centre with a drill chuck holding a 15mm (⅝in) drill. Drill to a depth of 15mm (⅝in), gluing in a protruding dowel.

◆ When the glue has set, turn the piece around in the lathe, exchanging the driving dog for a three- or four-jaw chuck and the drill in the tailstock for a revolving centre. Hold the dowel in the chuck, and support the other end with the revolving centre.

◆ Turn to an exact 85mm (3⅜in) diameter

◆ Measure from the headstock 52mm (2¹⁄₁₆in), and at that point turn down to 25mm (1in) diameter (*see* Fig 13.34).

◆ Join the large diameter at the headstock to the 25mm (1in) diameter part with a straight tapered cut (*see* Figs 13.35 and 13.36).

◆ Measure 75mm (3in) from the headstock, parting off at that point. Continue

Fig 13.33 Turning the base of the sycamore box.

Fig 13.34 Starting to produce the cone shape.

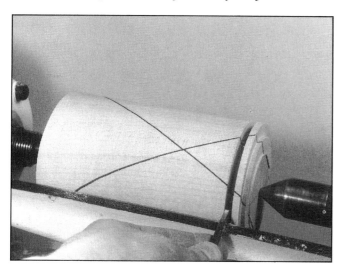

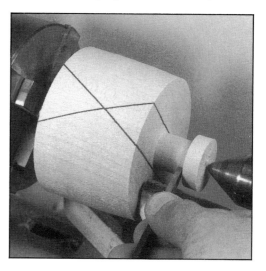

Fig 13.35
Turning down
the conical
sides.

Fig 13.36
Ready to turn
the point.

the tapered sides turning to a point – Fig 13.37 shows this cone being burnished with a handful of wood shavings.

Preparing the hub chuck for cone 1

◆   Drill into the hub to a depth of 40mm (1⁹⁄₁₆in), using a 25mm (1in) drill.
◆   Mark a 70mm (2¾in) diameter pencil circle on the face of the chuck.
◆   Turn a straight tapered cut from the pencil circle to the base of the drilled hole. Complete the pointed end of the angled

interior, following the slope of the side, with the angled tool.

Turning the inside of cone 1

◆   Trim the dowel level with the base of the cone.
◆   Apply double-sided tape evenly to the outer surface of the cone as before.
◆   Push the cone into the hub chuck, using the tailstock to apply even pressure.
◆   Turn a 2mm (³⁄₃₂in) internal step, 76mm (3in) diameter.

Fig 13.37 The point has been turned, and is burnished with a handful of shavings.

◆ Fit and turn the base as described for cone 4.

◆ Remove the base, and drill a 46mm (1¾in) deep hole, using a 25mm (1in) drill. Turn from the step to the base of the hole. Complete the internal conical hole using the angled tool, following the inner angled sides.

◆ Fit the base, and turn the edge to match the angled sides.

◆ Try cone 2 inside, fitting the base to make sure that the cone nestles snugly

Fig 13.38 The internal shaping checked with a card template.

inside. Adjust the internal shaping where necessary – Fig 13.38 shows the use of a template.

◆ Remove the hub chuck and all double-sided tape from the cone.

◆ I finished the cones with matt polyurethane varnish, as they will be handled frequently.

There are one or two points to consider: when turning the inside of the cone boxes, cut away little by little; as they are held inside the hub chuck by tape only, they can be 'snatched' out if the cut is too strong. Move the toolrest as far inside the hollow cone as possible to support the tool.

The hub chuck fit needs to be very good and ensure close contact; it can provide surprisingly good holding power. As an experiment, I turned the largest sycamore cone, held with the tailstock for additional support, using Blu-tak instead of double-sided tape. This had such a grip that it was very difficult to remove the cone when finished.

When turning the inside of inlaid or laminated cones, be careful, as the veneer inlay can sometimes grab the tool.

Keep the tools constantly sharp.

And finally, these pure, straight-sided cones are a wonder to handle, but can be really tricky if the joint between the base and top is too tight. It is then very difficult to get sufficient grip on the slick sloping sides to pull the base off.

CHAPTER 14

PHARAOH'S TOMB

HEN I TAUGHT WOODWORK, ONE OF THE PROJECTS I DEVISED FOR THE YOUNGER PUPILS WAS A SIMPLE MARBLE MAZE. THIS POPPED BACK INTO MY MIND WHILST I WAS TURNING SOME CONICAL SHAPES; THE TWO MELDED TOGETHER, AND OUT CAME THE THREE-DIMENSIONAL PUZZLE SHOWN IN FIG 14.1.

A series of drilled then plugged holes interlink inside the cone, to form a passage through the conical pyramid a little like the secret passages through the pyramids of Egypt. Place the ball bearing in the top hole and watch it disappear into the drilled chamber beneath (*see* Fig 14.2). Move the cone around to move the ball through the drilled tunnels to the exit hole at the base.

The ball can sometimes be heard rattling around inside, but where is it? Is it best to turn the pyramid to the right or to the left? Should it be turned upside down or sideways? Sometimes it appears at the start hole; other times it pops out of the exit. Whatever happens, it gives plenty of fun and pleasure, both in the making and in the using.

Preparation

◆ Have available a 6mm (¼in) ball bearing.
◆ Cut a 100mm (4in) cube from sycamore.
◆ Mark diagonals accurately to locate centres on the end grain faces of the sycamore cube.
◆ Mark one end grain face as the top, the

Fig 14.1 Pharaoh's tomb and intrepid ball bearing 'explorers'.

Fig 14.2 The ball bearing will be pushed into the hole and find its way through the internal passages.

Fig 14.3 Drilling the hole.

other as the base.

◆ Place the base down on the workbench, marking clearly the side facing the front as A, to its right face B, to the right face C and the remaining face D.

◆ Draw vertical centre lines down each face.

◆ Join these vertical centre lines across the base and top; they will run through the marked centre point.

◆ Have available the hub chuck used to turn the stacking cone boxes in Chapter 13.

◆ Cut a 60mm (2⅜in) long by 45mm (1¾in) square piece of sycamore for the top plug.

◆ Have ready some pieces of dark hardwood (I used rosewood) sufficient to turn five lengths 100mm (4in) long by 9mm (⅜in) diameter.

Drilling and plugging the holes

Hole 1

◆ At the top dead centre drill a vertical 9mm (⅜in) hole 75mm (3in) deep.

Hole 2

◆ Measure off face B 60mm (2⅜in) down the centre line from the top. At that point drill a 9mm (⅜in) hole at right angles to the

face 55mm (2¼in) deep (*see* Fig 14.3). Mark this position clearly as 2. This drilled hole will meet the first drilled hole.

Although the holes when drilled might be described as being at 'right angles to the face', it is far easier to arrange the block so that the hole can be drilled vertically. It is absolutely necessary that when each hole has been drilled it is cleared of sawdust by blowing through the hole, shaking, prodding, doing anything to release and remove any particles of wood left inside.

When the hole is clear, try the ball bearing in the passage: only when it makes its way easily through may the passage be sealed and the next hole drilled.

◆ Turn a dark hardwood dowel 25mm (1in) long and 9mm (⅜in) diameter. Chamfer the end of the dowel to fit into the hole.

◆ Glue the edges of the dowel (*see* Fig 14.4), fit it into hole 2 and hammer it down until level with the surface of face B.

When gluing the dowels, do **not** apply glue to the front end, where it may be forced down into the hole; this glue will set in the bottom of the hole, blocking the passage.

Be careful not to make the dowels so tight that they are difficult to push into place or so that any glue applied to the surface is

Fig 14.4 Fitting the plug.

squeezed off as the dowel is pushed into the hole. In the same vein, do not make the dowel too slack.

Hole 3

◆ Turn the sycamore block so that the base is uppermost. Measure on the centre line towards face D 15mm (⅝in) from the centre. At that point drill vertically down 60mm (2⅜in). This hole will meet up with hole 2. Remove the drill and clean out the sawdust as before; I used small angled riffler files to get around corners.

◆ Place the ball bearing in the start hole, and make sure that it runs freely and out of this hole, which should be marked as hole 3.

◆ When satisfied with the running, turn up a 30mm (1¼in) long, 9mm (⅜in) diameter dark wood dowel. Chamfer the end which will fit into the hole.

◆ Glue around the edges of the dowel and hammer it home until it is level with the base surface.

Hole 4

◆ Measure 40mm (1⁹⁄₁₆in) on face C, from the top down the centre line. Then measure 15mm (⅝in) horizontally towards face D. At that point drill square to the face 65mm (2⁹⁄₁₆in) deep, using a 9mm (⅜in) drill. This hole should meet hole 3; mark this new hole 4.

◆ Clean out the sawdust thoroughly and test with the ball bearing.

◆ Turn a 9mm (⅜in) dowel 40mm (1⁹⁄₁₆in) long from the dark wood, chamfering its end as before.

◆ Glue the dowel, hammering it until it is flush with face C.

Hole 5

◆ Measure 40mm (1⁹⁄₁₆in) on face B, from the top down the centre line. Measure 10mm horizontally towards face A.

◆ At this point drill 65mm (2⁹⁄₁₆in) deep at right angles to the face, marking this hole 5.

◆ Clean the sawdust out of the holes and test with the ball bearing.

◆ Turn a 30mm (1¼in) long, 9mm (⅜in) dowel, and chamfer its end.

◆ Glue the dowel, hammering it into the hole flush with face B.

Hole 6

◆ Turn the block so that the base is uppermost.

◆ Mark a line parallel to the centre line and on side A of the line, running from face B to D, 10mm (⅜in) away.

◆ Mark a line parallel to the centre line and on side B of the line, running from face A to C, 10mm (⅜in) away.

◆ Where the two lines intersect is hole 6; mark it as this.

◆ Drill vertically a 9mm (⅜in) hole, 70mm (2⅞in) deep. This will meet hole 5.

◆ Clean out the sawdust and test with the ball bearing.

◆ Turn a 25mm (1in) long, 9mm (⅜in) dowel, and chamfer its end.

◆ When you are certain that the runway is perfectly clear, glue and hammer the dowel in flush with the base.

Hole 7

◆ Measure 70mm (2⅞in) down the centre line from the top on face A. Then measure 10mm (⅜in) horizontally towards face B. At this point, mark hole 7 and drill a 9mm (⅜in) hole, 70mm (2⅞in) deep at 90° to the surface. This will meet up with hole 6.

◆ Clean out all the sawdust and test with a ball bearing. This is the last chance, so make sure all is clear.

◆ Turn a 30mm (1¼in) long, 9mm (⅜in) diameter dowel. Chamfer the end.

◆ Glue the dowel and hammer into hole 7 until it is flush with face A.

Hole 8

◆ Turn the base so that it is uppermost.

◆ Draw a line parallel to the centre line, running from B to D 15mm (⅝in) away, towards face C.

◆ Draw a line parallel to the centre line, running from face A to face C 10mm (⅜in) away, towards face B.

◆ At that point drill a 40mm (1½in) deep, 9mm (⅜in) hole. This will meet hole 7.

◆ Thoroughly clean out all sawdust, and then run the ball bearing through to test the hole. This is the most frustrating part yet, but you should be good at it by now.

◆ **Do not plug this hole**, as it is the exit hole.

All holes have now been drilled, and those which needed to be have been plugged. The internal ball bearing labyrinth is

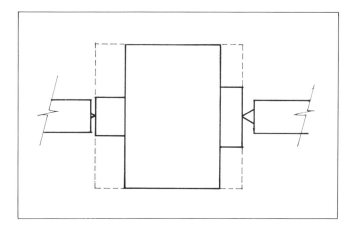

Fig 14.5 Turn a spigot at the headstock end.

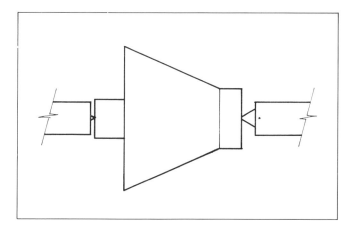

Fig 14.6 Turn down to part cone.

complete, and the conical shape can now be turned.

Preparation for the pyramid/cone

◆ Make sure that the centre is clearly marked on the base.
◆ Plane off all side corners in preparation for turning.
◆ Lathe speed 1000 rpm.

Turning

◆ Set the piece between centres, with the single drilled hole at the top centre supported by the revolving centre in the tailstock, and the driving dog located exactly on-centre at the base.
◆ Turn the whole cleanly to 95mm (3¾in) diameter.
◆ Measure in 20mm (¾in) from the shoulder at the headstock end, and mark a line around (see Fig 14.5).
◆ At this point turn that 20mm (¾in) width down to 25mm (1in) diameter.
◆ Measure in 15mm (⅝in) from the tailstock end, and turn down to an exact 40mm (1⁹⁄₁₆in) for the measured length.
◆ Join the larger diameter (95mm or 3¾in) at the headstock down to the start of the 40mm (1⁹⁄₁₆in) diameter at the tailstock with a straight sloping cut (see Fig 14.6).
◆ Remove this part from the lathe.
◆ Fit the 60mm (2½in) long by 45mm (1¾in) square piece of sycamore centrally

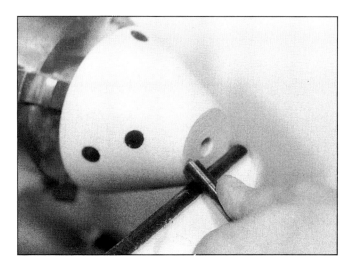

Fig 14.7 With the end block parted off, the partial cone held in a chuck has the end face turned square and true.

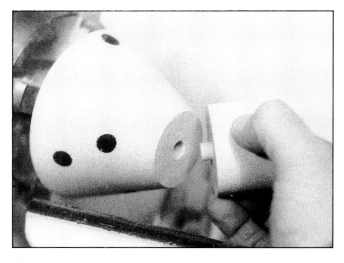

Fig 14.8 The end plug turned and about to be fitted.

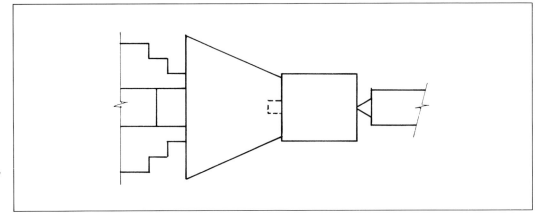

Fig 14.9 Fit end block into pre-drilled hole.

between centres.

◆ Turn as close to 45mm (1¾in) diameter as possible, with a 9mm (⅜in) diameter spigot, 9mm (⅜in) long at the tailstock end. The shoulder cut down to this spigot must be precisely square and flat.

◆ Remove this 'top' piece from the lathe, and exchange the driving dog for a three- or four-jaw chuck.

◆ Replace the larger turned part exactly the same way round in the lathe as it was before being removed. Support the central hole at the tailstock with the revolving centre while tightening the chuck jaws on the 25mm

(1in) turned end. This helps to ensure that the piece runs true.

◆ Once it is held firmly, part off the 40mm (1⅝in) part at the tailstock precisely square with the end face flat (*see* Fig 14.7).

◆ Take the newly turned 'top' piece and fit the turned spigot into the end hole, supporting the extreme end with the revolving centre (*see* Figs 14.8 and 14.9).

◆ Turn the majority of the side of this 'top' piece to follow the angled side of the larger cone (*see* Fig 14.10).

◆ Remove the cone and the partially finished 'top' from the lathe.

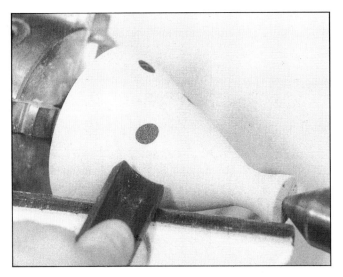

Fig 14.10 The end plug is being turned to flow into the conical shape of the main block.

Fig 14.11 The end plug in the chuck can be turned to a point.

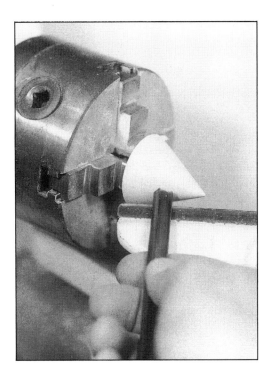

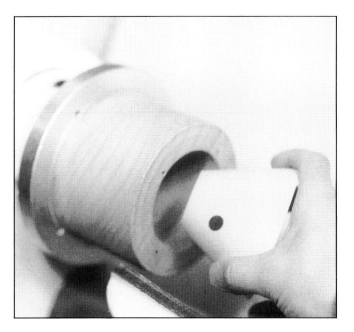

Fig 14.12 The base fitted into the prepared hub chuck.

Fig 14.13 The underside of the base is turned flat and the stub tenon turned off.

Fig 14.14 The base is turned flat and true.

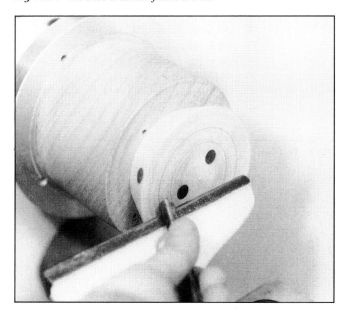

◆ Take the 'top' and hold the spigot in the three-jaw chuck to complete the turning of its conical end to a perfect point (*see* Fig 14.11).

Cleaning the base using the hub chuck

◆ Fit the hub chuck to the headstock.
◆ Turn or drill out a 40mm (1⁹⁄₁₆in) hole, 50mm (2in) deep.
◆ Mark in pencil on the face of the chuck an 80mm (3⅛in) diameter circle. Join the larger diameter to the base of the turned hole with a straight tapered cut.
◆ Fit the conical shape, with the top removed, into the hub chuck, making adjustments where necessary for a tight fit (*see* Fig 14.12).
◆ Fix the truncated cone into the chuck with double-sided tape, supporting the turned 25mm (1in) diameter end with the revolving centre.
◆ Turn the base of the cone square and true, turning away the spigot (*see* Figs 14.13 and 14.14).
◆ Remove the part from the hub chuck, taking off all pieces of double-sided tape.

Turning the feet

◆ Lathe speed 1500 rpm.
◆ From some of the remaining piece of the 9mm (⅜in) dark wood dowel, turn three feet, each with a 4mm (³⁄₁₆in) long, 4mm (³⁄₁₆in) diameter spigot; the main body begins at 9mm (⅜in) diameter and tapers to a point

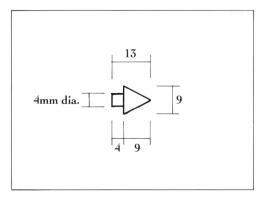

Fig 14.15 Turned feet.

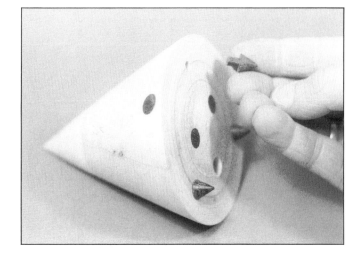

Fig 14.16 The turned feet are glued in place.

9mm (⅜in) away, as shown in Fig 14.15.

◆ Mark a 32.5mm (1¼in) radius circle on the cone base, using the dead centre of the base as the position to place a compass point.

◆ Leaving the compass set at the radius, 'walk' it around the marked circle. Mark the position for drilling at every second point; this gives three equidistant points.

◆ Drill a 4mm (³⁄₁₆in) hole, 4mm (³⁄₁₆in)

deep at these points; do not drill too deep, as a tunnel may be hit.

◆ Glue the feet into the drilled holes, having first cleaned off the pencil circle (see Fig 14.16).

The Pharaoh's tomb is now complete, and is shown in Fig 14.17. I finished the piece with a matt polyurethane.

Fig 14.17
The finished
piece.

LATTICE CIRCLES

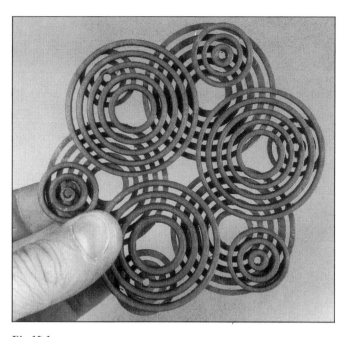

Fig 15.1
Lattice circles.

THIS INTRIGUING PIECE OF ECCENTRIC TURNING LOOKS QUITE FRAGILE, BUT IS MORE STURDY THAN IT APPEARS. IT IS TURNED FROM ONE PIECE OF WOOD, THE PARTS HOLDING TOGETHER ONLY WHERE THEY TOUCH (*SEE* FIG 15.1).

I first saw a similar piece to these lattice circles in a photograph of the work of a German turner born in 1855, one J. Saueracker. No explanation of how they were made was given.

If this is used as a turning exercise it will be found to be quick and relatively easy to produce, but the effect it can have upon the way of thinking about turned pieces is startling. The sudden realization that parts can be turned whilst others are left unturned, with areas cut through into one another and the overlapping of turned sections, causes all sorts of thought-provoking ideas to come to mind.

Besides the method described here –

completely opening both back and front – the solid 'webs' between the circles can be left in or, at the other extreme, all circles but those absolutely necessary to hold each to the other may be removed, leaving a skeletal structure.

Again, the choice of wood is important. A good, clear piece of close-grained wood is necessary. Here I have chosen applewood; this deep, dusky pink wood turns extremely cleanly and sharply, and it is a delight to turn, being moderately soft to cut.

Preparation

The basic preparation of the simple eccentric faceplate for these lattice circles follows.

◆   Measure the distance from the centre of your lathe to the lathe bed. If the distance is 100mm (4in) or more, then the work may be turned in the normal position at the headstock; if not, then the work will have to take place on the 'outboard' end of the lathe.

◆   Bandsaw a 20cm (8in) diameter circle from a 25mm (1in) thick piece of chipboard or MDF. Fix this to a faceplate centrally, and then fix on the lathe.

◆   If you are working over the lathe bed, slowly rotate the work by hand, making sure that it turns without hitting any part of the lathe bed or the toolrest.

◆   Turn on the lathe and turn the edge of the chipboard clean and true.

◆   Fix a drill chuck in the tailstock. Fit a 3mm (⅛in) drill into the chuck, then drill a hole through the centre of the chipboard circle.

◆   Remove the chipboard eccentric faceplate from the lathe and set it aside.

◆   Now turn three dowels 12mm (½in) long by 3mm (⅛in) diameter; these dowels will be used on the eccentric faceplate to locate the centre points.

◆   Turn a 50mm (2in) length, 9mm (⅜in) square of apple or similar close-grained wood down to round between centres.

◆ Take this piece and hold it in a drill chuck set in the headstock. Turn down 12mm (½in) of the unsupported end to 3mm (⅛in) diameter, and chamfer the end and part off the 12mm (½in) length. Repeat for the other two fine dowels.

◆ It is better to make these fine dowels marginally under the 3mm (⅛in) diameter than over, for when the workpiece hole is fitted on to them and the workpiece is turned finer, then tight-fitting dowels might become difficult to remove.

◆ Glue one of these fine dowels into the centre hole of the eccentric faceplate, leaving only 3mm (⅛in) showing.

◆ From a 6mm (¼in) wood chisel, grind a fine square-ended tool whose blade width will be 3mm (⅛in) for a length of 12mm (½in), as shown in Fig 15.2. Carefully grind the cutting edge square but to an angle of around 30°. Quench regularly to avoid overheating.

◆ Cut and plane the chosen wood to 30cm (12in) long by 100mm (4in) wide by 6mm (¼in) thick. Although it would be possible to work with wood straight from the bandsaw, it is far easier to work with planed wood, as then very little, if any, of the top surface will need to be turned away, ensuring a fully flat and true surface throughout the operation.

◆ The 30cm (12in) length is sufficient for three pieces, in case one is needed as a practice piece.

◆ Have ready 3 x 12mm (½in) No. 4 round-head screws and washers.

◆ Lathe speed around 750 rpm.

Marking the circles

Begin by marking accurately on to the 6mm (¼in) thick applewood the lattice circle

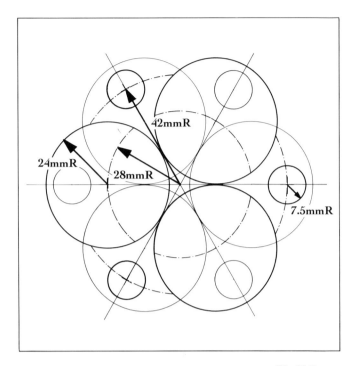

Fig 15.3
Layout for
lattice circles.

shapes shown in Fig 15.3.

◆ Draw a centre line down the length of the 100mm (4in) wide board.

◆ Set a pencil compass to 28mm (1⅛in) radius, positioning its point on the centre line 56mm (2¼in) away from the end of the board. Draw a 28mm (1⅛in) radius circle about that point.

◆ Place the compass point at the position that the circle crosses the centre line, and 'walk' the compass around the circle, giving six positions. The top one nearest the end of the board is 1, and working clockwise, the others will be 2, 3, 4, 5 and 6.

◆ Reset the compass to 24mm (1in) radius and draw circles this size at points 1 – 6.

◆ Reset the compass to 42mm (1⅝in).

Fig 15.2 Fine
square-end
tool.

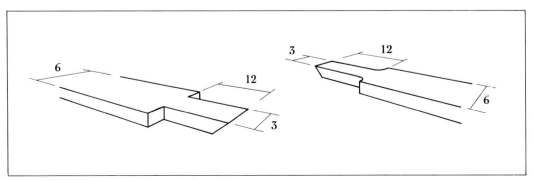

Place the compass point on the centre and draw a new circle. Where the larger circle cuts the centre line at the top end will be position A. Walk the compass around this new circle at its new setting to make six points in all, marking them from A clockwise, B, C, D, E and F.

Cutting the circles

◆ Bandsaw the outer shapes, carefully cutting on the waste side of the line (*see* Fig 15.4).

◆ Drill 3mm (⅛in) holes accurately at each of the points 1 to 6, A to F and the very centre (*see* Fig 15.5).

◆ Bring the eccentric faceplate to the workbench and place the cut shape on to it with the 3mm (⅛in) hole at point 1 over the dowel at the centre.

◆ Mark through positions F, B, 4 and D, being careful not to move the workpiece whilst doing this.

◆ Drill a 3mm (⅛in) hole at the point made through position D on the chipboard surface. Fit and glue one of the remaining 3mm (⅛in) dowels into this hole, leaving only 3mm (⅛in) showing above the surface.

◆ Make a small pilot hole to accept a No. 4 screw at positions F, B and 4.

◆ This practical method of locating the dowel and screw holes directly through the drilled holes ensures that any slight inaccuracies that might occur are worked out, and that the eccentric faceplate that you make will fit your piece of work.

◆ Reposition the cut shape in place, with hole 1 over the central dowel and hole D over the uppermost dowel. Fix screws with washers into holes F, B and 4, and tighten them down to secure the cut shape in position.

◆ Fix the faceplate on the lathe, bring the toolrest across and adjust it so that the 3mm (⅛in) square end tool's cutting edge is at centre height. Rotate the lathe by hand to make sure that nothing catches, for instance screwheads or the edge of the workpiece.

◆ Take the prepared 3mm (⅛in) square end tool; measure 3mm (⅛in) from its cutting edge back along the blade and mark this point with white typist correction fluid. This will mark the depth to which the tool will cut.

◆ When the lathe is turned on, it will be seen that the circle line around point 1 is clearly visible, but the rest of the work is a blur. Take the 3mm (⅛in) square end tool and position it on the toolrest so that the circle line is exactly in the middle of its cutting edge.

◆ Gently push the tool into the work, moving it very slightly side to side with an almost imperceptible motion, more like a nervous shake but sufficient to widen the groove that minute amount to stop the groove edges gripping the tool. Cut until the white mark on the tool surface is level with

*Fig 15.4
Cutting out
the shape.*

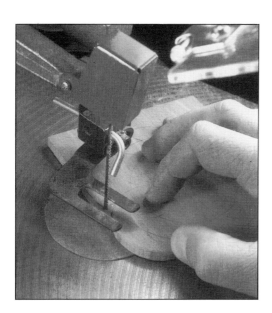

*Fig 15.5
Drilling the
centre holes.*

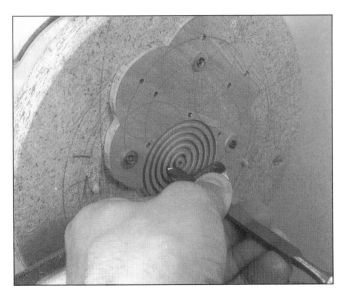

Fig 15.6 Turning the concentric circles with the majority of the work offset.

the top surface of the workpiece.

◆ Remove the tool and turn off the lathe. Measure 3mm (⅛in) bare from the last cut towards the centre of rotation, and mark this clearly in pencil. Mark the line fully as the work rotates.

◆ Bring up the tool and position it so that its edge is on the pencil line, and again cut a 3mm (⅛in) deep groove, widening it very slightly as before.

◆ Repeat the process until the outer edge and three grooves have been cut (*see* Fig 15.6.).

◆ Take particular care to slightly widen the final groove, as the central part is so small and fine that there may be short grain, causing it to break out with the slightest pressure.

◆ Round over the edge of each ridge, remove the toolrest and glasspaper any uneven or lifted edges with care.

◆ Turn off the lathe, undo the screws and remove the workpiece from the eccentric chuck.

◆ Reposition the wood, with hole 3 over the central dowel and hole F over the top dowel; screw it down using prepared screwholes; the odd numbered holes only fit over the centre dowel on this side.

◆ Repeat the process, cutting grooves as before (*see* Fig 15.7 for a simple template for making and checking the grooves). When complete, remove the workpiece and

reposition it with hole 5 on the central dowel and hole B on the top dowel. Screw down, and cut grooves as before.

◆ Remember to sharpen the tool regularly, and also check that the white correction fluid mark is adjusted if necessary (*see* Fig 15.8).

Cutting the secondary circles

◆ The centres for the secondary circles are marked A – F; it will now be necessary to position the remaining dowel and relocate the screwholes for this new placing of the workpiece on the eccentric chuck.

◆ Take the workpiece and place hole B upon the central dowel (the cut face still showing forward). Turn the workpiece so that it is 180° away from the top dowel already in place.

◆ Mark through position 5 to locate the new dowel, and positions A, C and E to locate the screwholes.

◆ Accurately drill a 3mm (⅛in) hole at the point marked under position 5, and drill pilot holes to take a No. 4 screw at the position marked under points A, C and E.

◆ Glue the 12mm (½in) long, 3mm (⅛in) diameter dowel into the drilled top hole, leaving only 3mm (⅛in) showing.

Fig 15.7 The template for marking ridges and grooves.

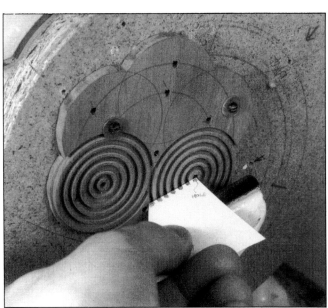

Fig 15.8 The fine square-ended tool.

Fig 15.9 Turning the three outer circles.

◆ The eccentric faceplate is now ready to accept the workpiece to turn the secondary circles.

◆ Sharpen the tool and check the white depth mark.

◆ Place the workpiece so that position B is over the central dowel and 5 on the new top dowel, and screw it firmly down, with the grooved surface facing out.

◆ Bring up the toolrest, adjusting it so that the tool cuts at centre height. Rotate the faceplate by hand to make sure nothing catches.

◆ Measure 11mm (just under ½in) from the centre of the drilled hole at position B, marking that position in pencil.

◆ Rotate the work by hand, holding the pencil at that point and drawing a circle on the workpiece. It will be seen that the circle will touch or nearly touch one part of the outer edge of the workpiece.

◆ Turn on the lathe, positioning the tool so that it will cut on the outer edge of the marked circle to the depth of 3mm (⅛in) (*see* Fig 15.9).

◆ Mark a point 3mm (⅛in) towards the centre from the first cut, and again cut a groove at that position to the depth of 3mm (⅛in), using the white mark on the tool as a guide.

◆ Take care to widen this groove so that

the centre part does not break out.

◆ Carefully round over the top edges of the ridges, remove the toolrest and rub any lifted or feathered edges with glasspaper.

◆ Turn off the lathe and move the workpiece around so that position D is over the central dowel. Fix down as before, and repeat the cutting operation as shown above. When complete, bring up position F over the centre dowel and repeat this cutting operation.

◆ All the turning on one side is now complete.

As the workpiece here is so light, little or no vibration will be caused by the work being set off-centre. If you do decide to work a larger or heavier piece, it may be necessary to fix a counterweight (other pieces of wood of similar weight and size) opposite the main bulk to balance and reduce vibration.

◆ Remove the workpiece from the eccentric faceplate and turn it over, positioning hole 2 on the central dowel.

At this point it is very important to check that the part now about to be turned is only partially turned on the underside. If by some mischance the previously turned section is

Fig 15.10 Using a triangular needle file to clean out the fine 'whiskers'.

replaced on its same centre (but of course on the underside), then all that will be produced will be a set of rings which will fall loose.

◆　Sharpen the tool.

◆　Repeat the whole process on this new face, cutting on centres 2, 4 and 6, but this time as each cut reaches its depth, a faint 'click – click' will be felt as the tool cuts into the underside grooves. If after reaching the 3mm (⅛in) depth mark this has not happened, just cut a fraction deeper.

◆　Do not be worried when cutting through to the other side; just take a careful light final cut, and all will be well.

◆　If at the bottom of the groove, where it intersects the underside groove, a flimsy wafer of wood shows, it may be pierced open and cleaned out with the end of a triangular needle file (*see* Fig 15.10).

◆　When the work on centres 2, 4 and 6 is complete, with the grooves cut and edges rounded and glasspapered, move on to the secondary circles on centres A, C and E as before.

◆　Now all that remains to be done is to remove the waste wood webs between the circles and the central 'pips' at positions 1 – 6, to give the open lattice effects.

◆　To remove the webs and pips, leave the workpiece on the eccentric faceplate. Take a

sharp 6mm (¼in) wood chisel and, working with the bevel down, carefully carve off the top surface to expose the rings beneath. For the smaller areas, sharpen the 3mm (⅛in) square end tool and use this bevel down. There is really only a small amount of waste wood to remove, but do so carefully and gently.

◆　A small hand-held electric drill holding a cutting burr will also remove the waste wood most satisfactorily (*see* Fig 15.11), but be careful that the tool does not grab at the waste wood, pulling it into some important part of the work.

◆　When one side is cleaned up, turn the workpiece over and clean up the other side.

◆　Finally take the work from the chuck, make sure all the grooves are clean and open, and then complete with the finish of your choice.

To make a finer, more delicate piece, make a narrower square-ended tool and cut more grooves and ridges – the only limitations are steadiness of hand and nerve.

Fig 15.11 Removing the webs between the turned circles.

CHAPTER 16

LATTICE LID BOX

Fig 16.1
Lattice lid
box.

HE LID OF THIS LATTICE BOX IS A PARTIAL SPHERE. A SERIES OF RIDGES AND GROOVES ARE TURNED ON THE INSIDE, AND ON THE OUTSIDE A GROUP OF CONCENTRIC GROOVES CUT THROUGH INTO THOSE UNDER-GROOVES, LEAVING OPENINGS WHERE THEY MEET (*SEE* FIG 16.1).

As these concentric circles interlink and the grooves beneath show through, a more complex pattern, somewhat reminiscent of swirling Maori face tattoos, emerges.

On this box, made from English walnut, four concentric circles interlink to form the pattern. There is no reason why more or less circles should not be used, or why the circles could not be arranged to fall on the same centre lines. To position them on different centre lines would require at least one more

angled chuck and careful planning. It might even be possible, with some thoughtful arrangement, to make the whole top more skeletal, using only the top circular ridges to hold the underside ridges in place, as described in Chapter 15; this box could be just the beginning of some rather intriguing pieces.

Preparation

◆ Cut on the bandsaw two pieces of good, clean, close-grained hardwood for the lid and the box, one 100mm (4in) diameter by 50mm (2in) thick, the other 100mm (4in) diameter by 40mm (1⅝in) thick. My choice was English walnut, which worked superbly, cutting cleanly and holding together well on the small delicate pieces.

◆ Three simple chucks are required, all wooden, screwed on to faceplates and turned to shape as described below. They may all be made ahead of time if you have sufficient

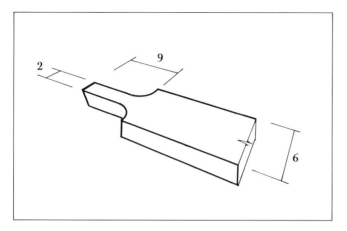

Fig 16.2 Square-end tool for the lattice lid box.

faceplates, or made as the work progresses, changing each on to the faceplate when required.

◆ The first chuck is very basic: a 100mm (4in) diameter, 12mm (½in) thick piece of wood is screwed centrally to a faceplate, with the surface turned so that it is flat and true. This will be used as a glue chuck, so pine will do.

◆ The second is 150mm (6in) diameter and 50mm (2in) thick. I used mahogany for this. This chuck will have a hollow cut into its face to support the lid during turning.

◆ The third is 110mm (4⅜in) diameter and 90mm (3½in) thick, cut from elm. This is just turned round and then cut at an angle to support the hollowed lid so that it is presented to the turner, enabling one part to be turned.

◆ A collar, used on the second and third chucks, is made from a piece 110mm (4⅜in) square and 6mm (¼in) thick.

◆ A square-ended tool, with a width of 2mm (³⁄₃₂in) for a length of 9mm (⅜in), should be ground from a 6mm (¼in) wood chisel (*see* Fig 16.2).

◆ Lathe speed 1500 rpm, reduced to 1000 rpm when cutting the group of concentric circles on the outside of the lid.

Turning the lid

◆ Take the 100mm (4in) diameter, 40mm (1⁹⁄₁₆in) thick piece of walnut and set it centrally between centres.

◆ Face off squarely on the tailstock side right up to the revolving centre.

◆ Remove this piece from the lathe, removing the driving dog from the headstock at the same time.

◆ Take the first basic chuck and fit it on to the headstock, making sure that the wood surface is flat and true.

◆ Apply PVA glue to the wood surface.

◆ Push a sheet of newspaper on to the glued surface of the walnut disc, pressing it firmly to it (*see* Fig 16.3).

◆ Locate the revolving centre, held in the tailstock, in the central hole left by the driving dog. Tighten the centre against the workpiece so that it is held under pressure whilst the glue sets.

This simple and often used paper/glue faceplate will allow the outside of the lid to be turned. When it is complete it can be split away, the paper cleanly parting when a chisel or a knife is forced into the glue line.

◆ When the glue has set, with the revolving centre still in place for support, turn the outside of the walnut disc to 82mm (3¼in) diameter.

◆ Remove the tailstock, bringing the toolrest across the face of the work. Turn the disc down to exactly 35mm (1⅜in) thick.

◆ Make two templates from card: the first a full profile of the top, the second a half profile of the top (*see* Fig 16.4).

◆ Use the card template to act as a guide when turning the outside of the lid to shape (*see* Fig 16.5).

Fig 16.3 Glue the walnut blank to the glue and paper wood chuck.

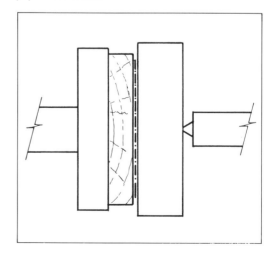

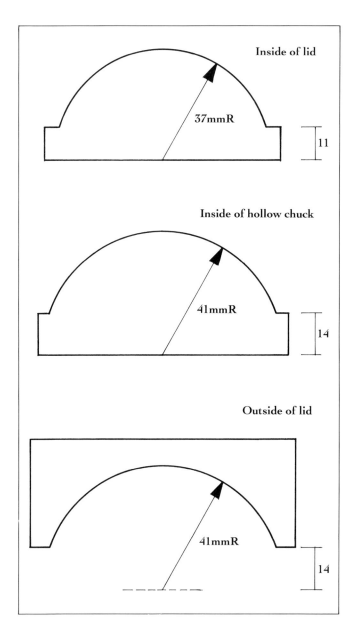

Inside of lid

37mmR

11

Inside of hollow chuck

41mmR

14

Outside of lid

41mmR

14

Fig 16.4 Templates.

◆ Locate the top dead centre of the piece. While the lathe is stationary, take a pencil compass set to 25mm (1in) radius and draw a pencil circle about that centre.

◆ Reset the compass to 35mm (1⅜in) radius and place the compass point on any part of the pencil circle just marked. 'Walk' the compass around the pencil circle; this will produce four points.

◆ At each of these points draw in pencil an 18mm (¹¹⁄₁₆in) radius circle. These four circles should just touch one another.

◆ Split the workpiece from the wooden faceplate along the glue line, using a knife or a chisel (*see* Fig 16.6).

◆ Remove the first faceplate/chuck from the headstock, replacing it with the second chuck. The first use to which this second chuck will be put is in the preparation of the collar from the 110mm (4⅜in) square, 6mm (¼in) thick piece. Draw diagonals on this piece to accurately locate its centre.

◆ Set a pencil compass to 47mm (1⅞in) radius and draw a circle about the marked centre. Where this circle cuts the diagonal lines drill a 3mm (⅛in) hole.

◆ Reset the compass to 55mm (2¼in), again drawing a pencil circle about the centre.

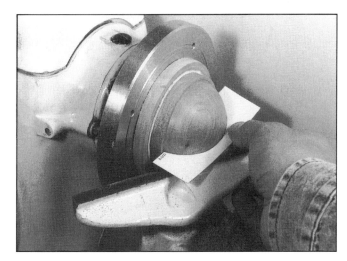

Fig 16.5 The outside of the lid held on a glue and paper chuck and turned to shape.

Fig 16.6 A knife and hammer splitting the glue and paper joint.

Fig 16.7 The collar centre being turned out.

Fig 16.8 Hollowing the chuck block.

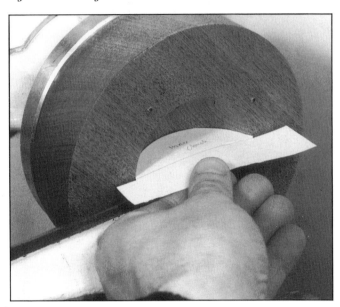

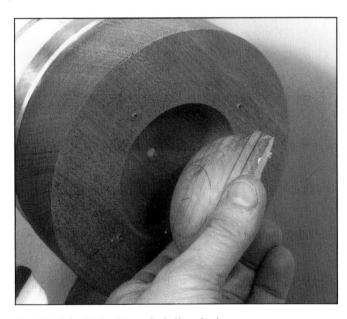

Fig 16.9 The lid fitted into the hollow chuck.

◆ Bandsaw to this outer circle, leaving a 110mm (4⅜in) diameter disc.

◆ At the centre point drill a 3mm (⅛in) hole. Five holes in all will now have been drilled.

◆ Locate the centre of the wooden chuck and, using a small screw fitted through the drilled centre hole, fix the disc centrally on to the chuck.

◆ Fix the disc firmly in place, using four more screws fitted into the four holes.

◆ Mark a datum line on the disc and on the chuck.

◆ Turn the outer edge of the disc so that it remains as close to 110mm (4⅜in) diameter, but is truly circular.

◆ Mark in pencil an 82mm (3¼in) diameter circle, cutting 3mm (⅛in) deep inside the line at this point.

◆ Mark a further pencil circle 75mm (3in) diameter, and cut through to the wood chuck inside this circle (*see* Fig 16.7). The collar is now the correct size, with an internal step cut into it. Remove the collar from the chuck; the central disc can be discarded.

◆ A hollow is now turned into the face of the second chuck to accept the dome-shaped lid. To ensure that the hollow is the correct shape, make a card template to the dimensions as shown for 'inner chuck' (*see* Fig 16.4).

◆ Using a 6mm (¼in) gouge and a round-nose tool ground from a 6mm (¼in) wood chisel, hollow out a 75mm (3in) diameter,

26mm (1in) deep shape until it conforms to the shape of the card template (*see* Fig 16.8).

◆ Test the turned lid in the hollowed shape, if necessary making adjustments for a perfect fit (*see* Fig 16.9).

◆ Push the turned lid into the hollowed-out chuck, bringing up the tailstock holding the revolving centre. Support the workpiece with the centre pushed against it.

Fig 16.10 Turning the underside of the lid to fit the collar.

Fig 16.11 The lid held in the hollowed chuck with screwed down collar.

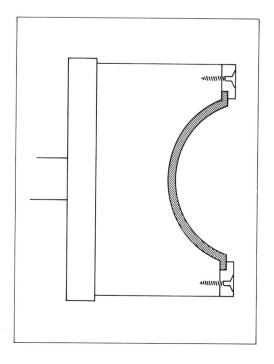

◆ Turn the outer rim of the lid until it is 3mm (⅛in) thick (see Fig 16.10).

Arrange the collar so that it is hung over the tailstock with the step facing the headstock. The collar may be brought up and fitted over the lid rim to test for fit when needed. When it fits snugly and with sufficient depth left on the rim for grip, screw the collar down (see Fig 16.11). The revolving centre can then be removed, as the lid will be held by the collar. Clearly mark a datum on the collar and the chuck, so that, should the collar be removed, it can be replaced in its original position.

◆ Make a template from card to the dimensions marked 'inner lid' (see Fig 16.4)
◆ Begin turning the inner shape of the lid, using the card template as a guide (see Figs 16.12 and 16.13).
◆ Once the internal shaping is accurately turned, the shell wall should be 5mm (⁷⁄₃₂in) thick.
◆ Remove the toolrest.
◆ Remove the revolving centre from the tailstock, replacing it with a drill chuck holding a 3mm (⅛in) drill. Bring this forward and drill through the centre of the lid. Withdraw the tailstock and bring the toolrest back across the face of the work.
◆ Begin marking a series of concentric

circles on the curved inside of the lid with a pencil, the first 2mm (³⁄₃₂in) away from the centrally drilled hole, and each successive circle a further 2mm (³⁄₃₂in) away from the previous one.
◆ Mark upon the surface of the 2mm (³⁄₃₂in) square-end tool a position 3mm (⅛in) away from its cutting edge (see Fig 16.14), using typist correction fluid for a permanent mark.
◆ This tool will be used to cut a series of

Fig 16.12 Turning the inside of the lid.

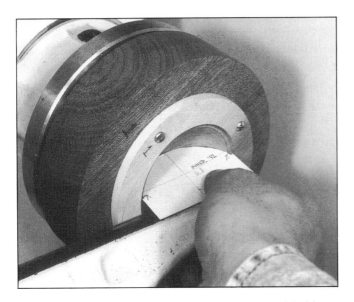

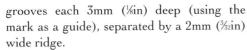

Fig 16.13 *Checking the internal shape of the lid with a template.*

Fig 16.14 *The inside of the lid marked out, and the square-end tool.*

grooves each 3mm (⅛in) deep (using the mark as a guide), separated by a 2mm (³⁄₃₂in) wide ridge.

◆ Begin with the first groove, which starts 2mm (³⁄₃₂in) away from the centrally drilled hole, and continue outward, leaving a ridge between each groove (*see* Fig 16.15).

◆ Arrange the tool so that its length would run through the imagined centre point of the

inner curve.

◆ Remember to keep the tool sharp and, if any amount of metal is ground away, to adjust the marked depth.

◆ When all the grooves have been cut, remove the piece from the lathe and set aside in a safe place (*see* Fig 16.16).

◆ The third chuck now needs to be worked on: fit the 110mm (4⅜in) diameter,

Fig 16.15 *Using the square-end tool to cut the internal grooves.*

Fig 16.16 The part-finished lid.

80mm (3⅛in) thick piece of elm centrally on the faceplate, turning it true. Mark a datum on the wood and on the faceplate so that it can be exactly relocated later.

◆ This chuck needs to be cut at a predetermined angle so that the lid may be held upon its angled face, using the collar made earlier. This presents part of the lid's curved surface for turning.

◆ The angle at which the chuck is cut is determined by drawing a section of the lid (*see* Fig 16.17). A centre line is drawn through the lid in line with the drilled hole, and the point upon the lid's curved surface which is to be turned 25mm (1in) away from that centre line is marked. A line is drawn through that point to the centre of the lid's curvature. This new line will be called the *turning centre*. If a further line is drawn at 90° to this turning centre, call this the *face line*. The angle at which the chuck needs to be cut will be shown between the base of the lid and this face line; in this case, the angle is 35°.

◆ Set the mitre guide of a bandsaw to 35°. Extend the length of the mitre guide with a piece of 50mm (2in) square timber; the chuck block can be firmly taped to this piece of wood, preventing any movement during cutting (*see* Fig 16.18).

◆ Mark a point 10mm (⅜in) from the base of the chuck block – the part with the screw holes in. This will be the starting position for

the bandsaw cut.

◆ Make sure that the screw holes of the chuck block are on the right when facing the bandsaw. Firmly fix the chuck block to the 50mm (2in) square piece of wood with masking tape. Line up the 10mm (⅜in) starting point with the bandsaw blade, then tape the

Fig 16.17 Layout of the hollowed lid set on the angled chuck.

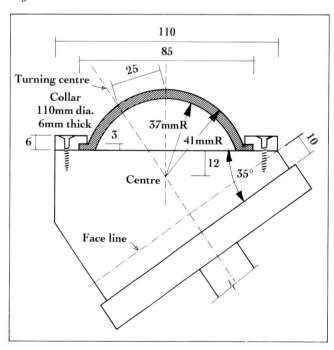

Fig 16.18 The 'third' chuck being cut at an angle.

Fig 16.19 The parts of the 'third' chuck.

chuck block to the square section of wood and begin the cut, cutting carefully and steadily.

◆ Refix the angled slice with the screw holes to the faceplate.

◆ The next stage will need a little care and dexterity: the domed lid will be placed upon the angled chuck, with the collar laid upon its rim (*see* Fig 16.19 for the parts). The centre of one of the pencil circles marked on

Fig 16.20 The lid held in place.

the outside of the lid can then be lined up with the revolving centre held in the tailstock (*see* Fig 16.20). There will be only one position where the domed lid can sit on the angled chuck, with the centre of one of the circles exactly touching the revolving centre (*see* Fig 16.21). Take time to find that position, and be ready with bradawl, screws and screwdriver to fix the collar down when the position has been reached. The edges of the collar should be evenly spaced on the angled chuck. In the photographs it will be seen that they just touch the edges; this is another good indicator which should help with the alignment of the collar and the domed lid. If parts of the collar foul against the faceplate, cut them off.

◆ With the revolving centre still touching the domed lid, revolve the lathe by hand to ensure that no part of the chuck or the work catches. The lathe can now be turned on and the work can be seen to spin on centre, being adjusted if necessary.

◆ One final point before starting to cut the rings on the lid: part of the top edge of the angled chuck may protrude a little, making it awkward to bring the toolrest close enough to support the tool. Carefully cut away any piece which may cause problems (*see* Fig 16.22).

Although I have had no difficulties when turning with this angled chuck, it might, at first, be a little worrying if you are unable to

Fig 16.21 The lid turned around to show how the one section remains on centre.

judge exactly where the whirling mass of wood actually starts. A ghost image will be seen; just turn carefully around the marked pencil circle (*see* Fig 16.23). Try testing the cut by first rotating the work by hand: this should help instil confidence.

Turning the ridges and grooves in the lid

◆ Begin by drilling a 2.5mm (³⁄₃₂in) hole at the centre of the pencil circle marked on the domed lid.

◆ Remove the tailstock and bring the toolrest back across the face of the work, rotating the work by hand to ensure nothing catches.

◆ Mark a series of concentric rings starting from the central drilled hole. The ridges will be 2mm (³⁄₃₂in) wide and the grooves 3mm (¹⁄₈in) wide. This will cause the final pencil circle to be larger than the circle initially marked upon the surface, causing the final groove, when cut, to break with the outer grooves of the circles on either side.

◆ Take the 2mm (³⁄₃₂in) wide square-end tool. Check that the 3mm (¹⁄₈in) distance marked from its tip is still accurate, adjusting it if necessary. Begin to cut the first groove closest to the centre. Cut to the 3mm (¹⁄₈in) depth, widening the groove to the prescribed 3mm (¹⁄₈in); this will ensure that the edges of this tool are not gripped and prevent it from being pulled into the work.

◆ The square-end tool must be aimed at the imagined centre of this partial sphere.

◆ As the tool reaches depth, a gentle 'click-click' will be felt where it begins to cut through into the groove below. Keep the cut gentle until the marked depth is reached. Turn off the lathe; any of the joining grooves which should be fully open can be cleaned out with a sharp triangular needle file.

◆ Continue cutting all the other concentric grooves, leaving the walls complete between them.

Fig 16.23 The grooves are cut through the surface. Note the whirling chuck 'ghost'.

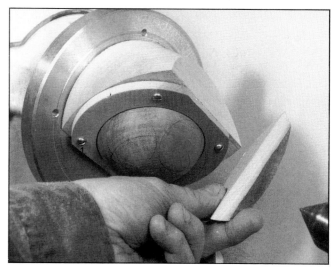

Fig 16.22 The top corner of the angled chuck removed to allow easier access for the tool.

Fig 16.24 The fourth circle set upon centre.

Fig 16.25 A triangular needle file cleaning through the open areas.

◆ It is most important that the final large groove is cut precisely to depth, as this will break into the grooves either side and the bases of each must align.

◆ If, during the cutting of these larger grooves, it is necessary to cut into the supporting collar to give the square-end tool access, cut this part slowly and carefully.

◆ When the first series of concentric grooves have been cut and their openings have been cleaned out with the triangular file, move on to the next circle.

◆ Sharpen the square-end tool regularly, adjusting the depth measurement if necessary.

◆ Undo the screws of the collar and twist the lid around so that the revolving centre correctly lines up with the centre of the drawn circle. When they are perfectly aligned, tighten down all screws.

◆ Drill the centre hole and turn the concentric grooves as before (*see* Fig 16.24). Before starting to turn, remember to rotate the work by hand to ensure that nothing catches on the lathe bed or toolrest.

◆ When all the concentric rings have been

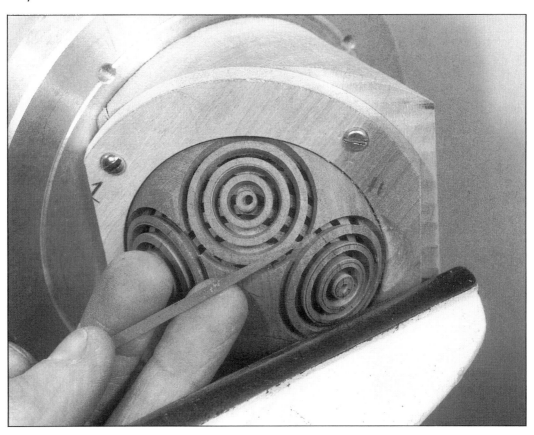

Fig 16.26 *The completed lid, showing the lattice effect.*

turned at all four centres, and when all the groove openings have been cleaned out (*see* Fig 16.25), the lid is complete, and should look as shown in Fig 16.26. A light glasspapering will remove any feathering from the groove edges.

◆ Remove the lid from the angle chuck

Fig 16.27 *The lid fitted into the recess in the base to check for fit.*

Fig 16.28 *Turning out the inside of the base.*

and set it aside in a safe place. Remove the angle chuck from the headstock.

Turning the base

◆ Take the remaining piece of walnut, fixing it to the first wood faceplate with a newspaper and glue joint. Use the revolving centre to add pressure to the joint while the glue sets.

◆ With the revolving centre still in place, turn the outside diameter to 90mm (3⁹⁄₁₆in).

◆ Remove the tailstock and revolving centre, and bring the toolrest across the face of the work.

◆ Face off the work and then turn an internal 83mm (3¼in) diameter step 3mm (⅛in) deep. Test the lid inside this step and adjust to fit (*see* Fig 16.27).

◆ Turn out the inside of the box to 75mm (3in) diameter to a depth of 38mm (1½in), using gouges and, for internal corners, a square-end tool (*see* Fig 16.28). Make sure not to disturb the turned step which the lid will sit on.

◆ Turn the outer shape to a gentle concave curve.

◆ Clean up the inside and outside of the box.

◆ When satisfied that the inner and outer faces of the box are finished, take a knife or a chisel and break the paper joint (*see* Fig 16.29).

◆ Using the wood faceplate, turn a jam-chuck to take the 83mm (3¼in) opening of the box.

Fig 16.29 *The base removed from the 'paper and glue' chuck.*

Fig 16.30 The base is reversed and held on a jam-chuck for turning the foot.

♦ Fit the box to the jam-chuck, testing and turning until a good tight fit is achieved.

♦ Bring the revolving centre up to support the base of the foot for the first cuts. Turn the foot of the base 4mm (⁵⁄₃₂in) deep, removing the revolving centre for the final cuts and the cleaning up of the inside of the foot (*see* Fig 16.30).

♦ Remove the box from the lathe.

♦ The lid now needs a small knob to complete the piece; turn a scrap of walnut, which can be held in a drill chuck fixed in the headstock, to the shape shown in Fig 16.31. Remember to undercut the shoulder which will sit upon the slightly curved top.

♦ The turned 3mm (⅛in) spigot can be glued into the centre hole in the top of the lid, but do not use too much glue as it can squeeze out, causing cleaning up problems.

I purposely kept the base of the box extremely plain so that it would be the lattice effect of the lid to which attention would be drawn. The finish I chose is equally simple: a matt polyurethane varnish, which enables the wood itself and not the finish to show.

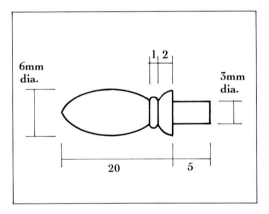

Fig 16.31 The lid knob.

CHAPTER 17

SPHERICAL JIGSAW

Fig 17.1
The spherical
jigsaw.

HIS PROJECT LINKED JIGSAWS WITH THE SPHERES I HAD BEEN TURNING, TO PRODUCE A TRULY THREE-DIMENSIONAL JIGSAW (*SEE* FIG 17.1).

The problem with this jigsaw was always how to firmly hold the sphere while cutting the interlocking parts. It had a simple solution: two wood endplates, each with a 25mm (1in) diameter central hole drilled through the inside edges of the hole (chamfered to prevent them digging into the surface of the sphere), and four bolts with wingnuts at each corner to make a cradle to hold the sphere firmly (*see* Fig 17.2). Chapter 2 shows jigs and chucks for detailed methods of constructing this cradle.

It was necessary to choose a good close-grained hardwood, as there would be many short-grained pieces in the centre of the cut out jigsaw. The wood requires an exaggerated grain, to give clues when fitting these awkward interlocking pieces back

together; I chose olivewood, and it was all that was required. It arrived with a label stating 'partially seasoned'. I was in such a rush that I began working with it the day it arrived. 'Partially seasoned' was stretching the truth, as the moisture span off when I began turning, with olivewood juice oozing

Fig 17.2
The cradle.

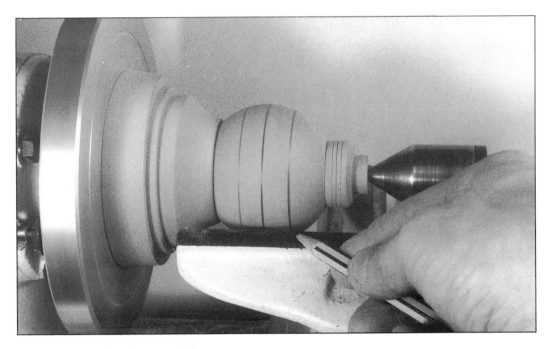

Fig 17.3 The turned sphere is marked out.

over the edge of the gouge; but what a joy it was to turn, with great streams of moist shavings rolling off the tool. Fortunately, I got away with it; having turned the sphere and cut the jigsaw, it dried evenly. I hope that if you choose wet olivewood you have as much fun as I did, but do not blame me if it cracks and warps!

Preparation

◆ Turn a 62mm (2⅛in) diameter sphere from the chosen wood, following the advice given in Chapter 6.
◆ Fit a fine-toothed blade into the fretsaw, jigsaw or scroll saw you intend to use.
◆ With the sphere held in the lathe, mark three lines around its circumference (*see* Fig 17.3): one centre line, the other two 9mm (⅜in) on either side; then turn the sphere through 90° and mark a further three lines similarly spaced. Using these lines as a guide, mark the interlocking shapes which the saw will follow to produce the jigsaw pattern, as shown in Fig 17.4.

Cutting the jigsaw sphere

◆ Place the sphere into the jig, fitting the saw blade inside the cradle before the bolts are pushed into place and tightened.

◆ The first set of lines must be arranged to run vertically and over the top whilst the second set must run horizontally around the sphere before you fully tighten the sphere in the cradle.
◆ Begin the first cut on one of the edge lines. The base of the cradle rests on the saw bed, with only the tip of the sphere base in contact (*see* Fig 17.5).

Fig 17.4 Layout of interlocking parts along drawn lines.

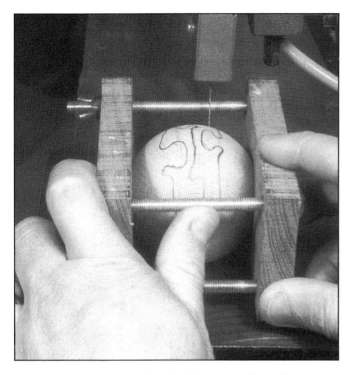

Fig 17.5 The sphere being cut in the cradle.

It has been a long time since I experienced such deep concern as I did with that first cut into the sphere. The scroll saw vibrated everything, and then, as the blade broke through the first cut, having negotiated every

twist and bend successfully, there was an almighty crack as the two parts of the cut, under compression from the cradle, snapped together behind the exiting blade. But learn from my experience: a little less tension in the cradle, a little less tension in the worker, and the worry soon disappears. Success breeds confidence.

◆ Once the first cut is made, 'nip' up the slack left from the saw cut by tightening the wingnuts – not too much – and then twist the cradle around to begin the second cut on the middle line without removing the saw blade from inside the cradle.

◆ Follow the marked lines, always allowing the saw to move freely and never twisting the work rapidly, as this would trap the blade and jam it in the wood, causing a breakage. Work gently and slowly, guiding the saw through the wood.

◆ On completion of the second cut, again 'nip' up the slack, turn the cradle around and begin on the third cut.

◆ When the third cut is complete, hold the parts together with small pieces of masking tape while the three horizontal uncut lines are brought to vertical.

◆ Continue cutting the remaining three lines, tightening the cradle after each cut.

*Fig 17.6
That exit cut!*

It is important that the cuts are made to be interlocking, for without this shaping, the parts would not hold together. Care must be taken not to allow the sphere to slip inside the cradle during cutting, as this may produce a tapered cut, making it next to impossible to take apart some pieces of the puzzle.

◆ With the triumphant final cut, carefully clean up the outer surface and polish the parts as you prefer. I left the olivewood parts naturally finished; their own slightly oily nature is a little like teak.

It is worth producing this piece for the exquisite sections formed, particularly in the centre; these sculptural pieces alone justify all the work involved.

Turning the stand

Having made this spherical puzzle, it is not easy just to lay it down and watch it roll in a wandering pattern until it settles in some fold or crease, so here is how to make a simple turned stand which will be useful both for display and containment.

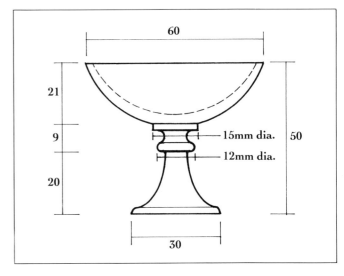

Fig 17.7 The stand.

Fig 17.8 Turning the spigot to hold the base top.

Fig 17.9 Turning the inside of the base top.

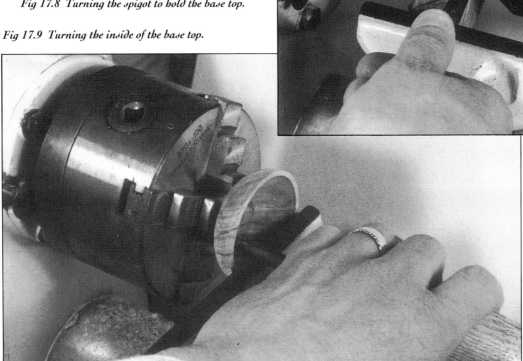

Fig 17.10 The piece supported on the shaped block held in the chuck, and the stub stem shaped.

Fig 17.11 The turned top removed from its shaped support, and the revolving centre.

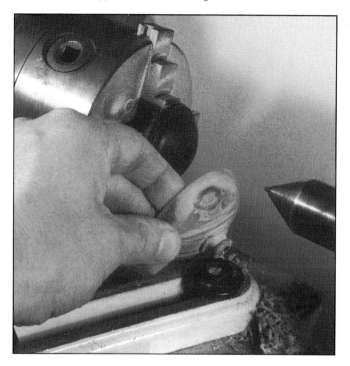

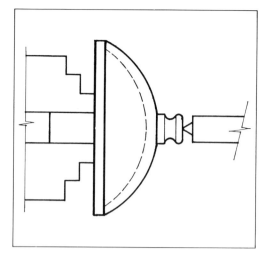

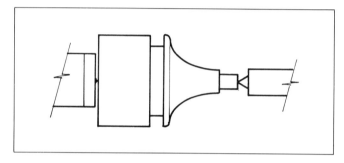

Fig 17.12 The base part turned between centres.

◆ Turn between centres a 65mm (2⅝in) diameter piece 30mm (1¼in) long of olivewood or wood that matches your sphere.

◆ Drill a 6mm (¼in) diameter hole 9mm (⅜in) deep at its centre, and fit the revolving centre back into the hole.

◆ Turn a 20mm (¾in) diameter boss 9mm (⅜in) long at the tailstock end, and shape the remainder with a clean gentle curve towards the headstock to the full diameter.

◆ Remove the piece from the lathe. Remove the driving dog, and replace it with a 3- or 4-jaw chuck. Hold the turned boss in the chuck, bring the toolrest across the face of the work and turn a hollow to a 62mm (2½in) diameter in the face of the work to snugly fit the sphere. A card template cut to this size and shape will help.

◆ Remove the work from the chuck and replace it with a scrap piece of wood, turning its end so that it will fit closely into the turned hollow. Reverse the work so that the turned hollow fits over the scrap of wood, allowing the boss to be supported by the

revolving centre and turned to shape. To increase the grip between the turned scrap in the chuck and the hollow part, fix a fine piece of glasspaper to the face of the scrap wood, using double-sided tape.

◆ Remove the work from the lathe and set aside.

◆ Any polishing should be done as the work proceeds.

Making the foot

◆ Turn up a piece 30mm (1⅜in) diameter 70mm (2¾in) long between centres.

◆ Turn a 6mm (¼in) diameter spigot 9mm (⅜in) long at the tailstock end to fit the drilled hole.

◆ Measure 20mm (¾in) from the edge of the turned spigot towards the headstock. At that point, using a parting tool, cut cleanly down into the work partway. From that position, cut down with a sweeping stroke towards the spigot with a 9mm (⅜in) gouge. Do not cut into the spigot diameter, but leave a small shoulder. When satisfied with

Fig 17.13 The turned foot ready to be parted off.

Fig 17.14 The finished jigsaw on the stand.

the shape of the curved line, part off.

◆ Replace the driving dog with a 3- or 4-jaw chuck holding the spigot in the jaws. Bring up the tailstock with revolving centre to support the work so that the base of the 'foot' may cleanly turned.

◆ When finished, remove the part from the chuck and glue the two pieces together.

◆ The stand is now completed, so place the finished sphere on top.

Treat the spherical jigsaw with care, for there may be some very fine pieces or some short-grained parts which can easily be broken, depending on how you have cut the parts. With planning, thought and care, the worst of these parts can be avoided.

It takes a little courage to allow the jigsaw to come to pieces for the first time; there is always the worry you might not get it back together. Well, that's what it's for – it's a challenge, so have a go, and if you can't fit it back together you can always make another one!

Fig 17.15
The jigsaw
in pieces.

Whistling top and magic trick

Whistling top and magic trick

Cone and slope

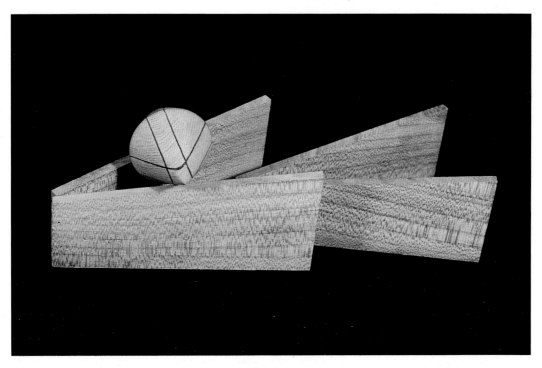

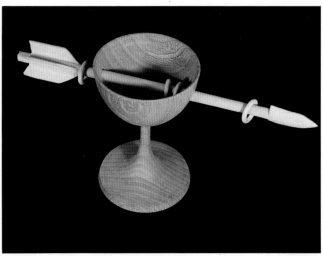

Goblet and arrow

Bottle and arrow

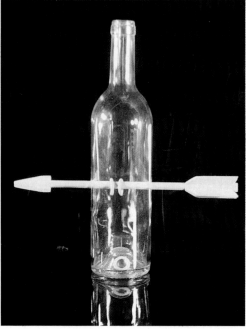

Tunbridge yo-yo

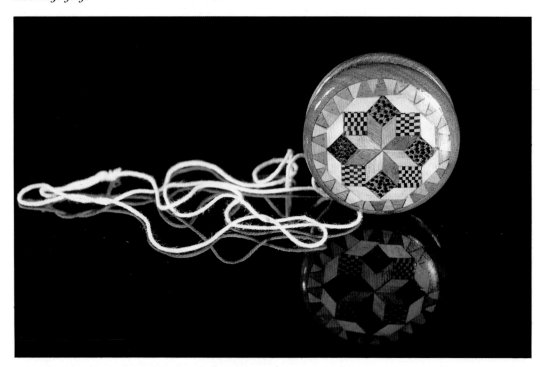

Tunbridge yo-yo

Stacking cone boxes

Stacking cone boxes

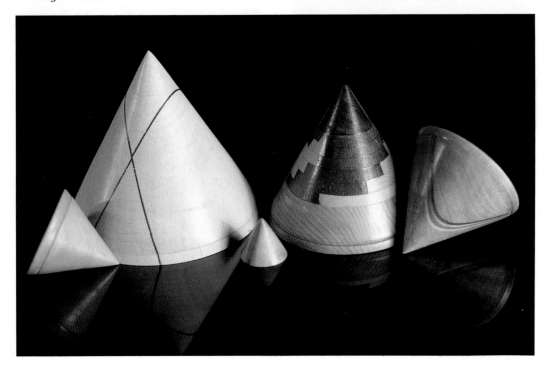

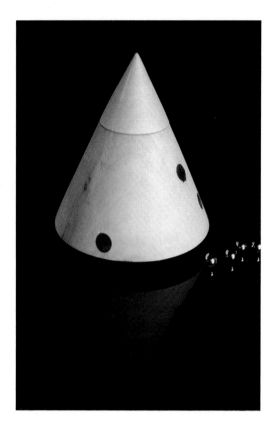

Pharaoh's tomb

Lattice circles

Pharaoh's tomb

Lattice circles

Spherical jigsaw

Spherical jigsaw

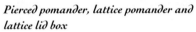

Pierced pomander, lattice pomander and lattice lid box

Pierced pomander, lattice pomander and lattice lid box

Singapore ball and captive cube in sphere

CHAPTER 18

PLUG CUT SPHERE

 WAS TURNING A SPIKED STAR INSIDE A SPHERE (*SEE* CHAPTER 23), AND I NOTICED THAT ONE OF THE FIRST CUTS I MADE PRODUCED A CENTRAL PLUG IN THE SPHERE'S SURFACE, WITH A DEEP GROOVE AROUND IT.

The thought suddenly hit me that the same cut could be produced with a tube-type plug cutter. If the plug cutter were set to cut to the correct depth, then the cuts made on other parts of the sphere would meet, leaving all the central plugs attached to one another, but free of the outer shell.

It was hard to complete that spiked star, as I was impatient to discover whether my theory would produce the result I had in mind. It worked, and the method follows.

As so little pressure is being placed on the central core as it is being cut, the choice of woods is quite wide. Any reasonably good quality wood, preferably free of major flaws, will work. I began with elm, and felt that it was too open-grained, but with care and good finish, that open grain can become a pleasant feature.

To make the piece a little more interesting, I have drilled holes through the centres of each plug which all meet at the centre, making the whole lighter, physically and visibly (*see* Fig 18.1).

Preparation

◆ Turn a 62mm (2⅜in) diameter sphere from the chosen wood (refer to Chapter 6 for turning spheres).
◆ Mark all 12 primary points and 20 constellation points (refer to Chapter 5).
◆ Have ready a 15mm (⅝in) diameter plug cutter (outside diameter 22mm or ⅞in) and a 9mm (⅜in) spur point drill.
◆ Turn 12 plugs from wood, 9mm (⅜in) diameter, 6mm (¼in) long. Drill the centre of

Fig 18.1 Plug cut sphere on stand.

each so that a screw may be twisted into it to act as a handle for removal.
◆ Make 36 supporting pieces 9mm (⅜in) long by 6mm (¼in) wide, the thickness being the same as the wall thickness of your plug cutter; bandsaw them as a long strip and cut each to length.
◆ Have ready the 62mm (2⅜in) diameter hemispherical chuck and the 12mm (½in) thick collar.
◆ Lathe speed 1000 rpm.

Turning the sphere

◆ Fit the sphere into the chuck with the collar loosely in place.

◆ Bring up the tailstock with the revolving centre so that its point touches one of the primary points marked on the sphere's surface.

◆ Tighten the tailstock so that the revolving centre pushes on the sphere, trapping it against the back of the chuck. The primary point is now held on centre.

◆ Tighten down the collar (*see* Fig 18.2).

◆ Withdraw the tailstock, and exchange the revolving centre for a drill chuck.

◆ Fit the 9mm (⅜in) spur point drill into the chuck, marking a point 32mm (1¼in) from the tip with white correction fluid.

◆ Bring the drill up to the work, turn on the lathe and drill to depth (*see* Fig 18.3).

◆ Withdraw the drill, turn off the lathe and fit one of the 9mm (⅜in) plugs (*see* Fig 18.4).

◆ Remove the 9mm (⅜in) drill from the chuck, and replace it with the plug cutter.

◆ Mark on the plug cutter's edge a point 13mm (½in) from the cutting edge with white correction fluid.

◆ Turn on the lathe, and steadily move the plug cutter into the work until the depth is reached (*see* Fig 18.5), withdrawing the cutter regularly to prevent overheating.

◆ Withdraw the plug cutter and switch off the lathe.

◆ Fit three of the prepared supporting pieces in the plug cut groove, spacing them equally around the groove – make sure that they are flush with, or just below, the surface.

The purpose of the central plug is to support the edges as the plug cutter cuts the outer groove. The supporting pieces ensure that the central plug is held firmly while each of the others are, in turn, cut through, released and supported. If not held in this manner, then the final cut breaking through would cause many of the plugs to be suddenly twisted and broken inside – *see* Fig 18.6 for the internal shaping.

◆ Continue working each of the remaining primary points in this way, making sure that the 9mm (⅜in) drill cuts into the central

Fig 18.2 Fixing the sphere in the hemispherical chuck, with the first primary point held on centre.

Fig 18.3 Drill out the first hole.

Fig 18.4 Plugging the first hole.

Fig 18.5 The marked plug cutter drills to depth.

portion already partially drilled.

◆ As the piece would look quite stark with plug cut centres, to finish the piece turn three concentric rings on the sphere's surface at each of the 20 constellation points.

◆ Mark on a plain card template a centre line, a point 1.5mm (¹⁄₁₆in) away, the next 3mm (⅛in) away and the third position 4.5mm (³⁄₁₆in) away. This is a guide; if you prefer different spacings, decide upon your own and mark them.

◆ Loosen the collar on the chuck and bring one of the constellation points to the front centre.

◆ Bring the tailstock up with the revolving centre in place, using it as before, to hold the constellation point, this time while the collar is tightened down.

◆ Remove the tailstock and centre. Bring the toolrest across and set it so that a fine parting tool will be set to cut at centre height.

◆ Revolve the work by hand to make sure that nothing catches, and when satisfied, turn on the lathe.

◆ Bring the card template up to the work, placing its centre line on the centre of the constellation point. Hold a pencil at each of the marked points, touching it against the sphere to mark three concentric circles.

◆ Cut a line on each of the three pencil lines with the corner of the fine parting tool (*see* Fig 18.7).

◆ Turn off the lathe, remove the toolrest and sand the work smooth.

It is necessary to work in an orderly manner on both primary and constellation points, remembering which you have cut or turned and where the unworked points are, as a large amount of time can be wasted searching for positions thought not to have been drilled or turned.

Fig 18.6 Internal hollow tube shapes produced by drill and plug cutter.

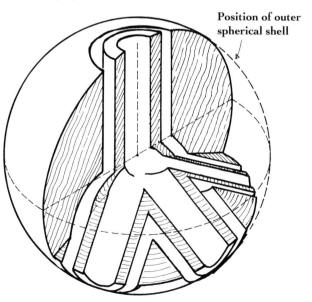

Position of outer spherical shell

Fig 18.7 Turning the concentric circle at the secondary points. Note the three pieces supporting the area cut out.

Fig 18.8 Removing the plugs.

◆ When all parts have been completed satisfactorily, it is time to remove the supporting pieces and the central plugs. A pair of tweezers can grip the edges of the supporting pieces to pull them out, and the central plugs are removed by twisting a screw into the small central holes and pulling (*see* Fig 18.8).

◆ If, when all 12 positions have had their supporting pieces and plugs removed, the centre does not loosen, it may well be held in place by a few whiskers of wood. Just work it lightly free, if necessary using a square needle file to reach the base of the groove to break free any small holding parts (*see* Fig 18.9). Be patient.

How to calculate the depth to which the plug cutter should cut

◆ The plug cutter will enter the main sphere in 12 positions. Where these cuts meet should form a smaller sphere, which we will call S.

◆ The area cut by the plug cutter is πr^2; π =3.142 (r is the radius of the plug cutter) – we will call this area A.

12 of these surface areas A of the plug cutter equal the surface area of the small internal sphere S. Therefore:

12A = S (the surface area of a sphere is calculated using the equation 4 π r where r is the radius of the sphere). Therefore:

12A = 4 π r.

Fig 18.9 A triangular needle file breaks through the 'whiskers' holding the central piece.

◆   By using a calculator and by putting first the radius of the chosen plug cutter to calculate its area, the surface area of the small sphere can be calculated and its radius may be further discovered.

◆   Using these measurements, a simple drawing will allow the depth to which the plug cutter should cut to be measured.

These calculations should give you freedom to experiment with other sizes of spheres and plug cutters, and maybe even increase the number of positions at which the plug cutter is used. Add to that the possibility that the plugs may be turned to shape or fitted with turned plug caps, and the variations are endless.

Turning the stand

For this stand I used a piece of branch wood from a laburnum tree; I knew that the branch had been growing almost vertical and would not bend after cutting or turning.

◆   Cut a 180mm (7in) length, 50mm (2in) square (a little larger in diameter if branch wood, to allow for removal of sapwood) piece.

◆   Set the piece between centres and turn to 50mm (2in) diameter.

Turning this damp branch was a real surprise. The first cuts through the damp bark produced huge peelings just like banana skins, in colour and texture. The shavings were almost queuing to peel off, and I really began to appreciate turning wet wood: instead of dry and powdery shavings falling warm or even hot upon the hands, cool tendrils settled in satisfying heaps.

◆   Measure 30mm (1¼in) from the tailstock, and at that point turn into the work to mark the position, using a parting tool.

◆   From that point measure a further 120mm (4¾in) towards the headstock and, again using the parting tool, cut into the work. This position marks the underside of the foot.

◆   Using a small gouge, turn from the marked point at the headstock down towards the tailstock in a sweeping stroke, carefully removing the bulk of the wood but leaving sufficient bulk at the headstock end from which to turn the foot.

◆   At the point first cut 30mm (1¼in) from the tailstock, then turn down to 5mm (⁵⁄₃₂in) for a length of 6mm (¼in)

◆   The main stem meeting that finely turned part should be 9mm (⅜in) diameter. Turn a small bead at this point.

◆   Now turn down to 6mm (¼in) at the headstock side of the bead, allowing this cut to sweep back towards the headstock, tapering gradually until it meets the main bulk of the base (*see* Fig 18.10).

Be careful when turning this wet wood, for the stem can easily be twisted off if too heavy a cut is made.

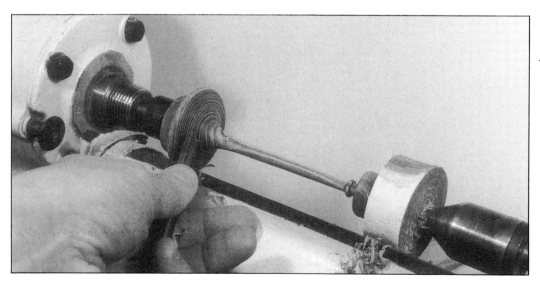

Fig 18.10 Turning the foot and stem of the base.

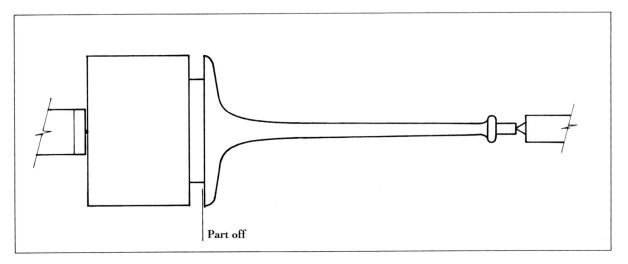

Part off

Fig 18.11 Base stem turned before parting off.

◆   The foot of the stand is rounded over and shaped before the underside of the base is slightly undercut and the whole piece cleaned up and finally parted off (*see* Fig 18.11).

It is best to leave damp pieces like this to dry slowly and evenly. If placed in a heavy paper bag with its end sealed, a small item such as this stand will dry evenly within a week or so.

Turning the top

Use the 30mm (1¼in) length sawn from the top end to turn the cup-shaped top. It can be

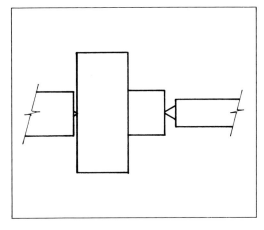

Fig 18.12 Spigot formed to hold in chuck.

Fig 18.13 The top is drilled through.

Fig 18.14 Turning the underside of the top.

Fig 18.15 The stand.

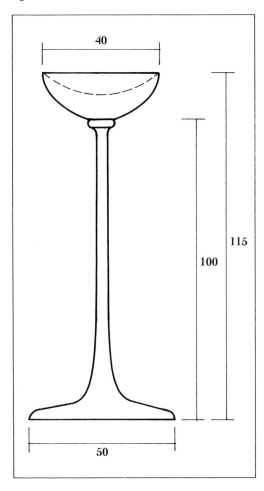

repositioned between centres to turn a spigot on one end, to enable it to be held by that spigot in a three- or four-jaw chuck (*see* Fig 18.12).

◆ With the part held in the chuck and supported with a revolving centre, turn the outside round and down to 40mm (1⁹⁄₁₆in) diameter.

◆ Withdraw the tailstock and bring the toolrest across the face of the work.

◆ Turn a hollow into the shaped top to support a 62mm (2½in) diameter sphere, using a card template if necessary.

◆ Exchange the revolving centre for a drill chuck holding a 5mm (⁵⁄₃₂in) drill. Withdraw the toolrest and drill into the workpiece (*see* Fig 18.13).

◆ Remove the piece from the chuck, and replace it with a 25mm (1in) diameter piece of wood (any type will do).

◆ Turn a 5mm (⁵⁄₃₂in) spigot on the end of this small piece, and shape the collar to support the already turned curved face of the top.

◆ Fit the top with its curved face butting against the curved shoulder into the now exposed end hole for support.

◆ Turn the underside of the top, gracefully curving under to match the inner curve, down to a 12mm (½in) diameter shoulder, 1.5mm (¹⁄₁₆in) wide (*see* Fig 18.14). Round the

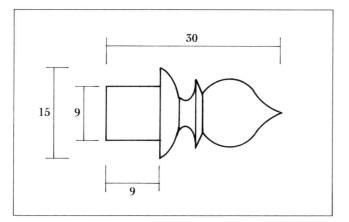

Fig 18.16 The finial.

shoulder over to form a bead.
◆   Clean up and store in the paper bag with the stem until dry.
◆   When both parts are dry, glue together and polish.

This light stand helps take away some of the heavy solidity of the plug cut sphere which it supports; *see* Fig 18.15 for dimensions.

Turning the finial

The sphere needs to be 'lifted' a little from an ordinary, quite heavy-looking piece. A turned finial fixed into one of the top holes will produce a lighter, more whimsical piece (*see* Fig 18.16 for dimensions). If the sphere is arranged well on the stand, the finial will appear to be the end of a piece running from the stand right through the sphere.

◆   Turn a small piece of laburnum, 45mm (1¾in) long and 18mm (¾in) square between centres to round.
◆   At the tailstock end turn a 25mm (1in) length down to 9mm (⅜in) diameter.
◆   Hold the 9mm (⅜in) diameter in a drill chuck fitted at the headstock end, with the 18mm (¾in) area left free for turning to the desired shape.
◆   Turn the finial with the toolrest close to the work and using gouges and a skew chisel, leaving an 18mm (¾in) diameter shoulder just before the 9mm (⅜in) spigot (*see* Fig 18.17). This shoulder should just seat nicely on top of one of the open plug ends for that final touch, as shown in Fig 18.18.

Fig 18.17 Turning the finial.

If a wood matching that of the plug cut sphere were chosen, a series of 12 spikes or finials could be turned and fitted, making a rather unusual spiked ball.

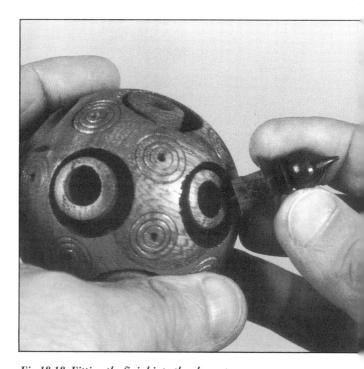

Fig 18.18 Fitting the finial into the plug cut sphere.

CHAPTER 19

PIERCED POMANDER

Fig 19.1 The blackwood pierced pomander.

challenging turnery project. The style chosen here allows for easy refilling, looks attractive and will, I hope, be a sufficiently interesting and stimulating piece of turned work.

I decided to use African blackwood for this piece, for several reasons. The main one was that I had heard it was a most excellent turnery wood and wanted to find out for myself. This pomander, having a fine shell wall, pierced throughout, would need a fine close-grained timber, a further reason for choosing blackwood. And finally I felt the simple shape of the finished piece would be enhanced by the pure stark blackness of the wood.

The piece of blackwood I chose was extremely tough and unforgiving, like dense plastic, grabbing the tool at every opportunity. An unpleasant first experience, but all changed later when turning the central spindle. The wood for the central spindle was from a different source, and I was delighted to find that this piece fulfilled all my expectations (*see* Fig 19.1). Blackwood, when it's bad, is very, very bad, but when it's good, it's superb.

Preparation

◆ Have available 3mm (⅛in) and 6mm (¼in) round-nose tools, plus the usual selection of turning tools.
◆ Grind away 2.5mm (³⁄₃₂in) from each side of a 6mm (¼in) wide wood chisel for a length of 6mm (¼in), leaving a 1mm (¹⁄₁₆in) wide cutting surface (*see* Fig 19.2).
◆ Have a three- or four-jaw self-centering chuck available.
◆ Select your wood for straightness of grain, and ensure that it is free from defects.
◆ Have ready the 62mm (2½in) diameter hemispherical chuck, the 6mm (¼in) thick collar with the 54mm (2³⁄₁₆in) diameter opening, and the 20mm (¾in) thick collar

HE DICTIONARY DEFINITION STATES THAT A POMANDER IS A BALL OF GOLD OR SILVER CONTAIN-ING AROMATIC SUBSTANCES, USED FROM THE SIXTEENTH CENTURY AS PRESERVATIVE AGAINST INFECTION. NO DOUBT POMANDERS WERE ALSO NECESSARY TO IMPROVE THE QUALITY OF THE AIR AT A TIME WHEN FEW WASHED OR BATHED.

Today, with the increased interest in potpourris, scented petals and leaves, pomanders can make an interesting and

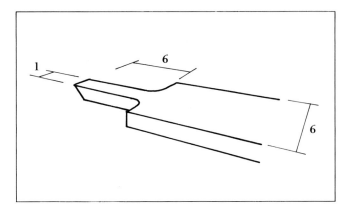

Fig 19.2 Ground square-end tool.

with the 48mm (1⅞in) opening.

◆ Lathe speed approximately 1000 rpm.

Turning the sphere

◆ Turn between centres a 70mm (2¾in) square by 120mm (4¾in) long piece of blackwood to 70mm (2¾in) diameter.

◆ Turn a 15mm (⅝in) long spigot on either end. The diameter of these spigots will be decided by the maximum opening of the three- or four-jaw chuck you will be later using: 25mm (1in) diameter is the largest that my four-jaw chuck will accept.

◆ Measure from the shoulder nearest the tailstock towards the headstock, marking a point at 31mm (1¼in); this is half the 62mm (2½in) diameter of the sphere. Turn the lathe

on, and holding a pencil at the point, mark a line round the work. Mark A to the headstock of this line, and mark B to the tailstock of this line (*see* Fig 19.3).

◆ Draw a horizontal datum line; this will help align the parts later. Now part off on the headstock side of the line. You may wish to saw off the last few centimetres or quarter inches of the parting, rather than using the parting tool the whole way.

◆ Remove the driving dog from the headstock and replace it with the chuck. Hold B in the chuck on the spigot, with the parted face showing forward. Face the work off clean, flat and square.

◆ Drill or turn a 25mm (1in) diameter hole 6mm (¼in) deep, using a sawtooth cutter or turning tool.

◆ Using the 1mm (⅟₁₆in) wide cutting tool, cut a 1mm (⅟₁₆in) wide groove to the same depth, the outer diameter of this groove being 60mm (2⅜in) (*see* Fig 19.4).

◆ Remove B from the chuck, and replace it with A, holding it in a similar manner as before. Face off clean and square.

◆ Turn a 25mm (1in) diameter spigot, 4mm (³⁄₁₆in) long, upon the face. Chamfer the top corner slightly to ease fitting. Try B against A to check the fit of the newly turned spigot into the hole in B, and adjust if necessary.

◆ Turn a 1mm (⅟₁₆in) wide and high ridge, with an outer diameter of 60mm (2⅜in).

Fig 19.3 Turn the block between centres, part into two equal parts. Note datum line.

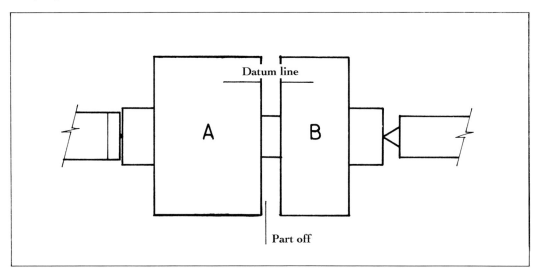

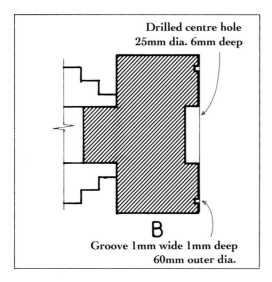

Fig 19.4 B in the chuck.

Fig 19.5 A in the chuck.

Slightly chamfer the corners of the ridge.

◆ From the inside edge of the ridge towards the spigot, remove 1mm (¹⁄₁₆in) depth of wood to level the outer edge with the inner. The central spigot will now be 5mm (³⁄₁₆in) high (*see* Fig 19.5). Fit B to A, and align the datum and make adjustments where necessary to ensure a good tight fit.

◆ Remove the parts from the chuck, and then remove the chuck and replace the driving dog. Reposition the fitted parts A and B with the driving dog marks locating back into the dog and the live centre fitting back into the centre hole in the end of the

mark. Tighten the tailstock.

◆ Turn the whole to an exact 62mm (2½in) diameter.

Refer to Chapter 6 on turning spheres and, using the joint line as the centre, turn the piece to an exact 62mm (2½in) diameter sphere, leaving only a little to part off at either end. Mark a pencil datum line across the joint of the sphere (*see* Fig 19.6).

◆ Gently saw through the waste wood at either end of the sphere, leaving a small 'pip' at either end.

Fig 19.6 Parts replaced between centres and turned to spherical shape.

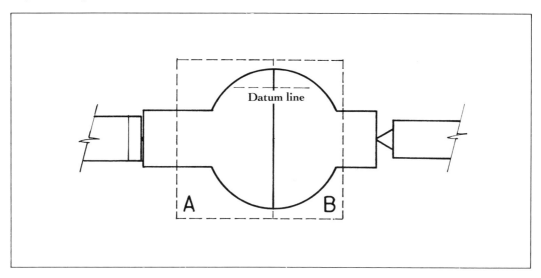

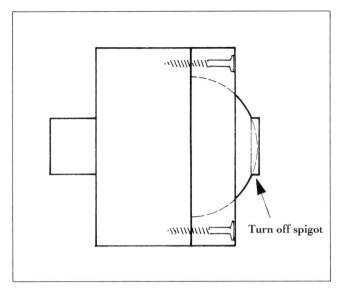

Fig 19.7 Hold A and B in hemispherical chuck.

♦   Separate and hold A and B in turn in the hemispherical chuck, using the 20mm (¾in) thick collar. Ensure that the 'pip' is facing out and is running exactly on centre (*see* Fig 19.7). Turn off the 'pips' so that both A and B are true hemispheres.
♦   Fit A and B, aligning the datum line. If

your joint is not sufficiently tight to hold together by itself, small pieces of masking tape will keep the two halves together while marking the primary and secondary points (*see* Chapter 5).

By now you will have discovered whether your choice of blackwood has been good or bad; the only real difference is the effort needed to turn it without the tools grabbing. If you have chosen a difficult piece, benefit by the experience, for woods you have considered awkward up till now will become childs' play, by comparison, in the future.

Preparation for hollowing the hemispheres

♦   Begin by turning 30 x 3mm (⅛in) diameter 3mm (⅛in) long dowels from a light-coloured hardwood. Hold the wood in a Jacobs chuck held in the headstock for ease of working.
♦   Mark a 57mm (2¼in) diameter circle on to card (cereal packets will do), marking the centre line then cutting the circle out. This

Fig 19.8 The chuck and blackwood half sphere, with depth markers of palewood.

Fig 19.9 The palewood depth markers.

will be used as a template.

◆ Have ready the 62mm (2½in) diameter chuck and the 6mm (¼in) thick collar with a 57mm (2¼in) diameter opening.

◆ 6mm (¼in) and 3mm (⅛in) round-nose tools will be needed.

◆ Lathe speed approximately 500 rpm.

Hollowing the hemispheres

◆ Fit the hemispherical chuck to the headstock.

◆ Drill a 3mm (⅛in) diameter hole 3mm (⅛in) deep at each of the primary points and secondary points on the blackwood sphere before fitting the sphere into the chuck. Mark the depth on the drill with white correction fluid.

◆ Glue one of the tiny white wood dowels into each of the holes, using superglue or similar. These will act as clear markers to show when the correct depth has been reached when hollowing out (*see* Fig 19.8).

◆ Separate the two halves of the sphere. Take one hemisphere and fit it into the chuck with its flat face to the front.

◆ Screw the collar on to the chuck, taking care to make sure that it is screwed down evenly. Make absolutely sure that all the screws are tight before turning the lathe on.

◆ Bring the toolrest across the face of the work, setting its height so that the round-nose tools are at centre height.

◆ Begin the hollowing with light cuts, testing regularly with the card template as a guide to where and how much wood needs removing. As the work is hollowed, move the toolrest closer to the working surface to reduce tool overhang. Keep looking for the white dowels to show through: this will indicate that the correct depth has been reached (*see* Fig 19.9). The edge of the collar also acts as a guide to the internal diameter of the work, as its diameter is the finished diameter of the hollow hemisphere. Use each of the round-nose tools as needed.

◆ It is an advantage to have a light which can be shone inside the work; it will make everything much more clearly visible.

◆ When completely satisfied that the inside is truly hemispherical and, most importantly, that the wall thickness is an even 3mm (⅛in), turn out, or drill out, the top hole to 6mm (¼in) diameter, as shown in Fig 19.9.

◆ The first hemisphere is now complete; just repeat the operation to hollow the second. Remember to turn or drill out the 6mm (¼in) top hole before removing it from the chuck.

Blackwood is deeply black and tough, and usually the turner ends up as black as the wood itself. It is too easy to be concentrating on the work as it progresses to forget to sharpen the tools. Do so regularly, for if you do not, the tool can quite suddenly be grabbed by the work, usually at precisely that most difficult moment, damaging the work beyond repair.

Preparation for piercing the sphere

◆ Have available the 3mm (⅛in) round-nose tool, which must be sharp.

◆ Have available the 1mm (¹⁄₁₆in) square-end tool, also sharp.

◆ You will need the hemispherical chuck and 20mm (¾in) collar (*see* Fig 19.10).

Fig 19.10 The hemispherical chuck and the blackwood hemispherical shells.

◆ Have ready a set of external callipers set at 12mm (½in).

◆ Set the lathe speed at 500 rpm.

As this hollow sphere is quite delicate, it will be helpful to give it some internal support when cutting the 12mm (½in) diameter holes through its surface. A foam material called Oasis can be bought in spheres of various sizes at most florists; buy one as near to 62mm (2⅜in) as possible, and carve, glasspaper or file it down to fit snugly inside the sphere (*see* Fig 19.11). This will support the walls, yet be so light that it will put no pressure at all on the sphere itself.

Piercing the sphere

◆ Place the filled sphere into the chuck, lightly tightening the collar down.

◆ Bring the tailstock with the revolving centre up to the work, touching against the centre of one of the white dowels nearest the joint line (*see* Fig 19.12).

◆ The sphere needs a firm grip in the chuck, as any movement could have disastrous results: fix small pieces of fine, evenly spaced glasspaper to the back of the chuck and inside of the collar, using double-sided tape.

◆ Carefully tighten the live centre against the dowel, forcing the sphere against the back of the hemispherical chuck.

◆ Tighten down the collar evenly, taking care to grip the work just enough to hold it firmly, but not so much as to crack its spherical shell.

◆ When bringing the tailstock towards the work to align the centre of the hole with the

Fig 19.11 The Oasis filling, the tools and the two half shells of blackwood.

Fig 19.12 Holding the joined halves of the sphere in the chuck to allow the holes to be pierced in the shell. The Oasis filling can be seen through the holes.

centre of rotation, place a hand on the lathe bed between the work and the tailstock. Now push the tailstock towards the work with the other hand; the hand on the lathe bed will gently break the forward movement of the tailstock, and will not allow the centre to be suddenly driven into the work. (It is called a disaster when you do it, but experience when you tell others how to avoid it.)

◆ Remove the tailstock and centre, bringing the toolrest across the work and setting it so that the round-nose and square-end tools are at centre height.

◆ Rotate the chuck by hand to make sure that nothing snags the toolrest. Turn on the lathe, bringing the round-nose tool to the white dowel. Cut into and through the wood surface, easing out the centre waste. Measure the opening frequently, with the callipers set to 12mm (½in). When close to size, bring the square-end 1mm (¹⁄₁₆in) tool to the work, squaring the edge of the hole and bringing it to the exact size.

◆ It is best to cut all the 12mm (½in) holes nearest the joint line (Equator) first, as this is the most fragile area. Move on to the next layers up (Tropics of Cancer and Capricorn), the finally the remaining top and bottom layers of holes. It will be found that the foam filling not only supports the sphere

while cutting, but also helps to keep the two halves aligned.

Preparation for the centre spindle

◆ Fit the driving dog into the headstock.
◆ Lathe speed approximately 1500 rpm.

Turning the centre spindle

◆ Turn a piece of 110mm (4³⁄₈in) by 25mm (1in) square blackwood between centres to 20mm (¾in) diameter.

◆ Turn the shaped part at the tailstock end as shown in Fig 19.13. Use a small gouge to cut the sweeping curve down to the rounded end. Cut down either side of the collar with a sharp skew, rounding over the side of the spherical end towards the collar. Make the sharply detailed cut between the two with the skew. Finally round over and down towards the tailstock, finishing off with a slight point.

◆ Undercut the inner shoulder so that it will fit snugly up to the sphere.

◆ Turn down from the inner shoulder

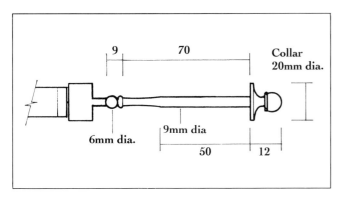

Fig 19.14 The collar.

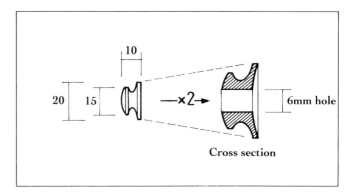

Cross section

Fig 19.13
The central
spindle.

towards the headstock to fractionally under 6mm (¼in), to within 6mm (¼in) of the driving dog.

◆ Measure 70mm (2¾in) from the inner shoulder towards the tailstock. At this point turn a small collar and a 6mm (¼in) rounded end (*see* Fig 19.14). Polish the top and bottom, and part off cleanly at the rounded end nearest the headstock.

◆ At the rounded end which has just been parted off, drill a 1.5mm (¹⁄₁₆in) hole down its length for 6mm (¼in) depth. Next drill a 2mm (⁵⁄₃₂in) hole across and through the rounded end. For a really clean hole, try using a round-nose dental burr.

◆ These holes will allow a fine cord to be passed through, knotted and pulled up to hang the finished pomander.

◆ To turn the top collar, set a piece of 25mm (1in) square by 50mm (2in) long blackwood between centres and turn down to a 20mm (¾in) cylinder.

◆ Remove the workpiece and driving dog, and fit a three- or four-jaw chuck.

◆ Hold the part in the chuck, the face off the end. Drill through the central axis of the piece with a 6mm (¼in) drill held in a drill chuck in the tailstock.

◆ Remove the drill chuck, and bring the toolrest across the end face of the work. Slightly hollow the face so that it will sit snugly against the sphere.

◆ Bring the toolrest around along the edge of the work, supporting the end of the work with the revolving centre.

◆ Using a gouge and skew, shape the collar as shown in Fig 19.15. Polish and part off.

I finished the sphere with several coats of tung oil buffed up to a dull sheen. It is a subtle finish, and durable as well.

To complete, slide one half of the sphere on to the spindle over the cord, followed by the second half and then the top collar (*see* Fig 19.16). Hang it up and fill it with pot-pourri.

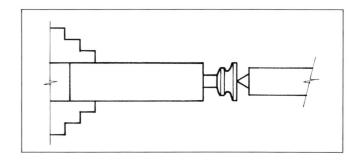

Fig 19.15 Turning the collar supported between chuck and revolving centre.

Fig 19.16 Drill one hole across the top of the spindle and one down to meet it. Knot the cord, thread through and up the centre hole.

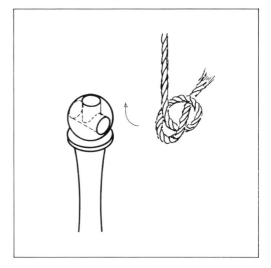

CHAPTER 20

LATTICE POMANDER

Fig 20.1 A pair of lattice pomanders, one in pieces ready to be filled.

THIS PIECE HAD BEEN AT THE BACK OF MY MIND FOR SOME TIME (*SEE* FIG 20.1); HAVING SEEN THE WONDERFUL EXAMPLES OF LATTICE WORK ON FANSTICKS (*SEE* FIG 20.2), AND FROM EXPERIMENTING WITH THE LATTICE CIRCLES, I JUST KNEW IT COULD BECOME THREE-DIMENSIONAL.

It was a combination of spherical work and two-dimensional lattice circles that threw out this idea. Being a pierced hollow sphere, it lends itself perfectly to holding scented potpourri – open and refill it whenever necessary.

A close-grained hardwood, such as the boxwood used here, is essential for a piece as delicate as this. As an experiment I tried using a good clear piece of yew, but at the final stages parts began to break out. African blackwood and ebony would work well, I know, and it would be best to choose a wood with little grain pattern, for it is the concentric grooves on the sphere's surface and the pierced effect which produce the interest; grain pattern would only interfere with the overall impression.

The procedure for making these lattice spheres is initially the same as that used for producing the pierced pomander, the difference being that the wall thickness of the hemisphere is increased to allow the internal grooves to be cut without slicing through the sphere's surface. In addition, only 12 primary points are marked upon the sphere surface: two top and bottom holes, and 10 others marking the centres for the concentric grooves.

Do not be put off trying the piece because of its apparent delicacy; taken stage

Fig 20.2 The lattice effect on a set of bone fansticks.

length of 6mm (¼in); this will leave a 2mm (³⁄₃₂in) wide cutting surface. Carefully grind the 6mm (¼in) sides so that they slope away from the top surface, then grind and sharpen the cutting edge. Keep the tool cool when grinding the shape, as overheating will destroy the temper.

◆ Grind away 2.5mm (⅛in) from each side of a 6mm (¼in) wide wood chisel, for a length of 6mm (¼in), leaving a 1mm (³⁄₆₄) wide cutting surface.

◆ Select your wood for straightness of grain, and ensure that it is free from defects.

◆ Have ready the 62mm (2½in) diameter hemispherical chuck, with the 6mm (¼in) thick collar with 54mm (2³⁄₁₆in) diameter opening and the 18mm (¾in) thick collar with 48mm (1⅞in) opening.

◆ Lathe speed approximately 1000 rpm.

Turning the hemispheres

◆ Turn a 70mm (2¾in) square by 120mm (4¾in) long piece of boxwood between centres to 70mm (2¾in) diameter.

◆ Turn a 15mm (⅝in) long spigot on either end; the diameter of these spigots will be decided by the maximum opening of the three- or four-jaw chuck you will later be using. 25mm (1in) diameter is the largest my 4-jaw chuck will take.

by stage, it is no more difficult than other pieces of turnery. More nerve-racking maybe, but the sheer pleasure and satisfaction of completing this work and mastering the skill is worth all the harrowing time spent at the lathe.

Preparation

◆ Grind 2mm (³⁄₃₂in) away from each side of a 6mm (¼in) wide wood chisel, for a

Fig 20.3 The block turned between centres. Note datum line.

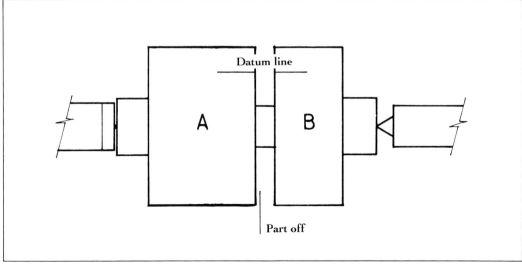

Datum line

A   B

Part off

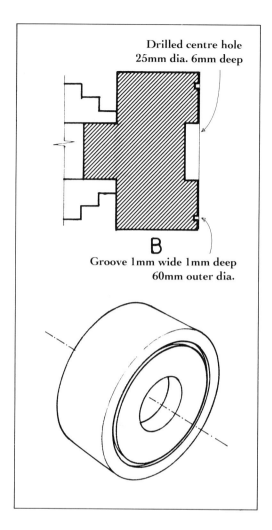

Drilled centre hole
25mm dia. 6mm deep

B

Groove 1mm wide 1mm deep
60mm outer dia.

Fig 20.4 A groove close to the outer edge and a hole in the centre of B.

Fig 20.5 A central spigot and outer ridge on the face of A.

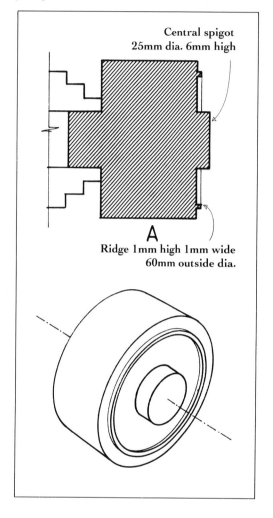

Central spigot
25mm dia. 6mm high

A

Ridge 1mm high 1mm wide
60mm outside dia.

◆ Measuring from the shoulder nearest the tailstock towards the headstock, mark a point 31mm (1¼in), half the 62mm (2½in) diameter of the sphere. Turn the lathe on and hold a pencil at that point, marking a line around the work. To the headstock of this line, the part is then marked A, and to the tailstock, the part is marked B.

◆ Draw a horizontal datum line, which will help align the parts later. Now part off on the headstock side of the line (*see* Fig 20.3). You may wish to saw the last little piece of the parting off, rather than using the parting tool the whole way.

◆ Remove the driving dog from the headstock, and replace it with the chuck. Hold B in the chuck with the parted face showing, and face off the work clean and square.

◆ Drill a 25mm (1in) diameter hole 6mm (¼in) deep using a sawtooth cutter (or the

hole may be turned out).

◆ Cut a 1mm (³⁄₆₄in) wide by 1mm (³⁄₆₄in) deep groove 60mm (2¹³⁄₃₂in) outer diameter on the outer face of the work, using the 1mm (³⁄₆₄in) wide tool (*see* Fig 20.4).

◆ Remove B from the chuck, replacing it with A. Hold in a similar manner, face off clean and square.

◆ Turn a 25mm (1in) diameter spigot, 4mm (³⁄₁₆in) long upon the face. Chamfer the top corner slightly to ease fitting, and then try B against A to see if the spigot fits the hole. Adjust if necessary.

◆ Turn a 1mm (³⁄₆₄in) high, 1mm (³⁄₆₄in) wide, 60mm (2¹³⁄₃₂in) outer diameter ridge on

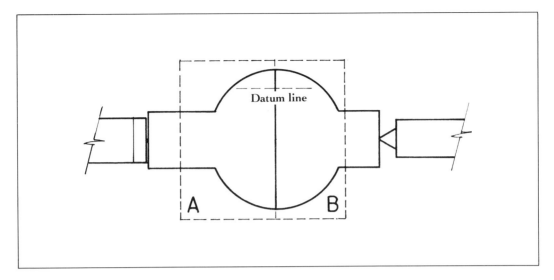

Fig 20.6 The parts fitted together for spherical turning.

the face of the work (*see* Fig 20.5). *Slightly* chamfer the corners of this ridge.

◆ From the inside edge of the ridge towards the spigot, remove the 1mm (³⁄₆₄in) depth of wood to level the outside edge with the inner. The spigot will now be 5mm (¹³⁄₆₄in) high. Fit B to A, align the datum and make adjustments where necessary to ensure a good tight joint.

◆ Remove the parts from the chuck, then remove the chuck and replace it with the driving dog. Replace the joined pieces between centres, with the datum lines together. Tighten the tailstock firmly (*see* Fig 20.6).

◆ Turn the whole to an exact 62mm (2½in) diameter.

◆ Refer to Chapter 6 on turning spheres. Using the join line as the centre, turn the work closely to a 62mm (2½in) diameter sphere, leaving only a little to part off at either end. Lightly pencil in a new datum line.

◆ Gently saw through the waste wood, leaving a small 'pip' at either end of each hemisphere.

◆ Separate and hold A and B in turn in the 62mm (2½in) diameter hemispherical chuck with the 18mm (¾in) thick collar. Ensure that the pip is facing out and is as closely on centre as possible. Turn off the pip so that each end of A and B is truly hemispherical (*see* Fig 20.7).

◆ Fit A and B, aligning the datum. If the joint is not sufficiently tight to hold together by itself, masking tape will keep the two halves together whilst the concentric groove centres (primary points) are marked. Refer to Chapter 5.

It always gives tremendous pleasure when turned joints fit so well that the joined sphere has to be knocked against a piece of wood to 'crack' it like an egg into two hemispheres –

Fig 20.7 A and B placed in the hemispherical chuck in turn.

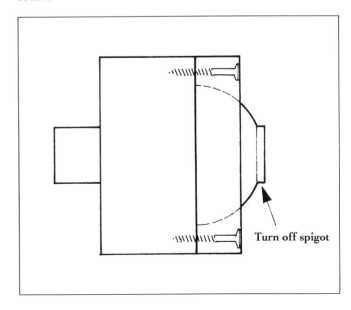

Turn off spigot

Fig 20.8 The turned hemisphere in the hemispherical chuck.

but be careful: too tight a joint might cause difficulty. Imagine having joined the two hollow hemispheres and the frustration of not being able to open them!

Preparation for hollowing the hemispheres

◆ Mark a 54mm (2³⁄₁₆in) diameter circle on to card or cereal packet. Mark the centre line, and then cut the circle out, to be used as a template.
◆ Have ready the 62mm (2½in) spherical chuck, with the 6mm (¼in) thick collar with a 54mm (2³⁄₁₆in) diameter opening.
◆ A 6mm (¼in) round-nose scraper will be needed.
◆ Lathe speed 500 rpm.

Hollowing the hemispheres

◆ Drill a 2mm (³⁄₃₂in) diameter hole 4mm (³⁄₁₆in) deep at each of the primary points. Use white correction fluid to mark the depth on the drill. These holes will act as guides when hollowing, as when they show through

the cut surface, you will know that the wall thickness is exactly 4mm (³⁄₁₆in).
◆ Separate the two halves of the sphere, and take one hemisphere and fit it into the chuck with its flat face to the front.
◆ Screw the collar on to the chuck, taking care that it is screwed down evenly – not one side more than another (*see* Fig 20.8). Also make sure all screws are tight.
◆ Bring the toolrest across the face of the work, setting its height so that the 6mm (¼in) round-nose scraper is at centre height when resting upon it.
◆ Begin the hollowing with light cuts, testing regularly with the 54mm (2³⁄₁₆in) diameter card template. As the work is hollowed, move the toolrest as close to the work as necessary.
◆ Keep looking for the drilled holes to show through, as this will indicate that the correct depth has been reached – these holes can be seen in Fig 20.9. The inner edge of the collar will also act as a depth guide – why else is it 54mm (2³⁄₁₆in) diameter? The wall of

Fig 20.9 The hemisphere is hollowed out.

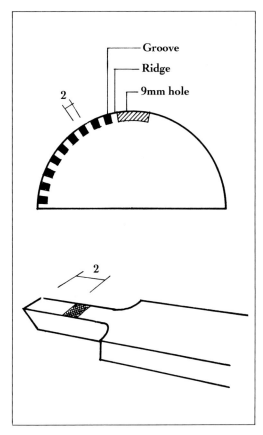

Fig 20.10 (Above) The card template set out.
(Below) Depth mark on the square-end tool.

Fig 20.11 Sectional view of the square-end tool
cutting the grooves.

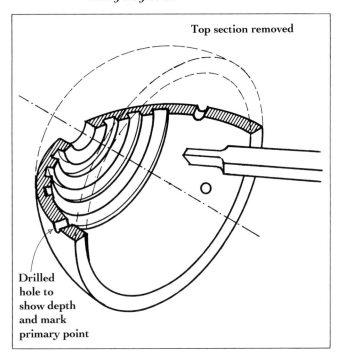

the hemisphere should be in line with its edge.

◆ When satisfied that the inside is hemispherical and, most importantly, that the wall thickness is an even 4mm (³⁄₁₆in), turn out the top hole to 9mm (³⁄₈in) diameter, or drill out to 9mm (³⁄₈in) diameter.

◆ It is important that the wall thickness is even, as it is so much easier, when cutting the outer grooves, to cut to one depth and expose all the grooves, rather than having to go back again and again to cut deeper, to expose one thicker section.

◆ Mark the 9mm (³⁄₈in) end hole on the card template, and mark from the edge of that hole a series of points, 2mm (³⁄₃₂in), 4mm (³⁄₁₆in), 6mm (¼in), continuing round until a quadrant is reached (see Fig 20.10 for this template). With the lathe stationary, place the template inside and line up the edge of the 9mm (³⁄₈in) hole to the same on the template. Using a fine, sharp pencil, transfer the 2mm (³⁄₃₂in), 4mm (³⁄₁₆in) and other points to the inner surface of the hemisphere. Remove the template and toolrest, and switch on the lathe. The pencil dots will appear as faint lines; mark them in fully with pencil.

Do not be disturbed if you come across a few inclusions and flaws when turning: continue turning until the correct wall thickness is reached. With luck, many of those troublesome parts will be turned away; if they are only minor, they may be strengthened by applying a small amount of superglue (cyanoacrylate) on and around the area.

Turning the internal grooves

◆ Replace the toolrest, bringing it as close to the inner surface as possible and adjusting it so that the 2mm (³⁄₃₂in) wide cutting tool's top edge is at centre height.

◆ Using white correction fluid, mark a point on the top surface of the tool 2mm (³⁄₃₂in) away from the cutting edge (see Fig 20.10). This will act as a depth guide.

◆ Turn on the lathe and bring the 2mm (³⁄₃₂in) tool close to the 9mm (³⁄₈in) hole at the base of the hemisphere. Leave the first 2mm (³⁄₃₂in) wide strip, lining the tool up with the

Fig 20.12 Using the fine square-end tool to cut the concentric grooves.

second of the 2mm (⁵⁄₃₂in) wide areas. Gently and slowly plunge the tool to its 2mm (⁵⁄₃₂in) depth. Withdraw and position it at the next but one 2mm (⁵⁄₃₂in) area so that a series of 2mm (⁵⁄₃₂in) ridges and grooves will be cut on the inside of the hemisphere (*see* Figs 20.11 and 20.12).

◆ Always ensure that the tool passes through the imagined centre of the hemisphere when the cutting edge is in contact.

◆ This first hemisphere can now be removed and replaced with the second one, and the process repeated. Fig 20.13 shows both hemispheres with finished internal grooves.

It is very easy to forget to sharpen the 2mm (⁵⁄₃₂in) tool when concentrating hard on ensuring that the gaps are kept equal, that the cut progresses steadily and to the correct depth and that the tool is angled through the centre of the hemisphere. Suddenly, and at precisely the wrong moment, the tool will let you know it needs sharpening, but it can be too late, and the damage will have been done. Think before problems arise and sharpen the tool regularly, but also remember to check that the 2mm (⁵⁄₃₂in) depth mark is corrected if necessary.

Preparation for the external grooves

◆ Change the 6mm (¼in) thick collar for an 18mm (¾in) thick collar with a 48mm (1⅞in) top opening.

◆ Sharpen the 2mm (⁵⁄₃₂in) tool.

◆ Lathe speed 500 rpm.

Fig 20.13 The two hemispheres with internal grooves cut.

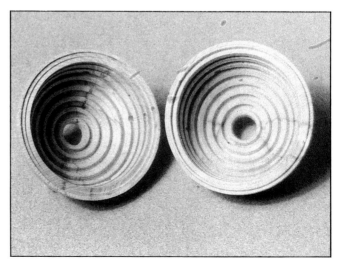

Turning the external grooves

◆ Fit the two halves of the sphere and align the datum.

◆ Place the sphere in the chuck, with the collar lightly held by the screws.

◆ If there is one area of the sphere's surface with minor faults or irregular grain, it is better to begin here, leaving the perfect patch for the end. Bring the chosen primary point to the front, but never the top and bottom 9mm (⅜in) holes. Draw the tailstock gently forward so that the centre fits into the 2mm (³⁄₃₂in) hole of the primary point. Tighten gently so that the sphere is forced against the back of the chuck; too much pressure may crack the work, so take care. Tighten down the collar evenly. Always check and double-check all collar screws are tight before continuing.

◆ Remove the tailstock and bring the toolrest across so that the 2mm (³⁄₃₂in) tool is at centre height.

If the sphere is slightly undersize and can move even a small amount when the collar is tight, this is the time to ensure a tight fit, for a slight slippage whilst cutting the concentric grooves can lead to damage. Small pieces of glasspaper, evenly spaced and fixed in place using double-sided tape inside the collar and chuck, are usually sufficient to remove slight movement.

◆ Turn on the lathe, ensuring that the 2mm (³⁄₃₂in) hole runs on centre. Mark a line 2mm (³⁄₃₂in) away from the hole's edge. Gently bring the tool up to the surface of the rotating sphere, and, slowly and carefully cut into the surface to the 2mm (³⁄₃₂in) depth, pointing the tool towards the centre of the sphere. The last part of the cut should be gentle. Turn off the lathe to see if the cut has pierced through; if not, turn on the lathe again and cut a little deeper. This first cut is quite simple, with no real pressure being applied.

◆ Move on to the second groove. Mark a circular path 2mm (³⁄₃₂in) away from the first

Fig 20.14 The two parts held together in the hemispherical chuck.

cut, and carefully cut the groove. When satisfied, move on to groove 3, then finally groove 4 (*see* Fig 20.14).

It is a magical experience as a faint heart-quickening 'click-click' sound tells that the tool has cut through and you may stop the lathe to look at the pierced section. Any pieces that have only partially been broken through can be opened out with a triangular needle file.

◆ When the first set of concentric grooves are cut, move on to the next primary point, setting up and cutting as before (*see* Fig 20.15).
◆ As work progresses, you might be tempted by your success so far to cut the lattice circles more quickly – always cut each circle with the same delicacy and care as the first, and don't forget to sharpen the tool regularly.
◆ When all 10 concentric circles are cut, remove the work from the chuck – for goodness' sake, don't let it slip now! – and place it in a safe part of the workshop.

Fig 20.15 Two concentric circles outer grooves meet. The internal grooves show through.

Preparation for making the spindle

◆ Fit the driving dog in the headstock.
◆ Lathe speed 1500 rpm.

Making the spindle

◆ Turn a piece of 110mm (4⅜in) by 25mm (1in) square boxwood (or matching wood) between centres to a 20mm (⅞in) diameter cylinder.
◆ Turn the shaped part at the tailstock end as shown in Fig 20.16, undercutting the

Fig 20.16 The central spindle.

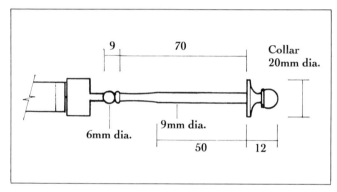

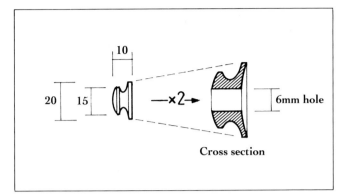

Fig 20.17 Turning the collar.

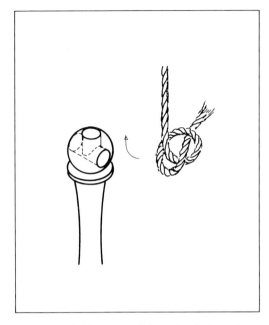

Fig 20.18 Drill across and down for the knotted cord.

inner shoulder so that it fits snugly up to the sphere.

◆ From the inner shoulder towards the headstock, turn down to fractionally under 9mm (⅜in).

◆ Measure 5mm (⁷⁄₃₂in) from the inner shoulder, and at that point turn down to 6mm (¼in) diameter towards the headstock.

◆ Measure 70mm (2¾in) from the inner shoulder, and turn the final top detail at that point. Polish and part off.

◆ Drill a 1.5mm (¹⁄₁₆in) hole down through the top of the spindle (*see* Fig 20.17), then drill a 2mm (³⁄₃₂in) hole across and through the top section of the spindle; small round-nose dental burrs are perfect for the job. These holes allow fine cord to be passed through, knotted and pulled up so that when the pomander is finished it can be suspended from the cord.

◆ To turn the top collar, set a piece of 25mm (1in) square by 50mm (2in) long boxwood between centres and turn down to a 20mm (⅞in) cylinder.

◆ Remove the workpiece and the driving dog; fit a three-jaw chuck.

◆ Fit the turned wood in the chuck, bring up the tailstock and face off the end. Remove the revolving centre and replace it with a drill chuck holding a 6mm (¼in) diameter drill. Drill through the centre of the workpiece.

◆ Turn the workpiece to shape, undercutting the face for a snug fit with the sphere. Bring up the tailstock for support, and complete the turning of the collar shape. Polish and part off cleanly (*see* Fig 20.17).

◆ Finally, slide the bottom half of the sphere over the cord on to the spindle, and

then the top half, followed by the collar, as shown in Fig 20.18. Open the sphere enough to fill it with potpourri, and hang as seen in Fig 20.19.

Fig 20.19 The pomanders in use.

CHAPTER 21

SINGAPORE BALL

O F ALL THE PIECES I HAVE MADE, I LIKE THIS ONE THE MOST. IT HAS A WONDERFUL LOOK AND FEEL, LIKE A GENTLE MEDIEVAL MACE HEAD WHERE THE POINTS DON'T REALLY WANT TO CAUSE ANY DAMAGE: THEY DROP BACK INTO THEIR HOLES ON CONTACT (*SEE* FIG 21.1). WHEN THE BALL IS MOVED, THE POINTS ON THE UNDERSIDE FALL FORWARDS, POINTS OUT, BUT THOSE ON THE UPPER SURFACE RETREAT INTO THEIR HOLES AND ARE ALMOST HIDDEN.

In Holtzapffel's book, *Hand or Simple Turning*, he describes these balls as being made by the Chinese in ivory and porcelain, and their shape as being derived from the lotus nut. He goes on to explain that, although it appears that the points have been turned and undercut in place, having forced one of them out and examined it, the grain direction did not match that of its surroundings. He surmised that the points were made separately and pushed into prepared hollows (*see* Fig 21.2). He finished his discourse by stating that the Singapore ball's manufacture requires no special instruction.

To maintain the illusion that the points were turned in place, and I feel that it is important to do so, be very careful in the choice of your wood. Make sure that if there is darker grain in the area of the hole, match it, or if there are a few pin knots close by, try and turn a point with a pin knot in it. Try to leave people guessing; make as convincing a piece as possible. That, in this case, is where the skill lies.

Preparation

◆ Turn a 62mm (2½in) diameter sphere from a close-grained hardwood (I used boxwood). Refer to Chapter 6 for instructions on turning spheres.

◆ Have available the 62mm (2½in) diameter hemispherical chuck and the 30mm (1³⁄₁₆in) thick collar.

◆ You will need a drill chuck which fits in the tailstock; this chuck must accept a 9mm (⅜in) drill.

◆ Have ready a 9mm (⅜in) drill and a 3mm (⅛in) drill to act as a pilot.

◆ Grind a tool from a 6mm (¼in) wood chisel to match the profile shown in Fig 21.3.

◆ Be careful not to overheat the tool when grinding; quench it regularly.

◆ Grind back a 30° cutting angle on the front and side of the tool.

◆ Lathe speed around 1000 rpm.

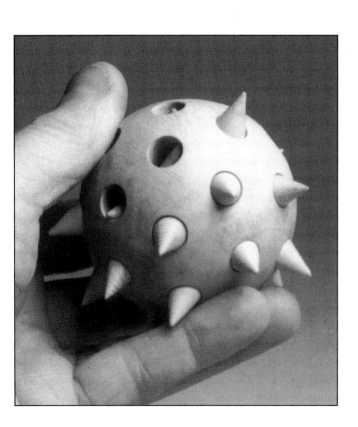

Fig 21.1 The Singapore ball.

Fig 21.2 The specially shaped tool, template and calliper, and a spare set of teardrops surround the finished ball.

Turning the sphere

◆ Refer to Chapter 5, and mark out the sphere with its 12 primary points and a further 20 constellation points (32 in all).

◆ Begin by fitting the sphere into the chuck, fitting the collar loosely.

◆ Bring one of the points marked on the sphere's surface (it does not matter which) to the front. Fit a revolving centre into the tailstock and push it gently towards the chuck.

◆ Touch the revolving centre on to the marked point on the sphere. Lock down the tailstock and tighten the revolving centre on to the point, pushing the sphere against the back of the chuck.

◆ Now that the sphere is held firmly with one point facing front and on centre, screw the collar down evenly.

◆ Make sure that the sphere is held firmly by the collar as the tailstock is drawn away from the work.

◆ Change the revolving centre for a drill chuck holding a 3mm (⅛in) drill.

◆ Mark a point 18mm (¾in) away from its tip on the drill with correction fluid.

◆ Turn on the lathe and drill the front point on the sphere to the marked depth with the 3mm (⅛in) drill. This will act as a pilot hole for the 9mm (⅜in) drill, which can now be fitted into the chuck.

◆ Mark on the 9mm (⅜in) drill a point 18mm (¾in) away from its tip, again with correction fluid.

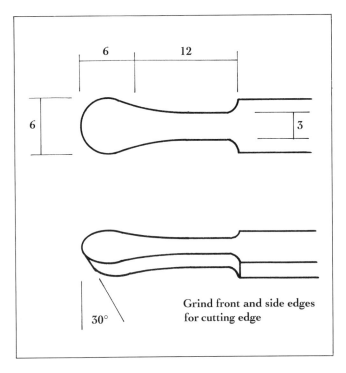

6

12

6

3

30°

Grind front and side edges for cutting edge

Fig 21.3 The profile tool.

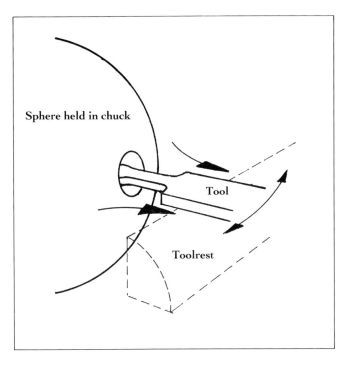

Sphere held in chuck

Tool

Toolrest

Fig 21.4 The cutting motion to produce the internal pear-shaped hollow.

◆ Mark on the profile tool, using correction fluid, a point 18mm (¾in) away from the front edge.

◆ Turn on the lathe and carefully push the tool into the drilled hole, making light contact with the hole's base.

◆ Move the front cutting edge of the tool so that it begins to cut the wood inside the hole, pulling it out towards the front, and reducing the amount cut as it approaches the opening. Try to imagine the shape being cut inside (*see* Fig 21.4, which shows the cutting motion).

◆ Repeat the cut until the inside is approximately pear-shaped; this can only be judged by feel, so turn off the lathe occasionally and decide whether the hole is the correct shape.

◆ The internal shape of the hole does not need to be exact, but it does need to maintain a similar shape in all 32 positions.

◆ At no time should the cutting edge of the tool make contact with the front opening of the hole, which must remain 9mm (⅜in) diameter.

◆ The hole has a small opening which,

◆ Using the pilot hole as a guide, drill a 9mm (⅜in) hole to the marked depth.

◆ Withdraw the drill and move the whole tailstock away from the work, bringing the toolrest across the face of the work.

◆ Position the toolrest so that the ground profile tool is at centre height.

Fig 21.5 The drilled hole is shaped internally with the specially ground tool.

partially filled by the tool, will quickly fill up with wood shavings. To remove these efficiently, take a straw, preferably a bendy one, place one end in the hole, **close your eyes**, and blow.

◆ When satisfied that the hole is the desired shape, move the toolrest away, loosen the collar of the chuck and bring another point forward. Again use the tailstock centre to hold the point on centre while tightening the collar down.

◆ Repeat the hole-cutting operation for each of the remaining 31 holes (*see* Fig 21.5).

◆ Although the holes may encroach upon one another during turning, do not be too worried. Do be aware, though, that too wide a cut in each hole may cause them all to join, which will make the centre break loose.

Preparation for the teardrop points

◆ Cut twelve 75mm (3in) lengths, 12mm (½in) square from wood which matches the turned sphere; this will allow enough wood for an occasional mistake.

◆ Turn these pieces between centres close to 12mm (½in) diameter, using a fine driving dog. These pieces will be held in a drill chuck fitting in the headstock, so if the drill chuck for your lathe only opens to 9mm (⅜in), turn a short spigot at the headstock end to that diameter.

◆ To act as a guide, mark out the shape and length (18mm or ¾in) of the teardrop on a piece of card – cereal packet will do.

◆ Lathe speed 1500 rpm.

As these teardrops only show their points and a little of their sides through the opening, it will be quite acceptable, and even helpful, to leave the tailstock point on their hidden rounded end.

Turning the teardrop points

◆ Using the card template, mark the length of the teardrop shape on the 12mm (½in) rod held in the drill chuck and revolving centre (*see* Fig 21.6). Cut down to 4mm (³⁄₁₆in) diameter at the point marked A in Fig 21.7, using a fine parting tool. Cut on the headstock side of the line.

◆ Turn this 18mm (¾in) length down to 9.3 – 9.5mm (around ¹³⁄₃₂in); this size will be decided by trail and error. It needs to be just over the 9mm (⅜in) size of drilled hole, and just enough to be able to press the teardrop hard into the hole, and enough that it should not come free. It depends on the exact size of the hole (which might vary slightly) and the density of the wood being used. The guide sizes shown in Fig 21.8 should be of help.

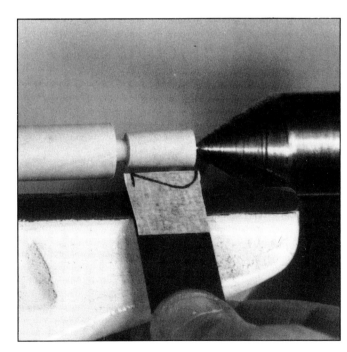

Fig 21.6 A template helps mark out the teardrop shape.

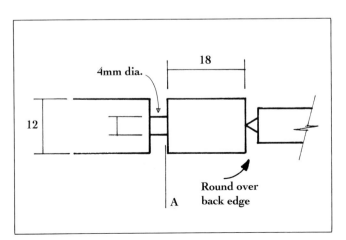

Fig 21.7 Turning a teardrop.

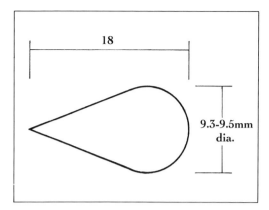

18

9.3-9.5mm
dia.

Fig 21.8 The teardrop dimensions.

◆ Shape from the top edge of the natural curve down towards position A, remembering that the final point of the teardrop will be at A.

◆ The outside diameter of the teardrop at the junction of the natural curve and the slope must not be reduced, otherwise the teardrop will just drop out of its hole.

◆ Clean up the shape so that the slope is straight and clear (see Fig 21.9), finally skimming down and parting off to a point, using a skew chisel (see Fig 21.10).

◆ Choose an area on the sphere which matches the colour and grain of the teardrop, and push the teardrop firmly into place. It should be moderately tough to push through the hole, not so much that it splits or permanently bruises the hole opening, but

Turn the teardrop and test, then set the callipers; maintain the calliper setting once you have reached the correct size.

◆ Round over the end near the tailstock with a skew chisel, producing a natural curve.

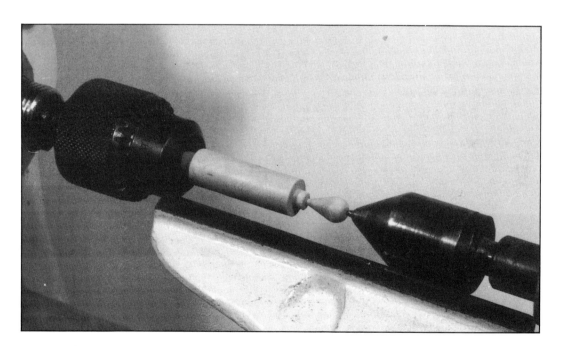

Fig 21.9 The turned dowel held between drill chuck and revolving centre.

Fig 21.10 The final parting cut.

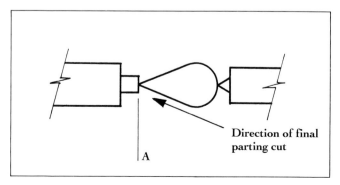

Direction of final parting cut

A

equally not so loose so that it falls out (*see* Fig 21.11).

◆ Be very selective in the wood grain and colour of the teardrop, and take every care to match the surrounding area on the sphere.

Turning the stand

For this stand I used privet, a small tree which has most often been tamed into garden hedges. When left to grow freely it produces a sizeable trunk. The wood is creamy white, smooth and clean-cutting, with streams and ribbons of shavings pouring off the turned work. The one drawback is that it is very difficult to season: the drying logs split and crack very easily and very quickly, no matter how carefully they are treated. Keep the wood in a place where it can dry out as slowly as possible.

◆ Turn a piece 120mm (4¾in) long by 55mm (2¼in) square between centres to round.

◆ At the tailstock end, measure 60mm (2⅜in) towards the headstock and at that point, again towards the headstock, turn down to 18mm (¾in) diameter (*see* Fig 21.12).

◆ Remove the driving dog from the headstock and replace it with a 4-jaw chuck.

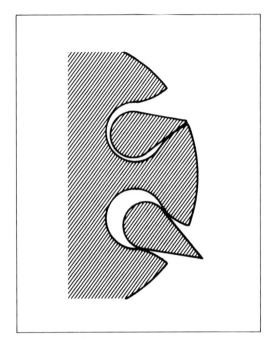

Fig 21.11 Teardrop fitting into the hollow.

◆ Withdraw the tailstock.

◆ Hold the 18mm (¾in) diameter part in the chuck, with the shoulder of the larger diameter pushed up against the jaws.

◆ Bring the toolrest across the end face and, using a round-nose tool, cut to a depth of 18mm (¾in).

◆ This internal shaping should resemble the inside of a trumpet bell, somewhat like a

Fig 21.12 Turning the stand.

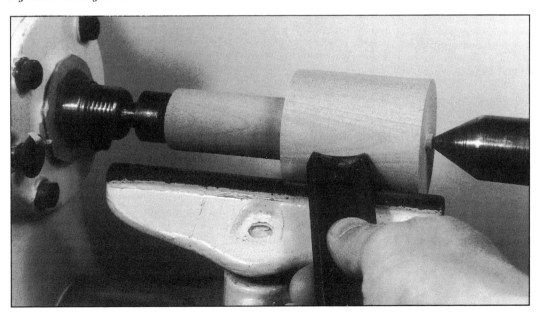

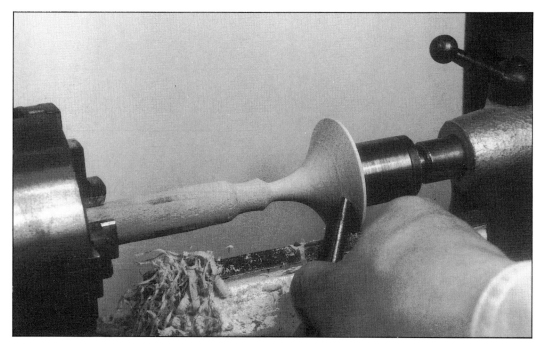

Fig 21.13 A sweeping cut with a gouge produces the trumpet bell shaping.

convolvulus flower. Use a gouge to remove the majority of the wood, but a narrow round-nose tool will be best to turn right down into the centre.

◆ Remove the toolrest once the internal shaping is exactly as desired, and finish the inside surface smoothly.

◆ Bring the tailstock, holding the revolving centre, back towards the work. Push the centre down into the hollow, marking the exact centre with its point.

◆ Withdraw the tailstock, loosen the chuck jaws and pull the work forward until only 9mm (⅜in) of the spigot is gripped lightly by the jaws.

◆ Bring the tailstock forward and push the revolving centre into the centre of the hollow, relocating the mark made earlier. Tighten the chuck jaws: this will ensure that the piece runs exactly on centre.

◆ Bring the toolrest across the length of the work, and with a sharp gouge shape the outside of the bell to create a fluent trumpet shape at the tailstock end of the work. This trumpet shape should echo the internal shaping, and the wall thickness should be around 3mm (⅛in).

◆ Sweep the gouge down along the stem, maintaining a fluent shape from the trumpet bell into the stem (*see* Fig 21.13).

◆ Measure 90mm (3⁹⁄₁₆in) from the lip of the bell towards the headstock. At that point turn down a small spigot 6mm (¼in) in diameter: this should be quite close to the overall diameter of the stem.

◆ Clean and polish the outer surface.

◆ Part off below the 6mm (¼in) spigot, leaving enough to fit into a 6mm (¼in) hole drilled into the chosen base.

Cutting the trumpet bell to shape

◆ The trumpet bell will be cut on the bandsaw to produce a three-pointed top.

◆ To calculate the distance that the bandsaw fence should be set away from the saw blade, measure the diameter of the trumpet bell. The diameter of the one described above was 54mm (2¼in). Divide this in half for the radius 27mm (1⅛in). Draw a circle of this size on paper with a pencil compass. Place the compass point anywhere upon the circle, and 'walk' it around the circle, marking where it touches. This will produce six points. Take one, miss one, take one, miss one, take one, miss one:

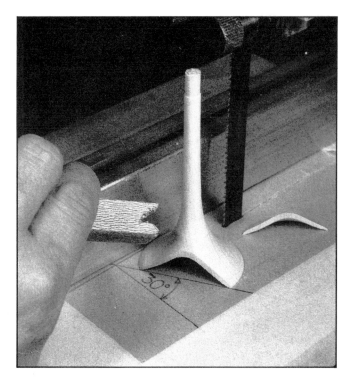

Fig 21.14 *The end of the trumpet bell is cut upon the bandsaw.*

line; push the uncut edge of the trumpet up against the fence, and make the second cut (*see* Fig 21.14).

◆ The second cut is aligned with the 30° mark. Push the uncut edge of the trumpet bell up against the fence, and make the third cut. Turn off the bandsaw.

◆ Clean up the tricorn end of the stand by rubbing its cut surface on glasspaper set on a flat surface.

◆ Polish the cleaned cut edges to match the rest of the stand.

◆ Select a suitable base, drill a 3mm (⅛in) hole and glue the turned end in place. This stand allows the sphere to be securely held, letting the majority of it be seen (*see* Fig 21.15).

Fig 21.15 *The Singapore ball on its stand.*

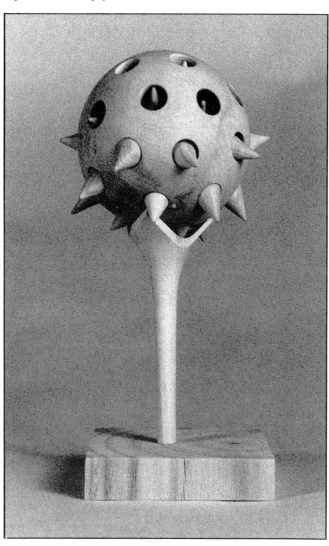

this will reduce it to three equally spaced points. Join these points to produce a triangle seated inside the circle. Choose one point and join it with the centre, continuing the line through to the opposite edge of the circle. Now measure the distance from that opposite edge where it touches the circle to the base of the triangle where the pencil line cuts through. In this case it will be 14mm (⁹⁄₁₆in).

◆ Set the bandsaw fence 14mm (⁹⁄₁₆in) away from the blade, then move it in another 3mm (⅛in), bringing the distance to 11mm (⁷⁄₁₆in). By experience I have found that cutting to the exact size makes the finished piece look a little thin; this extra allowance is just right.

◆ Slide a piece of card under the fence and into the blade, taping down the edges. Draw a line at 90° to the blade, and then another at 30° to that drawn line. This will be a guide for the second and third cuts.

◆ The first cut is made with the edge of the trumpet bell set against the fence. Turn on the bandsaw and, taking care to keep the fingers safely clear, cut the edge.

◆ The cut edge is then aligned with the 30°

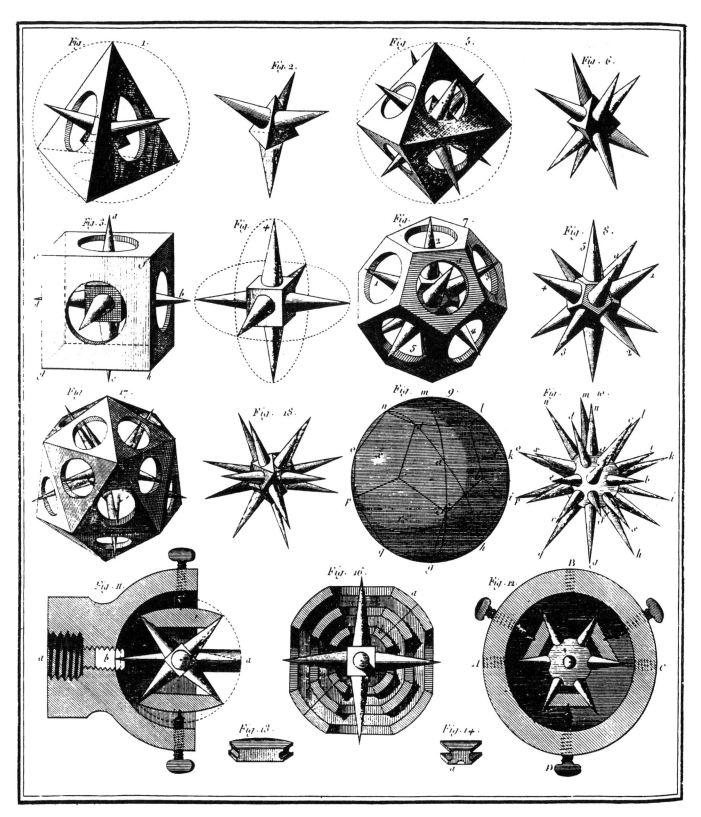

Examples of the kind of eighteenth- and nineteenth-century turnery which inspired some of the projects in this book (from *Manuel du Tourneur*, 1816).

CHAPTER 22

SPIKED STAR IN CUBE

HIS PROJECT LOOKS FAR MORE DIFFICULT TO PRODUCE THAN IN ACTUAL PRACTICE. USING SIMPLE TOOLS, ONLY ONE SPECIALLY MADE, A CUBE IS 'TURNED' AND A SIX-POINTED SPIKED STAR IS CUT INSIDE AND TRAPPED INSIDE THE SIX WALLS OF THE CUBE (*SEE* FIG 22.1).

Inspired by drawings in the book *Manuel du Tourneur*, by Hamelin Bergeron, published in 1816, I rushed headlong into the project. What I had not fully understood, but soon came to realise, was that although the chuck was only a simple square hole into which the cube fitted and was gripped, each time one surface of the cube was turned the fit became less tight and more off-centre. This problem was solved by cutting long thin wedges and tapping them in along the open edges of the cube, taking care to ensure they were centrally located each time. (It was fortunate that before I began I had marked diagonal pencil lines on each face of the cube, locating each face's centre.)

Before I began I also drew the cube and the spikes inside full-size, working out the dimensions to ensure that the depth to which the tools should cut was decided. This also gave the opportunity to best plan the shape of the spikes and to calculate the distance the angled tool should cut before it would break through the cube's face.

The wood I chose to work with was pear; it is an enormously satisfying wood to turn, clean and smooth cutting, producing an excellent surface.

One final point before beginning the work: as you cut out the cube, mark the end grain faces, as these are the two to be worked first. The edges of the chuck will fit snugly up, supporting edges which otherwise would be broken out. The side grain pieces can then be cut with little risk of edges

Fig 22.1 Spiked star in cube on its stand.

breaking out. This also relates to the internal cuts of end grain parts; they also have the benefit of support of surrounding wood to protect from break-out.

Preparation

◆ Make and have ready the square hole chuck described in Chapter 2.

◆ Carefully grind and sharpen the angled tool from a 15mm (⅝in) wood chisel, as shown in Fig 22.2. Paint the surface of the chisel with white correction fluid, so that the marked shape is clearly visible. When

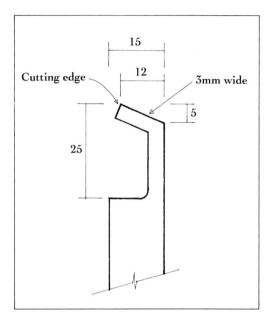

Fig 22.2 The ground tool produced from a 15mm wood chisel.

Fig 22.3 Grinding the special angled tool.

grinding away the waste metal, quench the tool in water regularly to prevent it losing its temper (*see* Fig 22.3).

◆ Have available a 3mm (⅛in) wide square-end tool and a 3mm (⅛in) round-nose tool.

◆ Cut a cube with length of side 55mm (2³⁄₁₆in) from the chosen wood. Remember to mark the two end grain faces and mark the diagonals locating the centre on each face.

◆ Turn five plugs, each 30mm (1³⁄₁₆in) diameter, 3mm (⅛in) thick, and each with a central 3mm (⅛in) hole and an off-set hole of the same size, to assist removal. These plugs should be turned from a 100mm (4in) long piece, 30mm (1³⁄₁₆in) diameter, drilled through the centre with a 3mm (⅛in) drill. 3mm (⅛in) pieces can then be parted off (*see* Fig 22.4). The off-set hole is drilled individually in each plug.

◆ Lathe speed approximately 500 rpm, and 300 rpm when the angled tool is in use.

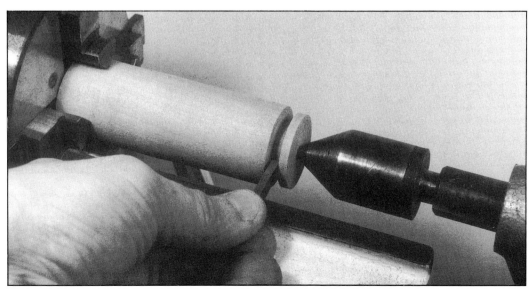

Fig 22.4 Turning the plugs.

Fig 22.5 The central spike is pre-turned with a square-end tool.

Beginning the work

◆ Place the cube in the square hole chuck with one of the end grain faces showing to the front. Tighten the screws on either side of the cut diagonal line on the chuck, to firmly grip the cube.

◆ Set the toolrest across the face of the work, adjusting it so that the 3mm (⅛in) wide square-end tool cuts at centre height.

◆ Using white correction fluid, mark a position 19mm (¾in) away from the cutting edge of the square-end tool. Remember that if the tool is resharpened, this distance must be checked and readjusted if necessary.

◆ Turn on the lathe, marking a 30mm (1³⁄₁₆in) diameter and a 10mm (⅜in) diameter on the face of the work in pencil.

◆ Carefully make the first cut on the inside of the larger diameter with the square-end tool, moving across to the outside edge of the smaller diameter.

◆ Continue to cut down until the white mark is reached on the edge of the tool, widening each cut as you progress so that the square-end tool is never gripped on its side by the wood (*see* Fig 22.5). This will leave a central core 10mm (⅜in) diameter, 19mm (¾in) long and a wide circular groove of the same depth up to the 30mm (1³⁄₁₆in) outer

diameter (*see* Fig 22.6).

◆ Now begin to cut the spike: the top centre of the core will be the tip, and the base edge of the core will remain unturned. Using the square-end tool, gently begin taking small stepping cuts down the core which start to produce the angle of the spike. Once the shape has been roughed out, complete with a fine slicing cut, using the corner of the square-end tool (*see* Fig 22.7). Try to make this a fluent single cut producing a clean surface from the top centre down to its base edge, as it is very difficult to clean up the shape afterwards. Do not allow too much tool contact with the work, as there is a danger of the spike twisting off. The actual shaping of the spike is purely up to you.

◆ Before undercutting the faces of the work, mark a 35mm (1⅜in) diameter upon the face in pencil. Cut down 1mm (½2in) on the outside of this line, using the freshly sharpened square-end tool, then turn away from the line towards the outer edge at the same depth (*see* Fig 22.8). Do not be concerned if you cut into the surface of the chuck, but do cut cleanly. Before rounding over the edges of this newly created lip, mark a line on the inside edge of the wide groove 3mm (⅛in) down; this will mark the starting

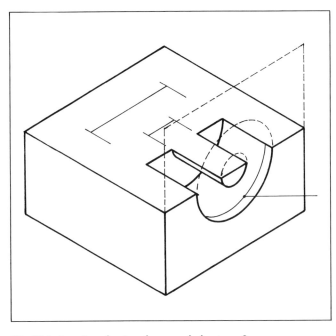

Fig 22.6 A section showing the central plug turned.

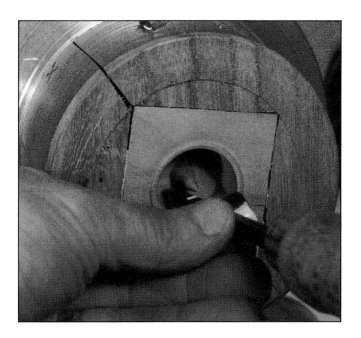

Fig 22.7 Turning the spike to a point with the square-end tool.

Fig 22.7 Turning the spike to a point with the square-end tool.

Fig 22.8 The spike turned and the collar around the hole.

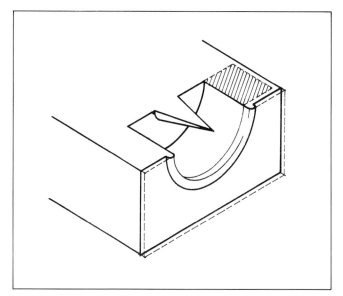

point of the undercut. Now carefully round over the edges of the lip.

◆ Reduce the lathe speed to 300 rpm before using the angled tool. Bring the angled tool up to the work, taking the first gentle cut at the 3mm (⅛in) marked pencil line (*see* Fig 22.9). Move it slightly towards the centre (into the depth of the work) to widen the cut, preventing the tool from being gripped and snatched into the revolving work and being careful not to knock against the spike.

◆ Continue with fine and gentle cuts, slowly moving the tool to widen the gap while judging the depth of cut against the distance the tool is moving in (*see* Fig 22.10). Remember that the cut must stop 3mm (⅛in) away from the faces of the adjoining four sides.

◆ Mark on the 3mm (⅛in) round-nose tool a point 19mm (¾in) from its cutting edge as a depth guide, using correction fluid. Use this tool to remove the waste wood below the undercut and to the sides of the wide groove, making light and gentle cuts at all times. The depth mark will act as a useful guide in preventing cutting into any areas which will eventually be turned as spikes.

As the waste wood is being cut away it will begin to clog up the inside of the hollow, and will be difficult to remove. An easy solution is to push a drinking straw into the hollow

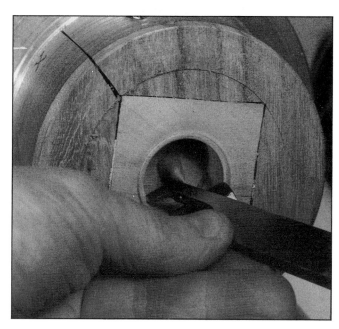

Fig 22.9 Carefully introducing the ground angled tool.

when the lathe is stationary, **close your eyes**, and blow. The shavings will be blasted out of the opening.

◆ When as much waste wood as possible has been removed, turn off the lathe, check

Fig 22.10 The angled tool undercutting the front edge.

that all is satisfactory and fit one of the plugs (*see* Fig 22.11). If there is a slight movement in the plug, Blu-tak will take up the slack and hold the plug in position.

◆ Loosen the chuck screws and remove the cube, turning it around so the other end grain face shows to the front. Tighten the chuck and repeat the spike cutting as before, finally fitting the plug.

Fig 22.11 Fitting the plug to support the spike; the extra hole in the plug is for easy removal.

Cutting the remaining four spikes

Cutting the first two spikes into the end grain faces is quite straightforward, but the remaining spikes require the cube to be set centrally each time before work begins. Fig 22.12 shows the internal layout of the spikes when completed.

◆ Place the cube in the chuck with an uncut face forward. Bring the tailstock, holding a centre, forward and position the marked centre of the cube exactly in line with the tailstock centre. Fix the cube tightly using fine wooden wedges, to ensure its centre remains 'on centre'. Tighten the chuck screws.

◆ Cut the centre core as before, and turn the face and lip. Mark the depth of the undercut into the edge of the wide groove before rounding over the lip.

◆ Be prepared to hit a void, a space cut by the tool on one of the other sides, on the third and successive spikes when using the

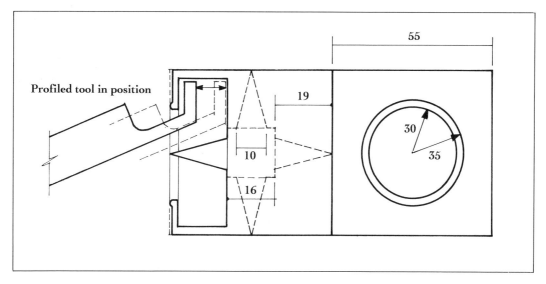

Fig 22.12 Internal layout of the star, and size of the turned lip.

angled tool. Hold the tool steady, and do not let the void throw the tool into a jumpy, bumpy cut. Remember to take light cuts: there is an overhang on the angled tool, and too much force on the cutting edge can cause it to be knocked downwards. Remember also to maintain the in-and-out movement to widen the cut; this will prevent the tool from being gripped. Blow out the shavings frequently so that the internal progress may be viewed, and continue removing the waste

Fig 22.13 The tool, the cube, the spiked star inside and the plugs.

with the round-nose tool.

◆ Remember always to take care not to knock the turned spike, as it may be damaged.

◆ A small web will be left in each of the internal corners; it is important, when removing the waste wood with the round-nose tool, that the corner web be turned out at the same time, thus making the shape as even as possible.

◆ As each face is turned, a thickness is removed, making it necessary to support the piece with more wedges: these hold the work firmly in place, preventing forward movement in the chuck, and also hold it firmly on centre. To judge concentricity, mark a pencil line whilst the work is rotating and adjust as necessary.

◆ When cutting the final hole, the last core cut will break through. Take particular care at this time and also when shaping the last spike, for all that now hold the centre parts are the five spike ends supported in the plugs.

◆ A further reason for turning the end grain faces first, which will be appreciated now, is that the grain direction of their spikes is lengthwise: this ensures that when turning the final point and cutting it away from the waste wood, the twisting action on the points supported in the plugs is held better in check with the additional support of these long-grained pieces.

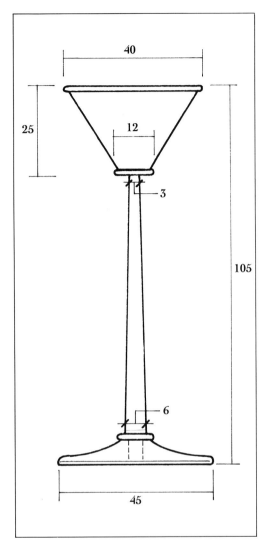

Fig 22.14 *The stand.*

◆ At times, cutting through into the void with the angled tool at full stretch and turning the corner webs out cleanly can be a little tense, but taking the cube from the chuck, removing the plugs one by one and seeing that spike centre loose inside gives one such a tremendous sense of achievement that all those moments of worry fall away (*see* Fig 22.13).

◆ Look carefully inside, and you will see that each of the spikes sits upon a square face of its own and on a smaller inner cube. If the faces of this smaller cube are all the same, this will be proof of the care taken throughout each of the stages.

◆ I finished the cube with tung oil, which worked quite well but is not the finish I would recommend for this piece. Two of the faces are end grain, and they soak up the finish, showing up much darker than the others. A friction polish as the work progresses may be a better finish.

Turning the stand

I chose pear for this stand, to match the turned cube, and instead of using an oil finish I used matt polyurethane. The difference was surprising: the oil darkened the pear, but the polyurethane kept it quite pale. The internal shaping of the top is such that the three-cornered end of the cube seats firmly inside the conical hollow. A small collar beneath the top relieves the starkness

Fig 22.15 *Turning the initial shape for the stand.*

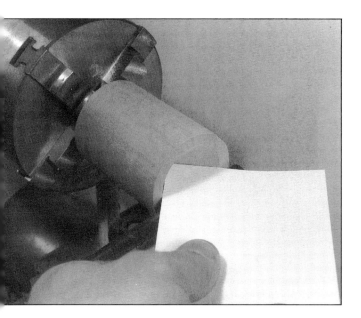

Fig 22.16 *Judging the internal shape with a corner of a piece of card.*

of the shaping before moving down towards the foot (*see* Fig 22.14 for the dimensions of the stand).

◆ Turn a piece of pear 130mm (5⅛in) long and 50mm (2in) square between centres to a cylinder whose diameter is as close to 50mm (2in) as possible.

◆ At the tailstock end, turn down to 15mm (⅝in) diameter for a length of 65mm (2⁹⁄₁₆in) (*see* Fig 22.15).

◆ Withdraw the tailstock and then remove the driving dog from the headstock,

replacing it with a three- or four-jaw chuck.

◆ Push the 15mm (⅝in) diameter length into the chuck until the larger diameter butts up against the jaws. Tighten the chuck.

◆ Bring the toolrest across the face of the work.

◆ Turn a 35mm (1¼in) diameter hollow into the end face of the work. This hollow is conical in shape, and a piece of card with a 90° corner can be used as a template to test when the shaping is correct (*see* Fig 22.16).

◆ When satisfied with the internal shaping, remove the toolrest and bring the tailstock, holding a revolving centre, towards the work. Push the centre into the hollow, which will make a central mark.

◆ Withdraw the tailstock and loosen the chuck jaws, pulling the work outwards until the 15mm (⅝in) part is held lightly in the jaws.

◆ Bring the revolving centre towards the work and relocate the marked centre inside the hollow.

◆ Tighten the chuck jaws. The piece should now run true and on centre.

◆ Reduce the diameter at the tailstock to 40mm (1⁹⁄₁₆in), and then turn the outer shape to reflect the inner, producing a conical end.

◆ Leave enough to turn a 12mm (½in)

Fig 22.17 Turning the stem.

diameter collar, about 1.5mm (1/16in) thick, just under the conical shaping.

◆ Turn down to 3mm (1/8in) diameter below the collar, and taper steadily towards the headstock.

◆ At a point 95mm (3¾in) away from the top rim measured towards the headstock, turn down a 6mm (1/4in) diameter spigot, having first turned a neatly shaped bead (*see* Fig 22.17).

◆ Clean up and part off, leaving a 9mm (3/8in) length of the 6mm (1/4in) spigot.

Turning the foot

◆ Cut out a 45mm (1¾in) diameter circle from a 9mm (3/8in) thick piece of pear.

◆ Drill a 6mm (1/4in) hole at the centre of the circle.

◆ Fit a turned 12mm (1/2in) dowel into the chuck, and turn a 6mm (1/4in) diameter spigot on its end.

◆ Fit the drilled hole of the pear disc on to this spigot (*see* Fig 22.18), and bring up the tailstock with revolving centre to support the end.

◆ Turn the outside diameter of this disc clean and true, then face off the surface closest to the tailstock flat and square.

◆ Remove the foot from the lathe and reverse it, bringing the tailstock and centre back for support.

Fig 22.18 The foot is fitted on to a turned spigot held in the chuck.

◆ Now turn the top surface of the foot in a pleasing fluent shape, leaving enough area on which the turned bead at the base of the stem may sit around the hole (*see* Fig 22.19).

◆ Clean up the foot and remove it from the lathe.

◆ Take the stem, apply glue to the 6mm (1/4in) spigot and press it firmly into the hole in the circular foot. When the glue is dry, polish the stand.

◆ Fit the cube into the stand, arranging the spike inside to its best advantage.

Fig 22.19 Turning the foot.

CHAPTER 23

SPIKED STAR IN SPHERE

OOKING THROUGH *MANUEL DU TOURNEUR* (*SEE* CHAPTER 15), IT IS FASCINATING TO SEE THE MANY VARIATIONS OF SPIKED STARS. SOME ARE CONTAINED IN VARIOUS POLYGONS, OTHERS FORM THE CENTRE PART OF CHINESE BALLS AND SOME, THE MORE DIFFICULT, ARE SPIKED STARS BY THEMSELVES, AGAIN IN A VARIETY OF FORMS.

Here is a relatively simple form, a spiked star held captive within a sphere (*see* Fig 23.1). It may be one of the simpler forms, but I feel that it is one of the most pleasing shapes. 12 holes each show a spike, and each spike is seated upon a pentagonal base, all part of the dodecahedral centre. These pentagonal bases and their centre are formed almost accidentally as the turning progresses; it is certainly predetermined, but can be a very interesting extra product when turning this interesting piece.

I have chosen to work in English beech purely as a demonstration, to show that a wood which would not normally be chosen for something as delicate as this can be turned effectively if care is taken; a more suitable wood for this project would be boxwood.

Preparation

◆ Turn a 62mm (2⅜in) diameter sphere (refer to Chapter 6).
◆ Mark 12 primary points on that sphere (refer to Chapter 5), making sure to clearly mark the end grain points.
◆ Turn from hardwood 12 plugs 25mm

(1in) diameter, 6mm (¼in) thick, with a 1.5mm (⅟₁₆in) hole drilled through the centre.
◆ Have ready a 3mm (⅛in) round-nose tool.
◆ Have ready a 3mm (⅛in) square-end tool and a 1.5mm (⅟₁₆) square-end tool.
◆ The hemispherical chuck to hold the 62mm (2⅜in) sphere will be needed, as will the 12mm (½in) collar.

Fig 23.1 Spiked star in sphere on stand.

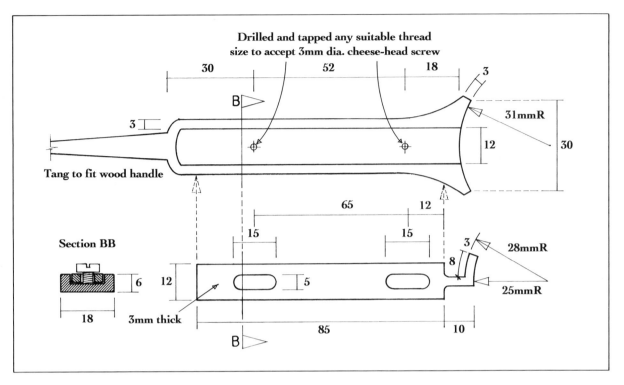

Fig 23.2 Undercutting tool and holder. Note the length of the cutter.

♦ The larger curved undercutting tool and holder will be required (*see* Fig 23.2) – this tool is described in detail in Chapter 3.

♦ Lathe speed 1000 rpm.

Beginning the work

♦ Hold the 62mm (2½in) diameter sphere in the hemispherical chuck, with one end-grain primary point facing forward.

♦ Bring the tailstock, holding the revolving centre, up to the work. Always place one hand on the lathe bed between the tailstock and headstock when pushing the tailstock forward; this will act as a brake, slowing the forward movement and preventing the revolving centre point accidentally being forced into the work.

♦ Line up the end grain primary points with the revolving centre and, keeping the two aligned, tighten down the collar evenly.

♦ Withdraw the tailstock and bring the toolrest across the face of the work.

♦ Adjust the height of the toolrest so that the 3mm (⅛in) square-end tool cuts at centre height.

♦ Rotate the lathe by hand to make sure

that nothing catches, then turn the lathe on.

♦ Mark a 25mm (1in) diameter circle in pencil about the first end grain primary point.

♦ Mark out a second circle 6mm (¼in) in diameter, concentric to and inside the first.

♦ Mark with white correction fluid a point 18mm (¹¹⁄₁₆in) from the cutting edge of the 6mm (¼in) square-end tool.

♦ Cut a hole fractionally under 25mm (1in) in the sphere, with a 6mm (¼in) spigot 18mm (¹¹⁄₁₆in) long remaining in the centre. Make sure that the base of the hole is perfectly flat.

♦ When cutting with the square-end tool, make sure that the cut is always widened so that the edges of the tool are not gripped, dragging the tool into the work and causing damage. Use the mark set on the tool to judge the depth of the cut (*see* Fig 23.3).

♦ Very carefully begin to turn the central spigot into a tapered spike, using the square-end tool (*see* Fig 23.4 for the section). Begin by turning a series of small steps, taper the tip to halfway, then cut from halfway down to the base (*see* Fig 23.5). Make sure that the tip is fully finished before working on the

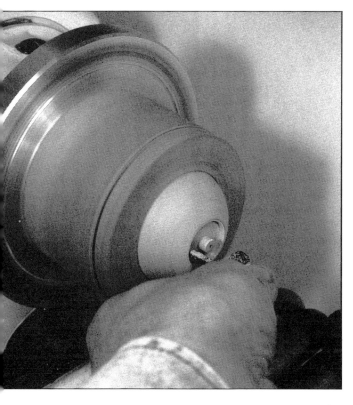

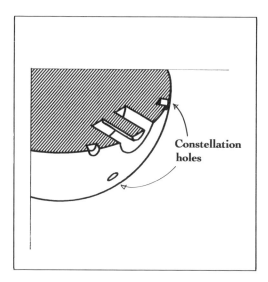

Fig 23.4 A section showing the start of cutting the spike.

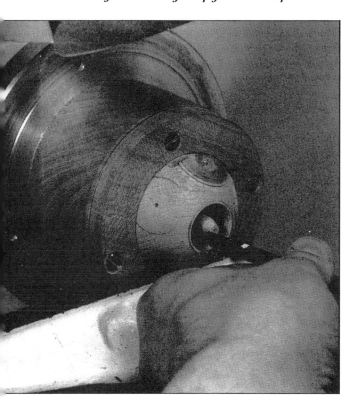

Fig 23.3 Using the square-end tool to cut the first area and produce a spike.

Fig 23.5 Turning the spigot down to a spike.

bottom part of the spike, as the thin end of the spike can easily break off if turned later. Also make sure that the spike flows in shape from tip to base; it cannot be altered later.

◆ Turn off the lathe when the spike has been satisfactorily completed (*see* Fig 23.6).

◆ The curved undercutting tool now needs to be set in the holder correctly:

◆ Draw a 31mm (1¼in) radius circle on paper with a pencil compass. Draw a 28mm (1⅛in) radius circle on the same centre. Place the tool holder so that its curved face rests against the larger circle, and adjust the curved undercutting tool so that its larger curved edge rests on the next circle. A 3mm (⅛in) gap will be seen between the holder and the tool. Lock the tool in position.

◆ Adjust the toolrest so that the tool in the holder is cutting at centre height.

◆ Care must be taken not to interfere with the spike and cause damage when inserting and removing this undercutting tool.

◆ Turn on the lathe and bring the tool holder towards the work. Carefully bring the undercutting tool into contact with the edge of the hole, avoiding the central spike. Make sure that the shoulder of the holder is rubbing against the surface of the sphere.

◆ Slide the holder to the left, keeping its shoulder rubbing on the spherical surface (*see* Fig 23.7). The undercutting tool is held 3mm (⅛in) away, and will cut a track beneath the surface; Fig 23.8 shows a

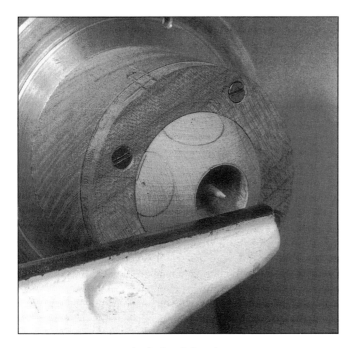

Fig 23.6 The finished spike.

sectional view.

◆ When the undercutting tool has cut to its full reach, carefully remove it; if it has become warm or even hot because of the friction during cutting, quench it in cold water. Remember to avoid hitting the spike.

Fig 23.7 Introduce the undercutting tool, carefully avoiding the central spike.

◆ Set aside the undercutting tool and turn off the lathe. Look inside the work: between the undercut and the hollow around the spike is a mass of waste wood which can now be turned out.

◆ Adjust the toolrest so that the 3mm (⅛in) round-nose tool is cutting at centre height. Rotate the lathe by hand to ensure that nothing catches, then switch on the lathe.

◆ Use the small round-nose tool to cut away as much of the waste wood as possible, while staying aware of the position of the spikes still to be turned (see Fig 23.9). Do not cut too deeply.

◆ When enough waste wood has been removed, bring the first plug forward for fitting.

◆ Check the plug's fit in the hole, widening the hole until a good tight fit is achieved. The taper on the spike which fits into the central hole will prevent the plug travelling down too far (see Fig 23.10).

◆ Turn the plug so that the sphere's profile is maintained; this will ensure that the chuck will grip the work satisfactorily.

◆ If during the turning the sphere begins to loosen in the chuck, apply small pieces of glasspaper with a double-sided tape backing to the inside of the chuck, and also to the

Fig 23.9 *The area around the spike to be cut back is pointed out.*

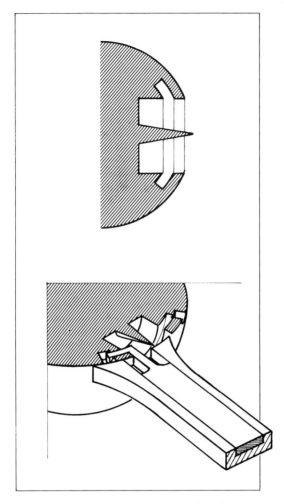

Fig 23.8 *A section showing the channel cut by the curved undercutting tool.*

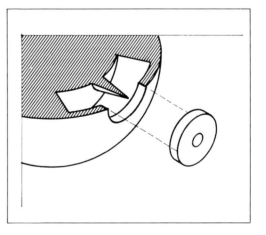

Fig 23.10 *A section showing the partial excavation, with formed spike and plug.*

Fig 23.11 *The area is marked for the lip to be turned.*

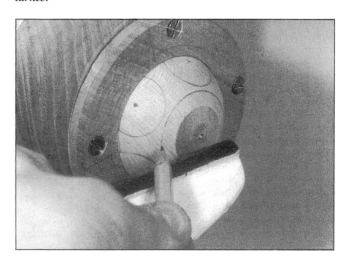

collar: this will dramatically increase the grip of the chuck.

◆ A small lip can now be turned on the outside of the 25mm (1in) diameter hole in the following way (*see* Fig 23.11):

◆ Take the 1.5mm (¹⁄₁₆in) square-end tool and mark a point 1mm (³⁄₆₄in) from the tip on its surface, using white correction fluid. Turn a groove down to the marked depth at a point 1mm (³⁄₆₄in) away from the rim of the hole, leaving a lip around the edge of the hole (*see* Fig 23.12).

◆ All the lips must be turned with this exact depth around them so that those areas match when they run into one another.

◆ Mark the letter E on the plug; this will help decide in which order to cut the other spikes after the other end grain spike has been cut. Cut all five around the first end

*Fig 23.12 The area surrounding the hole is turned
away with the small square-end tool.*

grain section, and then the next five around
the second end grain section.

◆ It will be found that these end grain
spikes are easier to cut, as they are being
turned with the grain. The reason for cutting
these first is twofold: firstly, the spikes are
held in the plugs, partially supporting the
rest of the internal work while it is being cut.
These two points are stronger and give
greater support. Secondly, when cutting the
faces upon which the spike sits (the base of
the hole), it is best to cut the end grain faces
first, as they are supported by the
surrounding wood, which prevents the edges
from breaking out. Fig 23.13 shows the
location of the spikes within the sphere.

◆ Having completed the first spike, loosen
the collar of the chuck and slide the sphere
around so that the second end grain point
comes to the front. Bring up the tailstock
holding the revolving centre, and line up the
end grain point with the centre.

◆ Tighten down the collar, keeping the
centres aligned evenly.

◆ Turn the spike, undercut, turn out the
waste, fit the plug, mark E for end grain and
turn the lip as before.

◆ Now move on to the next spike, working

the five in order around one end spike. Be
careful when turning these spikes, as they
are close to being short-grained.

◆ As these next spikes are turned, the
void, produced by cutting into the work for
the first spikes, will be hit (*see* Fig 23.14).
Make sure that the sphere is firmly held in
the chuck, or it may be jolted out of true.

Fig 23.13 The spike's location in the sphere.

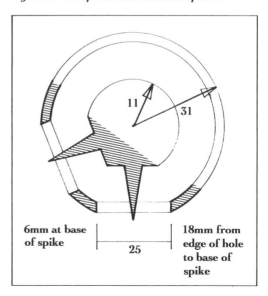

11

31

6mm at base
of spike

25

18mm from
edge of hole
to base of
spike

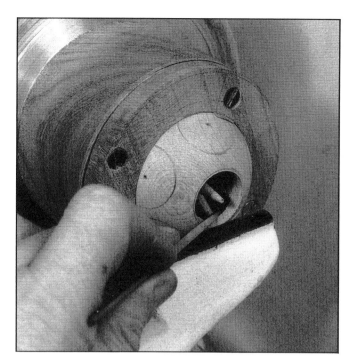

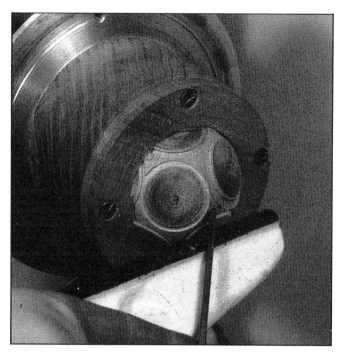

Fig 23.14 The void produced when cutting other spikes.

Fig 23.15 The unturned web between the holes is pointed out.

◆   Do not be disturbed by the 'clack-clack' of the tool hitting the wood and then the void; just work steadily and slowly. As more spikes are turned, the void will become greater and the amount of wood to cut will become less.

◆   Remember to keep the tools sharp to widen the gap around the square-end tool when cutting the first hole, and to completely turn the top half of the spike before turning down the lower half.

◆   Undercut carefully, and do not hit the spike.

◆   Fit the plug, turning it so that it follows the spherical shape.

◆   Turn the lip around each hole.

When cutting these spikes, the inside of the sphere will fill up with shavings. To remove these, push in a drinking straw and blow, but **close your eyes** first. Progress can only be seen in small stages, for when one part is finished only that small internal section can be viewed. The plug then fills that hole, ready for the next stage.

◆   Turn the final spike gently and with great care, for at the last cut the only things supporting the central part are the very tips of the spikes held in the plugs.

◆   Fill the final spike hole with a plug, and then turn it to match the spherical surface. Turn the lip around the outer edge of the hole.

It will be seen that there is a triangular section between each of these lipped holes left unturned. If these triangular sections are each brought to the front of the chuck in turn, centred, and the collar screwed down, they may be turned out to match the depth around the holes (*see* Fig 23.15). Any smaller unturned 'pips' can then be cleaned off with a carving gouge and then cleaned up further with needle files and glasspaper.

◆   When all the surface has been cut, cleaned and finished, the plugs can be removed. Drill two small holes either side of the central hole, fit screws into these holes and vertically pull out the plug (*see* Fig 23.16). But be careful; at this stage it would be a disaster to break off the tip of the spike.

Fig 23.16 Remove all the plugs once the sphere is complete.

It is a wonderful moment withdrawing the plugs. For the first time the complete spiked star can be seen, with each point sitting upon a pentagonal base. The truer the pentagon, the better the job.

Turning the stand

As the spiked sphere took on a pink shade when polished, the choice of wild service for the stand was suitable, not only because of the colour match but, being a finer-grained wood, it also accepted the small detailing of beads and coves more readily than beech. Fig 23.17 gives the dimensions of the stand.

◆ Cut two discs each 55m (2³⁄₁₆in) diameter from a piece of 25mm (1in) thick wild service, or a similar quality hardwood, and drill a 6mm (¼in) hole at their centres.

◆ Fit a drill chuck in the headstock of the lathe and hold a short 9mm (³⁄₈in) diameter dowel. Turn the exposed end of the dowel down to 6mm (¼in) diameter.

◆ Fit one of the discs on to the dowel: the centrally drilled hole push-fits on to the dowel.

◆ Bring up the tailstock with the revolving centre fitted, to support the exposed end. Tighten it firmly in place.

◆ Bring the toolrest across the work parallel to the lathe bed, and turn the disc edge flat and true.

◆ Square off the face closest to the revolving centre, taking particular care to make sure this face is perfectly flat or slightly

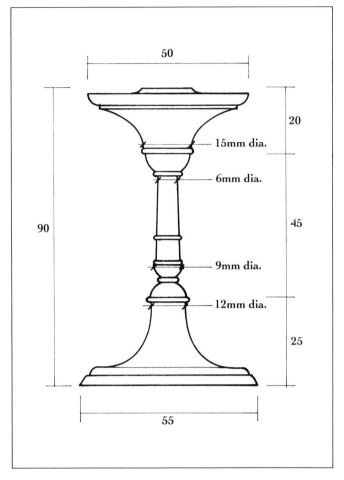

Fig 23.17 The stand.

Fig 23.18 Turning the foot of the stand.

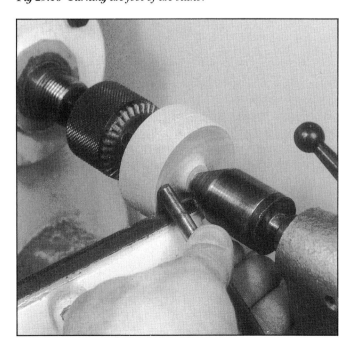

Fig 23.19 The underside of the top is turned.

indented, as this will rest upon the ground/table/shelf. Any convex curve will cause the stand to rock.

◆ Withdraw the tailstock, and reverse the workpiece in the lathe so that the faced-off end now rests against the drill chuck jaws. The revolving centre should again be pushed into the exposed drill hole to support the work.

◆ Turn the part closest to the tailstock down to 12mm (½in) diameter.

◆ The rim at the headstock end should be around 3mm (⅛in) thick.

◆ Turn the details on the foot, curving it gently up to meet the 12mm (½in) diameter end (*see* Fig 23.18). Turn a small bead closest to the revolving centre.

◆ Clean up thoroughly before removing from the lathe.

◆ Replace with the second disc, again supporting the end with the revolving centre.

◆ Turn the outer edge true, and make a curved turned-over edge closest to the tailstock, leaving a small island in the centre.

◆ When the shaping of the top face is satisfactorily completed, reverse the workpiece in the lathe and reposition it on the dowel held in the drill chuck; support the end with the revolving centre.

◆ Turn the tailstock end down to 15mm (⅝in) diameter.

◆ Turn the rim nearest the chuck so that a 5mm (5⁄32in) width remains; shape it as shown in Fig 23.17.

◆ Undercut and turn the piece towards the

15mm (⅝in) diameter end, making a sweeping fluent shape. Turn a small bead at the point closest to the revolving centre (*see* Fig 23.19).

◆ Clean up this top piece and then remove it from the lathe.

◆ The dowel held in the drill chuck can now be reversed and held on the 6mm (¼in) dowel. Trim it back until only 3mm (⅛in) of the 9mm (⅜in) diameter part is left. Shape this end to produce a flat cone, and drill a 3mm (⅛in) hole just a little over 3mm (⅛in) deep in the centre of that cone. This piece may now be removed from the lathe. The 6mm (¼in) end fits into the hole on the top of the top piece, so that the end of one of the spikes is held in it. This then supports the

Fig 23.20 The spindle held in position.

Fig 23.21 *Using a small skew chisel to turn the fine details.*

whole spiked star, holding it centrally inside the spherical shell when seated upon the stand.

Turning the central spindle

- ◆ Have ready a small driving dog.
- ◆ Turn a piece of service 70mm (2¾in) long, 15mm (⅝in) square between centres.
- ◆ Turn a 12mm (½in) length to 6mm (¼in) diameter at either end (*see* Fig 23.20).
- ◆ Remove the driving dog from the headstock and replace it with a drill chuck.
- ◆ Hold one of the 6mm (¼in) ends in the drill chuck, supporting the other end with the revolving centre.
- ◆ Turn the central spindle to the required shape with coves, straights and beads, as shown in Fig 23.21.
- ◆ Make sure that the top end of the spindle is shaped to run into and match the turned top, and that the lower end matches the fitting of the base of the stand.
- ◆ Clean up thoroughly, and then glue the spindle into the top and base. When the glue is set, polish the stand.

Fit the spiked sphere on to the stand, locating the end of one spike in the prepared hole. This will display the central spiked star at its best, held centrally within the delicate spherical shell (*see* Fig 23.22).

Fig 23.22 *The spiked star in a sphere on its stand.*

CHAPTER 24

CAPTIVE CUBE IN SPHERE

Fig 24.1 The captive cube in a sphere.

MOST OTHER ITEMS CAPTURED INSIDE A SPHERICAL SHELL CAN BE UNDERSTOOD OR PARTIALLY EX-PLAINED, BUT TO SEE A SOLID SIX-SIDED CUBE INSIDE A FRAGILE SPHERICAL SHELL BEGGARS BELIEF (*SEE* FIG 24.1). AFTER ALL, ONLY ROUND PARTS ARE 'TURNED', SO HOW COULD THAT CUBE BE TURNED INSIDE THE SHELL?

Well, the cube *was* 'turned': each of the six faces was presented to the front in turn, and was turned flat inside the sphere, which was held in a hemispherical chuck. Three specially made tools are needed to produce the internally turned cube: one is ground from a 12mm (½in) wood chisel; the second, a more complex undercutting tool supported in a holder, is described in Chapter 3 and shown in detail in Fig 26.2 (Tool 4) and Fig 24.2; the third is a square-end tool with a 3mm (⅛in) wide end ground for 9mm (⅜in) of its length.

The wood chosen for this project needs to be a close-grained hardwood, as the spherical shell walls are turned quite thin. I used boxwood.

Preparation

◆ Grind the angled tool to the dimensions shown in Fig 24.3 from a 12mm (½in) wood chisel.
◆ Paint the surface of the chisel with white correction fluid, and mark out the shape shown in Fig 24.4 in pencil on the white surface.
◆ Grind away the unwanted metal; do not

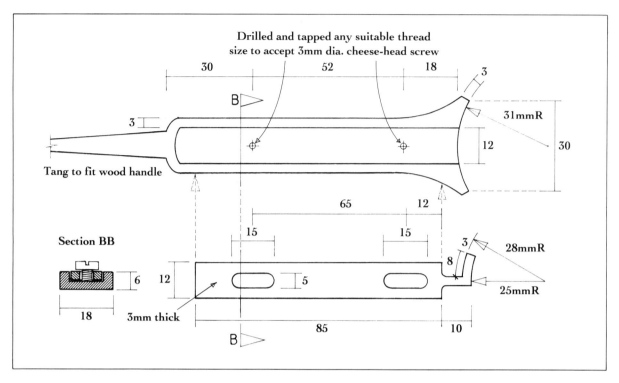

Fig 24.2 Undercutting tool and holder.

overheat the tool (*see* Fig 24.5), and have a container of water ready to regularly quench it. Don't forget to wear goggles.

◆ Grind the edges to form a cutting angle on the right-angled corner on the left-hand side of the tool, so that both edges are able to cut.

◆ If the tool overheats and the temper is lost, the tool will not retain its sharp edges; refer to Chapter 3 for how to re-temper.

◆ Turn a 62mm (2½in) diameter sphere from the chosen hardwood, referring to Chapter 6.

◆ Turn five plugs each 25mm (1in) diameter, 15mm (⅝in) long from hardwood, and drill a 2mm (³⁄₃₂in) hole through the centre of each. This will allow a screw to be threaded into the hole to help withdraw the plugs from the sphere when the work is complete.

◆ The larger undercutting tool and holder will be needed.

◆ Mark out the sphere with six main points and eight clearance points, as shown in Chapter 5. When marking these points, make sure that the two end grain positions are clearly marked.

◆ Have ready the 62mm (2½in) diameter

hemispherical chuck with the 12mm (½in) collar.

◆ Lathe speed 1000 rpm.

Fig 24.3 Grind from a 12mm wood chisel.

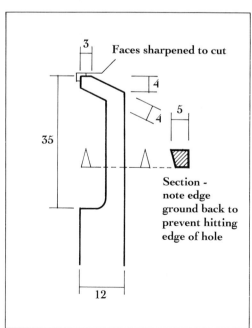

Fig 24.4 The tool marked out ready for grinding.

one of the clearance points, forcing the sphere against the back of the chuck. Lock the tailstock firmly so that the sphere cannot move, and tighten down the collar: this will ensure that the clearance point revolves on centre.

◆ Withdraw the tailstock and replace the revolving centre with a drill chuck holding a 15mm (⅝in) Forstner bit. Drill to a depth of 5mm (⁷⁄₃₂in), as shown in Fig 24.6.

◆ Centre and drill all eight clearance points as above.

◆ Bring the first main point to the front, making sure that it is one of the end grain points.

◆ Bring the tailstock holding the revolving centre to push against the end grain main point, forcing the sphere against the back of the chuck as the collar is tightened.

◆ Withdraw the tailstock and bring the toolrest across the face of the work.

◆ Mark a point 13mm (¹⁷⁄₃₂in) deep on a square-end tool, using correction fluid.

◆ Adjust the toolrest so that the square-end tool cuts at centre height.

Beginning the work

◆ Fix the sphere in the chuck bringing the revolving centre, held in the tailstock, up to the sphere's surface. Push the centre against

Fig 24.5 The tool ground to shape.

*Fig 24.6
Drilling the
clearance
holes.*

◆ Turn a 25mm (1in) diameter hole 13mm (¹⁷⁄₃₂in) deep, using the white measure mark on the tool as a gauge against the turned edge of the hole (*see* Fig 24.7).

◆ Make the hole diameter slightly under that of the 25mm (1in) turned plug so that it may be increased later, ensuring a good fit for the plug – *see* Fig 24.8 for a sectional view.

◆ Draw on paper a 31mm (1¼in) radius circle, using a pencil compass. Using the same centre, draw a 28mm (1⅛in) radius circle. Place the tool holder which holds the undercutting tool so that its curved surface rests against the larger circle, and adjust the curved undercutting tool so that its larger curved edge rests upon the next circle; a 3mm (⅛in) gap will be seen between the holder and the tool.

◆ Adjust the toolrest so that the tool in the holder is cutting at centre height.

◆ Turn on the lathe and bring the tool holder towards the work, with the undercutting tool in the turned hole and the curved shoulder of the holder running against the spherical surface.

◆ Slide the tool holder to the left, keeping it in contact with the spherical surface (*see* Fig 24.9). The undercutting tool will follow a curved path cutting beneath the surface, the

tool holder shoulder acting as a guide (*see* Fig 24.10). When the maximum distance possible has been cut, withdraw the tool along the same curved path.

◆ It may be necessary to withdraw the tool

Fig 24.7 Turning the first of the main positions.

Fig 24.8 A section showing the first hole cut. Note the drilled clearance holes.

Fig 24.9 Bring the undercutting tool from the right...

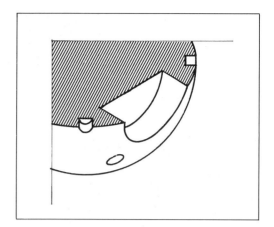

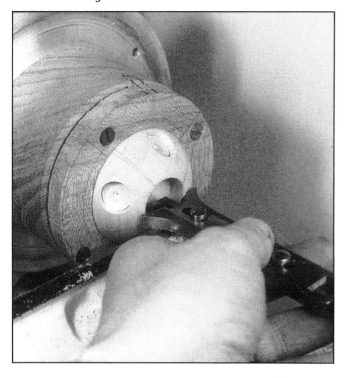

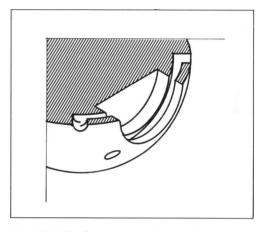

Fig 24.11 ... to the left. Note the cut into the clearance hole.

Fig 24.10 The first cut channel meets the clearance holes.

a few times to cool it in water before the cut is complete, as when the cutting edge is 'buried' deeply in the wood, friction can cause overheating.

It will be noticed that the undercutting tool will cut into the hollow clearance holes (*see* Fig 24.11), and that shavings will fall out of these clearance holes. The wood drilled away at these holes is at a point furthest away and most difficult to reach from any of the main points when using the undercutting tool, hence the necessity for drilling out the waste wood at these points.

◆   The hole turned at the main point will be seen to have a flat bottom and the curved path cut by the undercut tool will be close to the top. The bottom of the hole is part of the surface of one face of the cube. The extreme end of the curved undercut will be at the edge of the cube's face, so, using the angled tool ground earlier, the face of the cube can now be turned fully flat and true, as shown

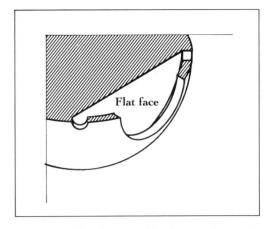

Fig 24.12 A flat face turned by the special ground tool.

sectionally in Fig 24.12.
◆   Readjust the toolrest so that the angled tool will cut at centre height.
◆   Turn the lathe on, keeping the long original shank of the chisel at 90° to the face of the work. This will present the ground cutting edge to the work precisely square.

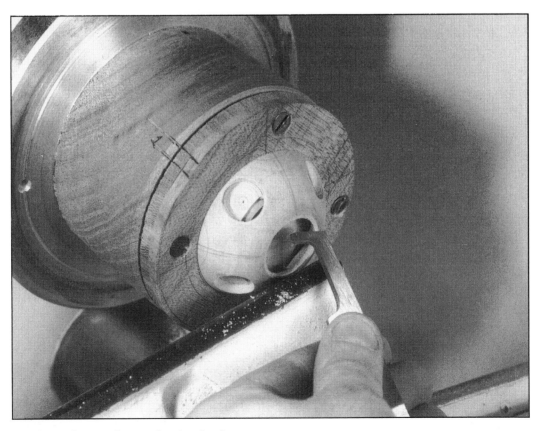

Fig 24.13 The specially ground tool used to flatten the internal surface.

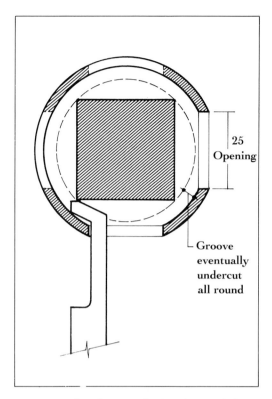

Fig 24.14 *The cube set inside the sphere, and the position of the special ground tool.*

Fig 24.15 *The fitted plug is turned to flow into the shape of the spherical surface.*

◆ Do not attempt to turn away all the waste wood in one deep cut. Turn small parts, working across into the curved undercut pathway and gradually working along the one face of the cube (*see* Fig 24.13).

◆ If the cut is watched as it progresses on the right-hand side of the work, it can be seen clearly and precisely how the tool is cutting, although the tool is over on the left side. Stop each time the tool reaches the curved pathway cut by the undercutting tool.

◆ Cut down until the whole flat face is turned to the same depth as the 13mm ($^{17}\!/_{32}$in) deep original hole. Fig 24.14 shows the proportions of the cube.

◆ Make sure that the flat surface is clean, with no circular marks or a central 'pip' to show that it has been turned.

◆ Remove the angled tool carefully.

◆ It will be noticed that this surface cut lines up with the centre of the base of the clearance holes, and that it is at this point still circular, not square (as the face of a cube should be).

◆ Take the 25mm (1in) plug, and turn out the hole for a snug fit.

◆ Turn a 1mm ($^{3}\!/_{64}$in) deep groove around the edge of the hole, using the 3mm ($^{1}\!/_{8}$in)

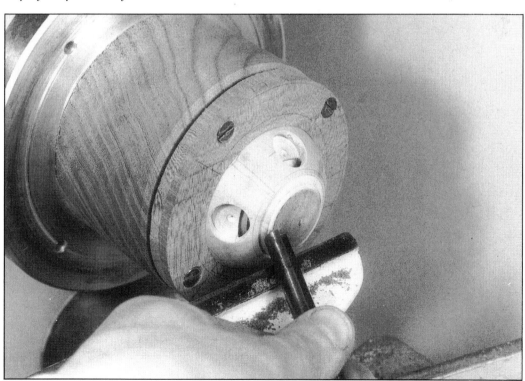

square-end tool, leaving a raised lip. Be careful when turning this lip not to invade the space around the clearance holes: leave enough space for their own grooves and lip around them, and make a judgement exactly how wide this groove may be turned without cutting into these areas around the clearance holes, while cutting as wide as possible.

◆ Take the plug and fit it firmly in the hole, pushing it down against the turned surface of the cube. Bring up the revolving centre in the tailstock to push it home.

◆ Turn the outside of the plug to follow the original curved surface of the sphere (*see* Fig 24.15).

The first main hole is now complete, and the collar may be loosened so that the second main part may be brought to front, again choosing the end grain position. It is most important to turn the end grain holes first, as they may be turned cleanly with their edges supported by the bulk of unturned wood. If they were turned at any time later, one or more of their edges would be exposed and could break out.

◆ Turn out the 25mm (1in) hole to a 13mm (¹⁷⁄₃₂in) depth as before, at the second main end grain point.

◆ Use the curved undercutting tool held in the holder to cut a curved pathway 3mm (⅛in) below the spherical surface.

◆ Use the ground angled tool to clean out the waste wood and to cut the flat face.

◆ Turn the main hole out to fit the plug.

◆ Turn the groove and lip around the main hole, and fully fit the plug.

◆ Turn the plug so that it follows the original curved surface of the sphere.

Having turned the two end grain areas, any of the four remaining main points may be worked in the same manner; now, as each surface is cut flat, the edges and corners of the cube will begin to appear, as can be seen in Fig 24.16.

As the work progresses, the cube will be held less and less by a little attached wood and more and more by the supporting plugs, so be aware that when undercutting the final main hole and when turning the final flat surface of the cube, all that now holds the cube are the plugs pushing against it. Turn with care, taking light, gentle cuts. These cuts will also be made into voids produced by earlier cuts, creating a gentle jolting cut, so do not allow the tool to be snatched.

Fig 24.16 Where three flat turned surfaces meet, a corner is produced.

Any woodshavings that accumulate inside the sphere and which make working difficult can be removed by placing a drinking straw into the work and blowing; always **close your eyes** when doing this.

With the final cut made, it will be very tempting to withdraw all the plugs to have a look at the cube. Be patient, and wait until all the grooves and lips have been turned around the clearance holes, as replacing all the plugs exactly as they were is virtually impossible.

Turning the lips on the clearance holes

◆ As the revolving centre can only be used as a guide, these holes need to be centred by careful judgement. Centre the clearance hole as closely as possible, lightly gripping the collar down. Turn on the lathe and gently touch a pencil point on the edge of the hole. The position that has the pencil mark on it is running furthest out, so push that point lightly inwards. Test again. Repeat until on centre, and then tighten down the collar evenly. Experience will speed up this centring method.

◆ When cutting the grooves around the clearance holes, make sure that they are all cut to the same depth as those around the main holes (*see* Fig 24.17); if they cut into one another, any discrepancy will be very obvious, and difficult to repair.

◆ When all the holes have been turned with grooves and lips, a small triangular web will be left proud between each area. Bring each of these webs (12 in all) to the front centre and turn them away to the same depth as the grooves. Any small 'pips' that remain may be trimmed away with a carving chisel, and the surface cleaned up with needle files and fine glasspaper.

Advice

It is best if the collar on the chuck is turned so that it is a little tight to begin with. Do not be concerned if there is a gap between it and the chuck; as the sphere's surface is turned away, the collar will slip down.

It may be necessary to attach small pieces of glasspaper with double-sided tape to the inside of the chuck and the collar, to increase grip.

Be careful when tightening the collar down on to the thin shell towards the end of

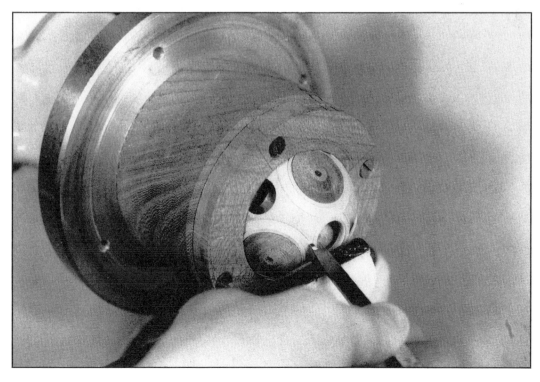

Fig 24.17 Turning the lip around the clearance hole.

the turning process: the collar must be sufficiently tight to grip the sphere, but not so tight as to crack it.

When drilling out the clearance holes, make an allowance for a spur point drill. If the spur is large, it may cut into what will be the corner of the cube; if that is the case, it may be better to turn out the clearance hole.

To complete the work once the surface has been cleaned, remove the plugs by tightening a screw into the drilled hole and carefully pulling. Be sure before removing the plugs that the surface is satisfactorily finished, as the plugs help support the delicate shell.

With the plugs removed, the cube will be seen in all its glory, locked inside the finely turned shell.

Any polygon may be 'turned'; it is just a matter of working out the exact positions for the main and clearance holes. A case of practical mathematics.

Turning the stand

The stand is made from wild service. It is close in colour to boxwood, but the slight change of colour makes it obviously separate.

◆ Turn a piece 120mm (4¾in) long by 55mm (2¼in) square round between centres.

◆ At the tailstock end measure 60mm (2⅜in) towards the headstock, and at that point, again towards the headstock, turn down to 20mm (¾in) diameter (*see* Fig 24.18).

◆ Remove the driving dog from the headstock, replacing it with a three- or four-jaw chuck.

◆ Withdraw the tailstock.

◆ Push the 20mm (¾in) diameter part into the chuck, either until the larger diameter butts up against the jaws, or as far as it will go.

◆ Bring the toolrest across the face of the work, and turn the work flat and true.

◆ Begin the internal shaping on the end face, cutting to a depth of 20mm (¾in). The internal shape should resemble the inside of a convolvulus flower or trumpet bell (*see* Fig 24.19). A gouge will remove the majority of the wood, but a narrow round-nose tool will be needed to turn right down to the thin centre.

◆ Remove the toolrest when the internal shaping is exactly as required and the surface is smoothly finished. Clean up and polish the internal face.

◆ Bring the tailstock, holding the revolving centre, back up to the work. Push

Fig 24.18 Turning the stand.

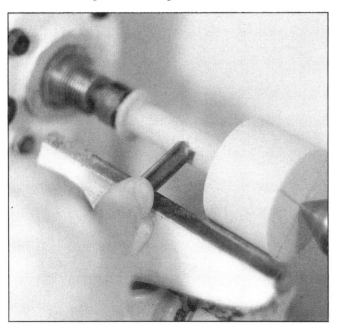

Fig 24.19 The end is hollowed with the stem held in the chuck.

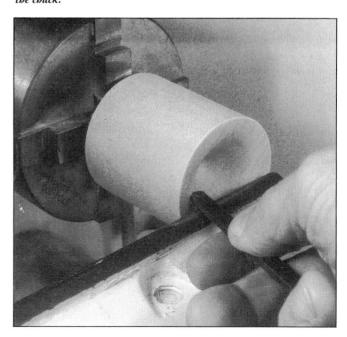

the centre down into the hollow, marking the exact centre with its point.

◆ Withdraw the tailstock, loosen the chuck jaws and pull the work out until only a 10mm (⅜in) part is gripped lightly by the jaws.

◆ Bring the tailstock forward and push the revolving centre into the centre of the hollow, relocating the mark it made earlier. Tighten the jaws; this will ensure that the piece runs exactly on centre.

◆ Bring the toolrest across the length of the work and, using a sharp gouge, shape the outside of the bell to create a fluent trumpet shape at the tailstock end of the work. Check the wall thickness regularly, turning down to 3mm (⅛in).

◆ Sweep the gouge down along the stem, maintaining a fluent shape from the trumpet bell into the stem (*see* Fig 24.20).

◆ Measure 90mm (3⁹⁄₁₆in) towards the headstock from the lip of the bell, and at that point turn down a small shoulder 6mm (¼in) diameter. This should be quite close to the overall diameter of the stem.

◆ Clean up and polish the outer surface.

◆ Part off below the 6mm (¼in) shoulder, leaving enough to fit into a 6mm (¼in) hole drilled in a suitable base.

Cutting the trumpet bell

◆ The trumpet bell will be cut on the bandsaw to produce a three-pointed top.

◆ To calculate the distance that the bandsaw fence should be set away from the saw blade, measure the diameter of the trumpet bell. The diameter of the one described above was 54mm (2¼in): divide this in half for the radius 27mm (1⅛in). Draw a circle of this size on paper, using a pencil compass. Place the compass point anywhere upon the circle and 'walk' it around the circle, marking where it touches. This will produce six points. Take one, miss one, take one, miss one, take one, miss one: this reduces it to three equally spaced points. Join these points to produce a triangle seated inside the circle. Choose one point and join it, with the centre continuing the line through to the opposite edge of the circle. Now measure the distance from that opposite edge where it touches the circle, to the base of the triangle where the pencil line cuts through; in this case it will be 14mm (⁹⁄₁₆in).

◆ Set the bandsaw fence 14mm (⁹⁄₁₆in) away from the blade, and then move it in another 3mm (⅛in), bringing the distance to

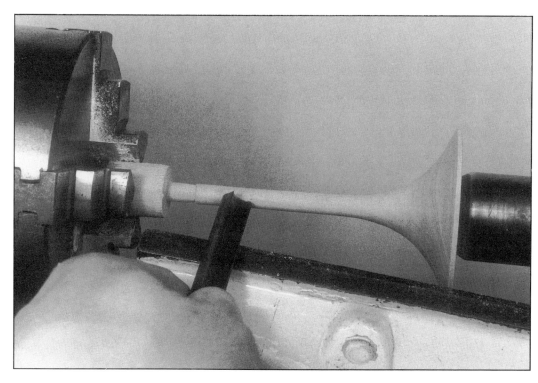

Fig 24.20 The trumpet end and stem are turned.

11mm (⁷⁄₁₆in). I have found that cutting to the exact size makes the finished piece look a little thin and skinny. That extra allowance is just right.

◆ Slide a piece of card under the fence and into the blade, taping down the edges. Draw a line at 90° to the blade, then another at 30° to that drawn line: this will be a guide for the second and third cuts.

◆ The first cut is made with the edge of the trumpet bell set against the fence (*see* Fig 24.21). The bandsaw is turned on and, taking care to keep the fingers safely clear, the edge is cut.

◆ The cut edge is then aligned with the 30° line, the uncut edge of the trumpet is pushed up against the fence, and the second cut is made.

◆ The second cut is aligned with the 30° mark. The uncut edge of the trumpet bell is pushed up against the fence, and the third cut is made. Turn off the bandsaw. Fig 24.22 shows the bell after the third cut has been made.

◆ Clean up the tricorn end of the stand by rubbing its cut surface on glasspaper set on a flat surface.

◆ Polish the cleaned cut edges to match the rest of the stand.

◆ Select a suitable base; I chose a small section of bark-covered pear. Drill a 3mm (⅛in) hole and glue the turned end in place.

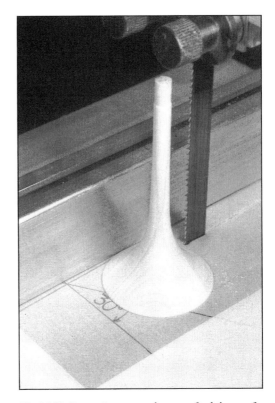

Fig 24.21 Preparing to cut the top end of the stand.

It might be fun to turn a few of these trumpet shapes deeper, wider or longer, cutting curves into the bell end rather than straight lines, and discovering other interesting shapes which may be used as stands.

Fig 24.22 The three edges of the top cut.

CHAPTER 25

LIDDED BOX IN SPHERE

 N HOLTZAPFFEL'S BOOK *HAND OR SIMPLE TURNING*, THERE IS A DESCRIPTION OF THE MAKING OF A LIDDED BOX TURNED WITHIN A SPHERE, BUT THIS RELIES UPON SPECIAL METAL CHUCKS.

Here a lidded box can be turned inside a sphere (*see* Fig 25.1), using simple wooden supporting dowels held in a four-jaw chuck. If it was decided that no chucks were to be used at all, a simple substitute would be to turn a Morse taper in wood, to fit directly into the headstock. This could then be turned out to fit the spigot, which is a supporting part of the box, as described below.

Turning a lidded box is quite straightforward, but when the tools cannot either be seen cutting or be allowed to move in the most convenient way because the openings in the sphere are so restrictive, this simple piece of turnery becomes extremely challenging.

Preparation

◆ For this project, the largest number of 'special' tools used in this book will be required. All are simply ground from 6mm (¼in) wood chisels. One other special tool will be of help; the ground angled tool described in Chapter 24.
◆ A 3mm (⅛in) wide square-end tool and a 3mm (⅛in) wide round-end tool are simply ground from a pair of 6mm (¼in) wood chisels.
◆ Two angled tools facing towards the left, one round-ended, the other square-ended, are ground to present a cranked 3mm (⅛in) face to the work.
◆ The final tool ground from a 6mm (¼in) wood chisel is an angled square-end tool facing right, again with a 3mm (⅛in) wide cutting edge.

When grinding these tools, take particular care not to overheat them, as this will cause them to lose their temper. Quench them in

Fig 25.1 Lidded box captive in a sphere.

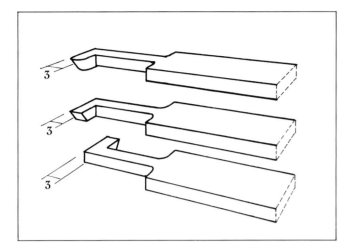

will be used to fix on to the spigots turned at either end of the sphere.

◆ Turn a 62mm (2⅜in) diameter sphere from boxwood or a similar hardwood, referring to Chapter 6.

◆ Mark 12 primary points (*see* Chapter 5) on that sphere, making sure to clearly mark the two end grain points.

◆ A simple 'saddle' will also need to be made; a description will be given later, when it needs to be used.

◆ Lathe speed approximately 1000 rpm.

Beginning the work

◆ Fix the sphere into the hemispherical chuck, with one end grain primary point facing forward.

◆ Bring the tailstock, holding the revolving centre, up to the sphere.

◆ Press the centre against the end grain primary point, pushing the sphere against the back of the chuck. Tighten the collar down evenly once the sphere is held firmly.

water regularly. The dimensions for the three angled tools are shown in Fig 25.2.

◆ The larger curved undercutting tool and holder described in Chapter 3 will again be needed (*see* Fig 25.3).

◆ The hemispherical chuck with 12mm (½in) collar will be required.

◆ Turn 10 plugs 25mm (1in) diameter, 6mm (¼in) thick from hardwood.

◆ Turn two dowels 35mm (1⁵⁄₁₆in) long and 18mm (¾in) diameter from hardwood; these

Fig 25.3 The undercutting tool and holder.

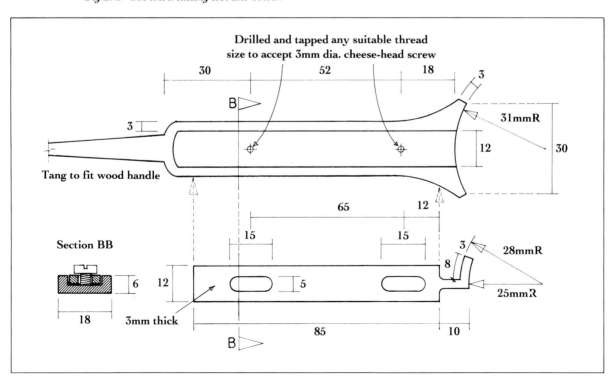

◆ Withdraw the tailstock, bringing the toolrest across the work and adjusting it so that the 3mm (⅛in) square-end tool will cut at centre height.

◆ Mark a point 6mm (¼in) from the cutting edge of the square-end tool, using white correction fluid.

◆ Turn on the lathe and mark in pencil a 25mm (1in) diameter circle with an inner 12mm (½in) concentric circle on the sphere's surface.

◆ Using the 3mm (⅛in) square-end tool, cut away the area between the larger and smaller circle, to the marked 6mm (¼in) depth upon the tool's shank. This will produce a 25mm (1in) diameter, 6mm (¼in) deep groove, with a central 12mm (½in) diameter spigot.

◆ Turn a 3mm (⅛in) wide groove 1.5mm (¹⁄₁₆in) deep, leaving a 1.5mm (¹⁄₁₆in) lip round this hole, using the square-end tool.

◆ Turn off the lathe, loosen the collar and bring the second end grain position to front.

◆ Bring the tailstock, holding the revolving centre, up to locate the second end grain primary point, locking it in position with the sphere pressed against the back of the chuck while the collar is screwed evenly down.

◆ As before, remove the tailstock and bring the toolrest across; set it so that the square-end tool cuts at centre height. Cut the 12mm (½in) diameter central spigot with a 25mm (1in) diameter, 6mm (¼in) groove around it. Turn the lip as before.

◆ Each of the 10 remaining primary points will be worked in the following manner:

◆ Loosen the chuck collar.

◆ Bring the primary point to front.

◆ Bring the tailstock bearing the revolving centre to fix the primary point on centre, pushing the sphere to the back of the chuck while the collar is evenly screwed down.

◆ Withdraw the tailstock and centre, bringing the toolrest across and adjusting it so that the 3mm (⅛in) square-end tool cuts at centre height.

◆ Cut just slightly under a 25mm (1in) diameter hole, 6mm (¼in) deep.

◆ The curved undercutting tool now needs to be set in the hole correctly.

◆ Draw a 31mm (1¼in) radius circle on paper, using a pencil compass; using the same centre, draw a 28mm (1⅛in) radius

circle. Place the tool holder so that its curved face rests against the larger circle, and adjust the curved undercutting tool so that its larger curved edge rests upon the next circle. A 3mm (⅛in) gap will be seen between the holder and the tool.

◆ Adjust the toolrest so that the tool in the holder is cutting at centre height.

◆ Turn on the lathe and bring the tool holder towards the work. Carefully bring the undercutting tool into contact with the inside edge of the hole, making sure that the shoulder of the holder is rubbing the surface of the sphere.

◆ Slide the holder to the left, keeping its shoulder rubbing on the sphere's surface. The undercutting tool will be held 3mm (⅛in) away, cutting a curved track beneath the surface, as shown in Fig 25.4.

◆ When the undercutting tool has cut to its full reach, carefully withdraw it; if it has become warm or even hot due to friction during cutting, quench it in cold water.

◆ It will be noticed that the undercutting tool will cut into one of the end grain holes, just touching the outer edge of the spigot (*see* Fig 25.4). When all these primary points have been undercut, the spigot will have an area around it cut free from the surrounding wood.

Fig 25.4 The undercutting tool used in the primary hole.

Fig 25.5 The points where the undercutting tool meets.

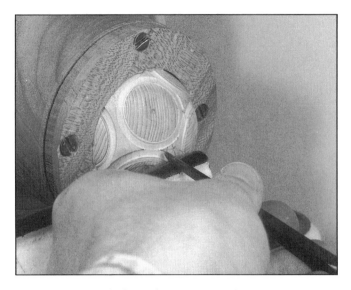

Fig 25.6 Turning the lips and turning away the webs between.

◆ Take a 25mm (1in) diameter, 6mm (¼in) thick plug, and fit it into the hole. If the plug does not fit easily, turn the edge of the hole until the fit is firm.

◆ If any of these plugs are particularly tight, mark them as such so that they may be recognised later; when they are removed, it is easier to remove that tight ones first when most of the thin shell is supported by the rest of the plugged holes.

◆ Turn the outside of the plug to maintain the external curve of the sphere.

◆ Care must be taken when undercutting the final hole, as all that holds the inner 'ball' will be the pressure from the plugs in each of the primary holes (*see* Fig 25.5).

◆ When turning and fitting each hole with a plug, turn around the edge of these holes a 3mm (⅛in) groove, 1.5mm (1/16in) deep, leaving a 1.5mm (1/16in) lip (*see* Fig 25.6), using a 3mm (⅛in) square-end tool.

◆ It is important to ensure that these grooves around the lips are cut at exactly the same depth, as they will meet, and where they meet they must match. The unturned areas between these joining grooves may be turned out by bringing each in turn to front centre and cutting them back, using the square-end tool. Any small 'pips' which remain may be cut out with a carving gouge (*see* Fig 25.7) and the surface then cleaned up with a needle file and glasspaper.

◆ Once all the areas around the lips have

been cut and cleaned up, the plugs may be removed. Twist a screw into the centre of the plug, choosing the tighter ones first, and pull on the screw to lift the plug clear. Pull vertically and slowly so that the edge of the hole is left undamaged. When all the plugs have been removed, it will be noticed that the centre is a loose sphere with spigots at either end.

Fig 25.7 The webs may also be removed with a carving gouge.

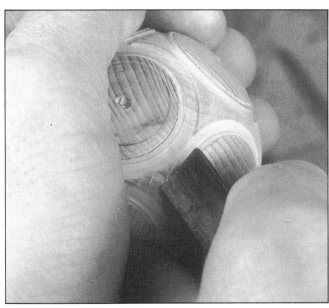

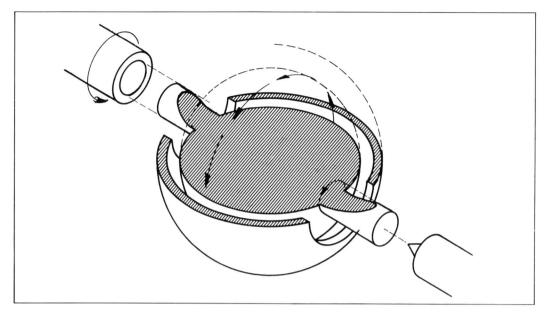

Fig 25.8 Sectional view showing the central block rotating and the outer shell remaining stationary.

Making the supporting saddle

Specific instructions for making the saddle cannot be given, as lathes vary so much, but some basic details will be common, and these are set out below. Fig 25.8 shows the use of the saddle.

◆ Cut a piece of hardwood at least 75mm (3in) wide and 12mm (¼in) thick.
◆ The length will depend upon (a) whether the lathe bed is square or round (if round, extra length is needed to straddle the round bed), and (b) the centre height of the lathe. 12mm (½in) should be added to this dimension to give support to the shell at the back, away from the toolrest but above centre height.
◆ Remove the hemispherical chuck from the headstock, replacing it with a driving dog.
◆ Place the prepared piece of wood (cut to fit the lathe bed if necessary) on the lathe bed so that its narrow edge faces the worker when standing in front of the lathe, and letting the wood just touch the driving dog. Bring up the tailstock, holding the revolving centre, so that the centre presses against the wood, then tighten it home. This will give an

impression of the driving dog centre on one side and the revolving centre on the other. Using either of these points as a centre for a pencil compass, draw a circle 31mm (1¼in) radius. Cut carefully to this line; trim the front edge so that the toolrest may still be brought close to the work, but leave the back edge to support the spherical shell.

Preparing to turn the box

◆ Remove the driving dog from the headstock, and replace it with a three- or four-jaw chuck (you may wish to turn directly from the headstock, using a wood mandrel with a Morse taper).
◆ Take one of the 35mm (1⅜in) long, 18mm (¾in) diameter dowels, and hold it in the chuck.
◆ Bring the toolrest across the face of this dowel, and adjust the rest so that the square-end tool cuts at centre height.
◆ Turn a 12mm (½in) hole 6mm (¼in) deep into the face of the dowel.
◆ Remove the toolrest, bringing the sphere up to the dowel. Fit the 12mm (½in) spigot into the turned hollow, adjusting until the fit is exact.
◆ Glue the spigot into the hollow, supporting the loose outer shell on the cradle and pushing the revolving centre into the

Fig 25.9 The shell supported on a saddle, allowing the inside block to revolve freely.

Fig 25.9 The shell supported on a saddle, allowing the inside block to revolve freely.

Fig 25.10 The revolving central block is turned to shape.

centre hole of the spigot at the opposite end. This will keep the piece on centre (*see* Fig 25.9).

◆ Leave overnight for the glue to set.

◆ The turned 18mm (¾in) dowel is wide enough to take a hole to accept the spigot and small enough to rotate inside the 25mm (1in) hole turned in the end of the spherical shell. This will allow the central mass of wood to turn within the shell while the shell remains stationary upon the cradle.

◆ Tape the cradle to the lathe bed and tape the shell to the cradle. With the outer shell supported and firmly taped to the saddle, the inner sphere can freely rotate within.

Beginning the internal shaping

◆ Always rotate the work by hand before switching the lathe on, and make absolutely sure that nothing is touching the outer shell before the lathe is turned on.

◆ Bring the toolrest forward and set it so that the tools cut on centre height.

◆ Make the first cut using the round-end tool to turn the inner piece true (*see* Fig 25.10).

Fig 25.11 Cross section showing the lidded box turned from the inner block.

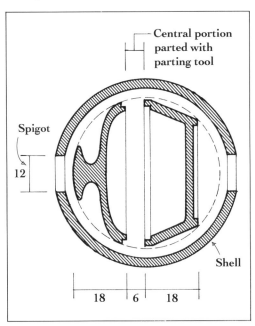

Fig 25.12 The two pieces are separated.

◆ Bring one of the shell windows so that the tool will have access to the inner sphere. Tape the shell to the sphere to hold it in this position. The windows can be repositioned and the shell retaped whenever necessary, to allow the tool access to other areas.

Although there is a dimensioned drawing for the inner lidded box (*see* Fig 25.11), circumstances may cause the turnery to alter slightly as the work progresses. Turn to exact dimensions if you can; if the dimensions need to be altered because the inner sphere has to be turned smaller to make it truly round, for example, be prepared to alter them.

◆ With the lathe stationary, measure 20mm (¹³⁄₁₆in) in towards the tailstock from the point where the dowel touches the inner sphere.
◆ Adjust the shell so that a window will allow a 3mm (⅛in) square-end tool to make a cut at this point.
◆ Cut a 1.5mm (¹⁄₁₆in) wide step at this point, approximately 45mm (1¾in) diameter.
◆ Cut a 4mm (⅛in) wide groove deep enough to be the start of a parting cut at the tailstock side of the step. The measurement, at 4mm (⅛in), is slightly wider than the square-end tool, so that when the cut is made the edges of the wood will not grip the tool.
◆ Part the top from the base (*see* Fig

25.12), and tape the tailstock end of the work to the back of the shell, to prevent it interfering with the turning.
◆ Excavate the inside of the top (*see* Fig 25.13), using the simple angled or hooked square-end tool.

View the work through any window available. This continually changing viewpoint can be very frustrating, as no one cut may be seen from beginning to end without the bars between the circular windows obstructing the view. Always adjust the windows so that the tool may work freely, and tape the shell in place firmly. (The tape holding the shell has been removed to make the picture clear in some of the photographs in this chapter.)
    Remember to: always rotate the work by hand before switching on to make sure nothing catches; clean out accumulated shavings before they cause problems; withdraw the tools carefully – a clumsy move can cause great damage; keep tools sharp.

◆ Continue to turn out the inside of the top with the tools described earlier, using those which will do the job effectively. Cut lightly, as there will be a larger than usual overhang from the toolrest.

Fig 25.13 Using the angled tool to hollow out the inside of the lid. Note the taped base.

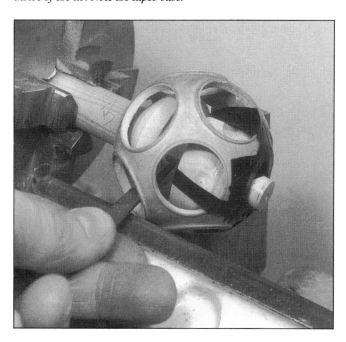

Fig 25.14 *The knob of the lid turned.*

Fig 25.15 *Parting the lid.*

◆ If necessary re-turn the step so that it is true, clean and square.

◆ Once the inner shaping is completed, begin the outer shaping of the lid. Turn the outer shape so that it complements the inner, maintaining an even wall thickness.

◆ Turn the knob down to 18mm (¾in) close to the dowel. Turn the curved shaping under the knob using the round-nose tool (*see* Fig 25.14), taking small, gentle cuts.

◆ Glasspaper may be used at this stage if required; press it against the work with the back of one of the tools while holding the other end in the fingers to prevent it being dragged in.

◆ Before turning the top of the knob and parting off, make absolutely sure that the inner and outer shaping of the lid is precise.

◆ Part off the top of the knob with a good clean cut (*see* Fig 25.15). The finished lid can be seen in Fig 25.16.

◆ Turn off the lathe and turn the workpiece around in the lathe, re-setting the next piece of dowel in the chuck and preparing as before. When gluing the base in place, the lid may be pushed up against it and a piece of scrap wood pressed against the lid knob so that the tailstock may apply pressure without marking the top of the knob (*see* Fig 25.17).

◆ Leave the glue to dry overnight.

◆ Tape the lid to the tailstock end of the shell.

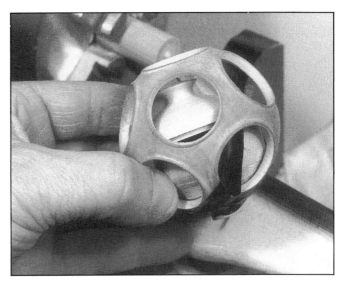

Fig 25.16 *The completed lid.*

◆ Adjust the shell so that the inner block may rotate inside without damage. Tape the shell to the saddle.

◆ Always move the shell so that the windows are positioned enabling the tool to move as freely as possible.

◆ Begin to cut the recess in the base to take the step joint in the lid, using the hooked square-end tool. The lid may be held close to the base, with the lathe stationary, so that the size of the recess may be judged; an initial cut can be made and the lid tested in it, continuing until a good firm fit is achieved.

Fig 25.17 Turn the piece around, push the parts together and support the end of the lid with a shaped piece of wood.

◆   Begin hollowing out the base, cutting to about 9mm (⅜in) deep, using any of the various tools to produce the hollow (*see* Fig 25.18).

◆   Push the top on to the base and, using a specially turned scrap of wood, support the lid with the help of the revolving centre in the tailstock.

◆   Turn the outer shape of the box so that the lid flows into the shape of the side (*see* Fig 25.19). This part may be quite awkward,

Fig 25.18 The lid is withdrawn so that the inside of the base may be hollowed.

Fig 25.19 Turn the outside profile and edge of the base.

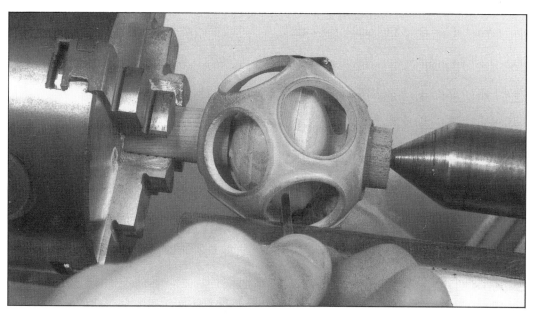

Fig 25.20 The underside of the base now needs its foot turning before parting off.

Fig 25.21 The lidded box complete.

as the windows have to be continually readjusted to allow the tool access.

◆ Once the outer surface is turned, the lid may once again be removed and taped to the shell while the underside of the base is turned.

◆ Using the hooked tool which angles to the right, cut a foot on the base, undercutting with great care (*see* Fig 25.20).

◆ Continue the careful work on the foot, cleaning up cautiously.

◆ Part off cleanly from the supporting dowel, and cut any remaining 'pip' from the surface with a carving gouge to complete the job. Fig 25.21 shows the completed box inside the sphere.

Before starting this piece, it is important that you have a very clear idea of the shape of the box which is to be turned; but you must also be prepared to make alterations if necessary. What appears to be a very simple turned box captive within a sphere is made more difficult by the constraints of that surrounding sphere.

If you have enjoyed turning the box, why not try other items? The list is as long as your imagination.

Turning the stand

The stand here is made from English boxwood to match the sphere. There is a

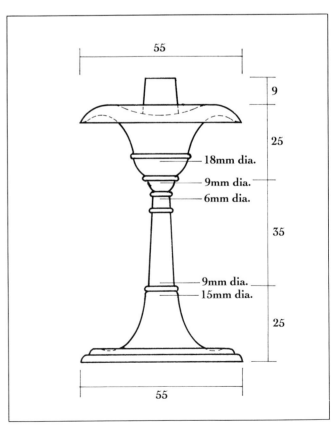

Fig 25.22 The stand.

central plug on top of the stand which lifts the box so that it may be more clearly seen trapped inside the spherical shell. The dimensions are given in Fig 25.22.

◆ Cut two 55mm (2³⁄₁₆in) diameter discs from a 25mm (1in) thick piece of boxwood.
◆ At the centre of each disc drill a 6mm (¼in) diameter hole all the way through.
◆ Fit a drill chuck into the headstock, and fit a short 9mm (⅜in) dowel into that drill chuck. Turn a 6mm (¼in) diameter spigot on the exposed end of that dowel.

Do not be tempted to use a piece previously turned for a similar job; although the part may appear to be held on centre, it is not always possible to replace it so that it is truly central. If it runs out of true, it will cause many problems when turning the top and base of the stand.

◆ Fit one of the boxwood discs on to this 6mm (¼in) diameter spigot, bringing the tailstock, holding the revolving centre, up to support the end.
◆ Bring the toolrest across and turn up the edge so that it is round and true.
◆ Turn the face at the tailstock end flat, or possibly a little concave (*see* Fig 25.23); if it is turned a little hollow it will sit more evenly upon a flat surface.
◆ Once the base end has been turned, remove the piece from the lathe and reverse it upon the dowel, bringing the revolving centre back to support the end.
◆ Turn the end at the tailstock to 12mm (½in) diameter, and turn a small bead at the point closest to the revolving centre.
◆ Turn at the headstock so that a 5mm (⁵⁄₃₂in) wide lip remains; turn a slight slope and step on that lip.
◆ Turn a sweeping cut towards the tailstock from that step, meeting the turned diameter, but not cutting into the bead.
◆ Turn in at the inner edge of the turned step at the headstock end, so that step now becomes a raised ring or bead, then continue that sweeping cut towards the tailstock (*see* Fig 25.24).
◆ When satisfied with the shaping, clean up and remove from the lathe.
◆ Replace with the second disc, turning it round and true.

Fig 25.23 Turning the top of the stand.

◆ Turn a curved hollow at the tailstock end, making the curve run into the centre. The tailstock may temporarily be removed to make the cut flow right to the centre.
◆ Reposition the tailstock, and work upon the edge.
◆ Turn a gentle curved lip on the edge.
◆ Clean up the inner surface and edge and reverse in the lathe, supporting once again between the dowel in the chuck and the revolving centre.

Fig 25.24 Using a small skew chisel to detail the underside of the top.

Fig 25.25 Turning the base.

◆ Turn down to 15mm (⅝in) diameter at the tailstock end.

◆ Undercut the curved rim at the headstock end so that the edge has a constant thickness, reflecting the curve of the top.

◆ Turn a fluent curve towards the tailstock (*see* Fig 25.25).

◆ Turn a series of beads into that curve, then re-turn the curve so that it remains fluent but leaves the beads standing proud.

◆ At the tailstock end turn a curve to flow over towards the centre, with a final bead at the extreme end where it meets the revolving centre.

◆ Turn a simple plug with a 6mm (¼in) diameter spigot at one end; this spigot is held in the drill chuck at the headstock while the exposed end – about 15mm (⅝in) diameter and 15mm (⅝in) long – is shaped. This will be fitted into the hole in the top of the stand to raise the turned box.

Turning the central spindle

◆ Use a small driving dog.

◆ Set a 70mm (2¾in) long by 15mm (⅝in) square of box between centres.

◆ Turn a 12mm (½in) long, 6mm (¼in) diameter spigot at either end.

◆ Remove the driving dog and replace it with a drill chuck.

◆ Hold one end of the turned spindle in the drill chuck, supporting the other with the revolving centre.

◆ At the headstock end turn to 12mm (½in) diameter, to match the base. At the tailstock end turn to 15mm (⅝in) diameter, to match the top.

◆ Turn a small bead at either end, and in between a series of flats, beads and coves to make a decorative stem (*see* Fig 25.26).

◆ When complete, clean up, remove, and glue all the parts of the stand together. Polish when the glue is dry.

Fig 25.26 Cutting the details into the stem.

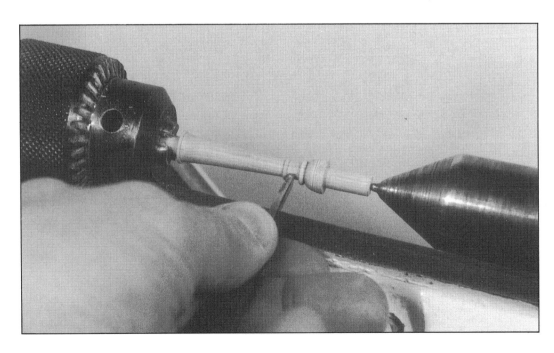

CHAPTER 26

CHINESE BALLS

F ALL THE MYSTE-RIOUS OBJECTS PRODUCED BY ORIENTAL CRAFTS-MEN, THE CHINESE BALL, THAT SET OF BALLS WITHIN BALLS, HAS RETAINED ITS MYS-TERY THE LONGEST (*SEE* FIG 26.1).

Seen in their many various forms, from the simplest turned type to the most intricate, each ball covered in complex pierced work or carving, they hold a tremendous fascination over the viewer, yet their production is basically simple.

These balls may be made more easily by increasing the size of the holes drilled at the primary points, or more complex by adding a spiked star to the centre of each primary point, or even more difficult by increasing the number of balls held inside the major sphere. Whichever set of Chinese balls are made, the method remains the same.

Preparation

◆ Choose a flawless piece of boxwood or similar quality hardwood, and turn a 62mm (2½in) diameter sphere from this.
◆ Have ready the four special undercutting tools and their tool holder, plus the profile tool which shapes the holes at the primary points; all these tools are shown in Fig 26.2.
◆ The hemispherical chuck with the 12mm (½in) thick collar will be needed to hold the turned wooden sphere; this can be seen in Fig 26.3.
◆ A drill chuck to fit the tailstock and four drills will be required. Drill sizes: 3mm (⅛in), 4mm (⁵⁄₃₂in), 6mm (¼in) and 9mm (⅜in).
◆ Lathe speed 750 rpm. This is a guide only, as the speed may be increased or decreased to suit the turner.

Beginning the work

First drill 12 equally spaced conical holes into the prepared sphere. At each of these holes, when positioned so that they rotate on centre, a curved undercutting tool will be introduced to begin the shaping of the inner sphere. Beginning with the smallest inner sphere and working outwards, each is completely finished before moving on to the next. Each of the conical holes is filled with a conical wooden plug, which supports the part or fully turned inner spherical shells while work continues.

◆ Turn 12 conical plugs, each 22mm (⅞in) long, 18mm (¾in) diameter at the larger end,

Fig 26.1 Two Chinese balls with their stands.

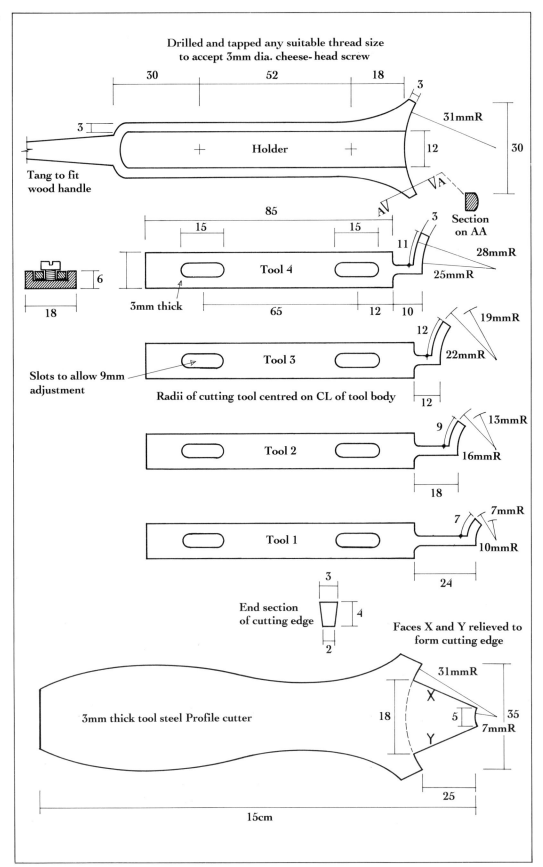

Fig 26.2 The undercutting tools and profile tool.

Drilled and tapped any suitable thread size to accept 3mm dia. cheese-head screw

30

52

18

3

31mmR

Holder

12

30

3

Tang to fit wood handle

A

A

Section on AA

85

15

15

3

11

28mmR

6

Tool 4

25mmR

18

3mm thick

65

12

10

19mmR

12

22mmR

Tool 3

Slots to allow 9mm adjustment

Radii of cutting tool centred on CL of tool body

12

13mmR

9

Tool 2

16mmR

18

7mmR

7

Tool 1

10mmR

24

3

End section of cutting edge

4

2

Faces X and Y relieved to form cutting edge

31mmR

X

35

18

5

3mm thick tool steel Profile cutter

7mmR

Y

25

15cm

*Fig 26.3
Sphere, tools,
plugs and
chuck.*

and 6mm (¼in) at the smaller (*see* Fig 26.4). Be prepared to alter the taper on these plugs, as although the conical hole in which they fit is produced using the same profile tool, the shape of the hole may vary slightly; the profile tool will be cutting into end grain, and then it will be cutting into side grain. A slight unnoticed movement in the wrist can also cause some variations. So work carefully and be prepared to adjust the plugs accordingly.

◆ Take a length of 25mm (1in) square wood and fit it between centres.

◆ Turn down to 18mm (¾in) diameter.

◆ Measure 22mm (⅞in) towards the headstock from the tailstock.

◆ At that point on the headstock side of the line, turn down to 6mm (¼in) diameter, using a parting tool.

◆ Join the 18mm (¾in) diameter at the tailstock to the 6mm (¼in) diameter, 22mm (⅞in) away, with a straight tapered cut.

◆ Part off or saw off at the 22mm (⅞in) point.

◆ Make 12 conical plugs in this manner.

As the hemispherical chuck in which the sphere is held whilst working may be removed from the headstock at any time

without disturbing the work, the conical plugs may be turned to exactly fit the hole as it is produced. If you are confident that each hole will be exact, produce all the plugs at one time.

Working on the sphere

◆ Mark 12 primary points upon the sphere, noting the two end grain positions (refer to Chapter 5).

◆ Mark the constellation points about each of the primary points; there will be 20 in all (*see* Chapter 5).

◆ Place the sphere in the hemispherical

Fig 26.4 Turning the plugs to fit the tapered holes.

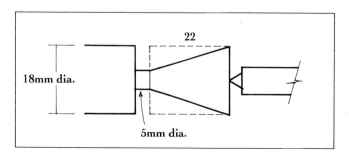

Fig 26.5 The profile tool.

chuck, with one end grain primary point to the front.

◆ Bring the tailstock forward, holding the revolving centre. Push the point of the revolving centre on to the exact centre of the end grain primary point, forcing the sphere against the back of the chuck.

◆ Tighten the collar down on to the sphere, tightening the screws down evenly.

◆ Withdraw the tailstock and replace the revolving centre with a drill chuck holding a 9mm (⅜in) drill.

◆ Mark a point 18mm (¾in) away from the cutting tip of the drill, using white correction fluid.

◆ Turn on the lathe and plunge the drill into the sphere to the marked depth at that first end grain primary point.

◆ Turn off the lathe and withdraw the tailstock and drill.

◆ Bring the toolrest across the face of the work; the toolrest is adjusted so that the top surface of the profile tool is at centre height when resting on it.

◆ Turn on the lathe and push the profile tool into the drilled hole, widening it out until the curved shoulders touch the surface of the sphere (*see* Fig 26.5). It may require a little effort to push the tool into the drilled hole, and some friction may result, causing the tool to heat. If this happens, quench the tool in cold water, dry it off and return to the work.

◆ The plugs will need to be fitted once the first undercutting tool has been used, so move on to the next end grain position and repeat the operation.

◆ When both end grain points have been drilled out and profiled, move to the remaining 10 primary points, making sure that the end grain points are still marked.

◆ When profiling the other primary points it may be noticed that in one hemisphere, around an end grain point, one particular primary point will be easier to cut than the others. If this is the case, mark it clearly as such; if no difference is noticed, wait until the undercutting tools are first used.

◆ Having cut all the primary points, the constellation points may now be drilled.

As each shell is cut with the undercutting tools, it will be noticed that there is one point which is most difficult to reach. That point is at the extreme edge of the cutting range of the undercutting tools, located exactly equidistant from the centres of any three adjacent primary points. It is this point also where the constellation point falls. Drilling these constellation points not only adds to the appearance of the sphere, but also fulfills an important function (*see* Fig 26.6): that point most difficult to reach is drilled away, allowing the undercutting tool to do its job far more efficiently.

◆ Bring the first of the constellation points to the front, and fix it in position, using the revolving centre held in the tailstock. Lock down the collar (*see* Fig 26.7).

◆ Drill out all the remaining 19

Fig 26.6 Cross section through the sphere, with primary and constellation holes drilled.

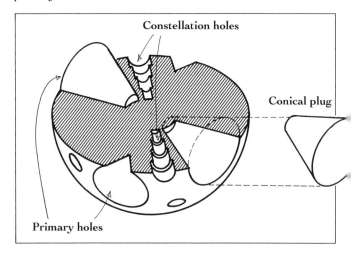

Constellation holes

Conical plug

Primary holes

Fig 26.7 Holding the sphere on centre and tightening the collar.

Fig 26.8 Adjusting the first undercutting tool.

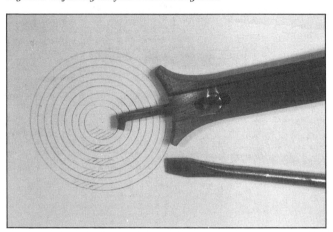

constellation points, using the following drills to the marked depths:

◆ First 9mm (⅜in) drill to a depth of 4mm (⁵⁄₃₂in).

Second 6mm (¼in) drill to a depth of 10mm (¹³⁄₃₂in).

Third 4mm (⁵⁄₃₂in) drill to a depth of 16mm (¹¹⁄₁₆in).

Fourth 3mm (⅛in) drill to a depth of 22mm (⅞in).

Using the undercutting tool

◆ Bring the first end grain primary point to the front and tighten down the collar on the chuck, using the revolving centre to hold it on centre.

The reason for working the end grain positions first is that, when the outer balls are being cut, the end grain parts are the weakest. It is far better to cut these first when supported by the bulk of wood around them than when unsupported.

◆ Fit the smallest undercutting tool into the holder.
◆ To adjust these undercutting tools to cut at the correct depth, it is necessary to draw out a series of concentric circles representing a cross section of the finished shells (*see* Fig 26.8).

The curved shoulder of the holder is rested on the outer edge of the circle and the undercutting tool pushed until it reaches the circular path it is required to cut. The screws holding the tool to the holder may then be tightened, locking it in place. It is important that these tools are positioned exactly in place or possibly a little closer to the centre; if they are adjusted so that they move even slightly towards the outer edge, the final gap which is left to cut the final shell will slowly become so small that the outer shell may become dangerously thin.

Fig 26.9 Push the undercutting tool in on the right...

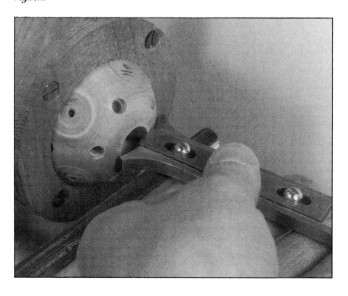

Fig 26.10 ...then bring it across to the left.

◆ Bring the toolrest across the face of the work and adjust it so that the undercutting tool cuts at centre height.

◆ Turn on the lathe.

◆ With the undercutting tool moved to the extreme right of the hole, push it inwards until the curved shoulder of the holder rubs the surface of the sphere (*see* Fig 26.9). Do

not be alarmed if the tool needs to be pushed in to reach its full depth; as there will be slight variations in the exact sizing of the profile tools, the size of the hole cut and precise size of the undercutting tool, this may happen.

◆ Now, with the holder's shoulder rubbing the sphere's surface, slowly bring the tool and holder across to the left (*see* Fig 26.10). The tool will follow a curved path concentric to the outer surface of the sphere.

◆ When the undercutting tool has cut to its full distance move it back to the right, keeping the shoulder of the holder rubbing the sphere's surface.

◆ When the tool is fully back, withdraw it and turn off the lathe.

◆ Remove the toolrest and fit the first plug (*see* Fig 26.11).

It is necessary for the outer edge of the plug to maintain the shape of the sphere, as this will ensure that the whole sphere will be firmly held in the chuck. If one plug protrudes, it may make it more difficult to grip the sphere evenly, and may throw it out of true when turning.

◆ Bring the tailstock holding the revolving centre up to the plug, holding it in position while the surface is turned to match the curve of the sphere (*see* Fig 26.12).

◆ Withdraw the tailstock and replace the

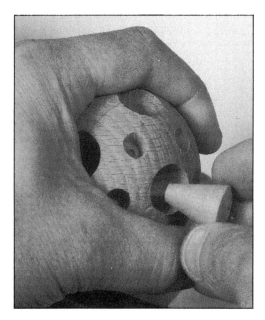

Fig 26.11 Fitting the conical plug.

Fig 26.12 The outside of the plug is turned to the spherical surface.

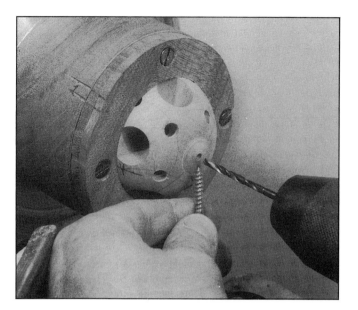

Fig 26.13 Drill the centre of the plug to accept a screw.

Fig 26.13 Drill the centre of the plug to accept a screw.

Fig 26.14 A section through the sphere showing the first undercutting tool making a cut.

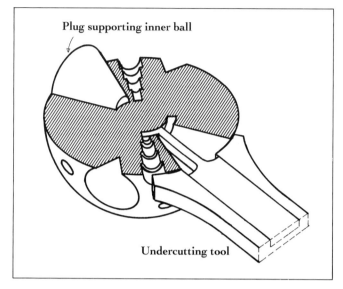

centre with a drill chuck holding a 3mm (⅛in) drill.

◆ Drill out the centre of the plug to a small depth (*see* Fig 26.13); this provides a starting hole to take a screw, which will be used as a handle to remove the plug. It is surprising how tenaciously a taper can grip.

◆ Mark a single line, indicating that the first undercutting tool has been used, on the end of the plug. This will save time searching to discover which holes have and which have not been worked. Also mark on a piece of paper that the first undercut has been made.

◆ Loosen the collar and bring the second end grain point to front; centre it using the revolving centre in the tailstock, then lock down the collar and undercut as before. Fig 26.14 shows a sectional view.

◆ Fit the plug, and mark a single line on the plug and mark on the paper that the second undercut has been made.

If the work now begins to follow a logical sequence, it will be much easier and less troublesome: having dealt with the two end grain points, work firstly the five primary points about one end grain point, then the other five primary points around the other end grain position. Mark on each plug a single line to show that the first undercut has been made, and also mark on the paper. When all 12 primary points have been undercut, the next size undercutting tool will replace the first.

◆ Fit the second undercutting tool in the holder, adjusting it to the correct position using the drawn concentric circles, and making absolutely certain that it is correctly positioned. Fig 26.15 shows a sectional view of the second undercut.

◆ Bring the first end grain point to the front, fix a screw into the plug and withdraw it.

Fig 26.15 The second undercutting tool in use.

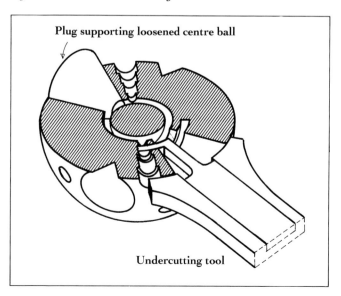

From now on the tailstock will need to be carefully brought forward: place one hand on the lathe bed between the tailstock and headstock, to act as a brake when it is being pushed forward. As each undercut is made the sphere will become more and more delicate, and it would be more than unfortunate if the revolving centre were allowed to hit the sphere and damage it.

◆ Use the revolving centre to fit into the conical hole to hold it on centre whilst the collar is screwed firmly down.

◆ Withdraw the tailstock.

◆ Bring the toolrest across the work, and turn on the lathe. Hold the undercutting tool to the extreme right and push into the conical hole until the shoulder of the holder rubs the sphere's surface.

◆ Bring the tool across to the left, with the holder shoulder still rubbing the spherical surface. The curved tool will again follow a pathway concentric to the sphere's surface.

◆ Once the tool has cut to its full distance bring it back across to the right, with the holder shoulder still rubbing, then withdraw it.

◆ Turn off the lathe, replace the plug and mark a second line on the plug to show that

the second undercut has been performed at that position, then mark on the paper that the first of the second series of undercuts has been worked.

◆ Now move to the next end grain point, and centre and undercut there. Mark the plug and the paper. Work the five primary points around it, marking on the plugs and on the paper.

◆ Complete by moving to the next five primary points.

It was mentioned earlier that one of the five primary points about each end grain will cut more easily than the others. By now this position will be obvious; identify it with a mark and from now on make this position the last of the five to be cut. As each undercut is made it is supported by surrounding wood, except for that final cut. If this final cut is made at one of those easy cutting positions, some of the problems will be removed.

◆ A few tips before moving on to the third undercutting operation:

● The pressure of pushing sideways with the undercutting tool, combined with the wood dust falling through the

Fig 26.16 Sharpening the undercutting tool still held in the holder.

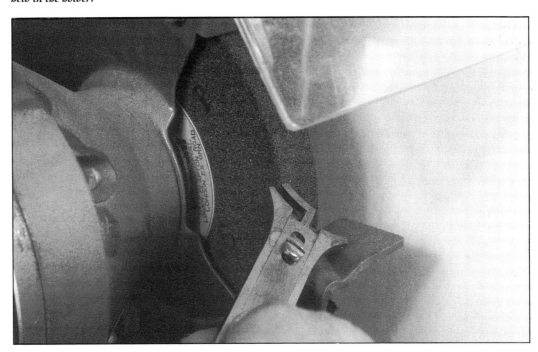

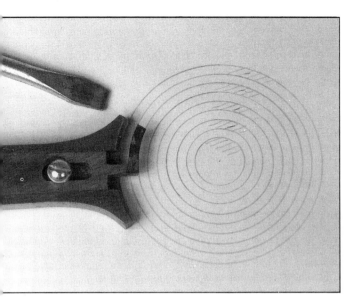

Fig 26.17 Setting the final undercutting tool.

Fig 26.18 The third undercutting tool withdrawn to show the undercut pathways.

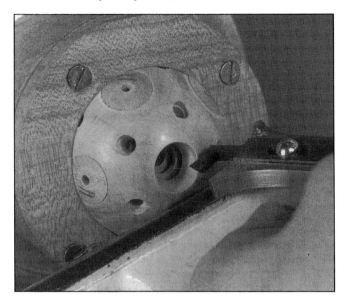

constellation holes, can cause the inside of the chuck to lose its grip. To combat this, apply pieces of fine glasspaper to the inside of the chuck and collar, using double-sided tape.

● Remember to keep the tool sharp; after six or more cuts it may become blunt or at least the edge will be dulled slightly. Sharpen regularly but **do not remove it from the holder**: sharpen the tool still in the holder (*see* Fig 26.16), as it would be almost impossible to replace it exactly in the same position. Blunt tools cause friction, which may overheat the surrounding wood, causing it to crack.

● As the tool is held deeply in the wood when cutting, it may become warm or begin to overheat, particularly on the final cuts. Remove the tool regularly during these cuts, and quench it in cold water to avoid losing the temper.

● Do not overtighten the collar on the delicate shell for the final cuts, but equally do not leave it too loose. Strike a fine balance.

● Keep that record on paper of the number of undercuts. You will know exactly when each shell is finished, and it will be too late at the end, when it is discovered one hole has not been worked with the second or third undercutting tool. Work systematically.

● To clear wood dust from the primary points, push in a drinking straw, **close your eyes**, and blow.

Begin undercutting, using the third tool set in position on the drawn concentric circles (see Fig 26.17).

◆ Begin at one end grain position (*see* Fig 26.18).

Fig 26.19 The undercut pathway has reached into the constellation hole.

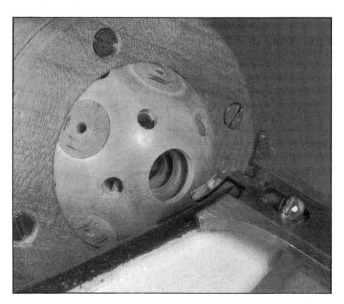

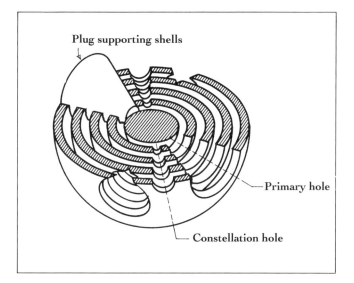

Plug supporting shells

Primary hole

Constellation hole

Fig 26.20 *Cross section of the sphere, with all the curved pathways cut.*

show that the third undercut has been made on each, and also mark on the paper as a tally.

◆ Move to the final outer shell.

By now the importance of the constellation holes will be understood (*see* Fig 26.19): they allow some of the wood dust to escape, and perform the vital task of cutting away the waste wood from that awkward position furthest away from the primary points.

◆ The tool can now be clearly felt cutting into the wood and then the void, with a 'click, click'. Keep the cuts slow and gentle, quenching the tool regularly.

◆ Work the end grain points first, then the five points around them.

◆ Sharpen the tool frequently and cool it regularly.

◆ The final cut is slowly and gently made at one of those easy cutting primary points. Fig 26.20 shows a section with all the cuts made.

◆ Move to the next end grain position, working the five primary points around it. Then finish the next five primary points, remembering each time to finish on the easy cutting positions.

◆ Mark on the plug end with a third line to

Fig 26.21 *Turning the lips around each primary hole.*

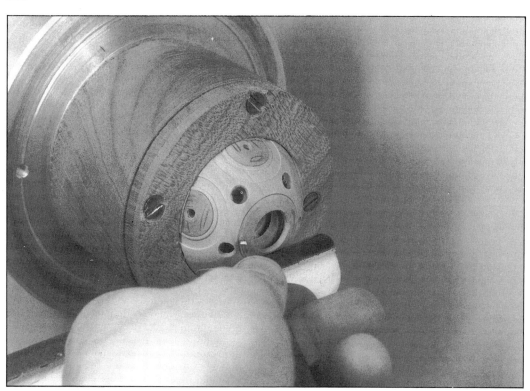

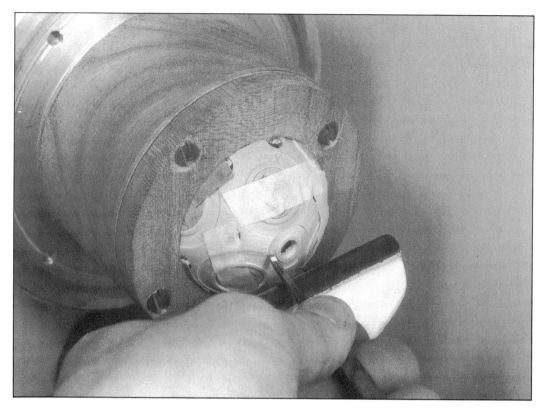

Fig 26.22 The plugs are held in with tape as the lips are turned around the constellation holes.

◆ Do **not** remove all the plugs to see the loose balls rattling around inside. The lips around the hole need to be cut first, and if the plugs are removed, the probability of ever replacing them exactly is 12^4 to 1 against (I think).

Cutting the lips

◆ Begin cutting the lips around the primary end grain points first, as before.

◆ Bring each point to the front as before, this time removing the plug.

◆ Set the toolrest at 90° to the axis of the work.

◆ Using the pencil, mark a circle around the primary point so that it leaves sufficient space around adjacent primary and constellation points for a small lip to be turned about them.

◆ Cut 1mm (⅟₃₂in) deep, 1.5mm (⅟₁₆in) away from the edge of the first primary hole using a 2mm (³⁄₃₂in) square-end tool (*see* Fig 26.21).

◆ Continue this cut until it reaches the drawn pencil circle.

◆ Round over the lip.

◆ Glasspaper lightly around the edge to remove any remaining pencil lines.

◆ Mark and turn a lip at each remaining primary point.

◆ Bring each constellation point to the front, centring it with the tailstock and revolving centre and remembering to place one hand on the lathe bed to act as a brake.

◆ Fix the plugs in place with small pieces of masking tape to prevent them flying out once the lathe is turned on (*see* Fig 26.22).

◆ Position the toolrest so that there is sufficient gap between it and the work so that, should a plug come loose, it can fall freely away and not become trapped between the work and toolrest, causing damage.

◆ Turn a lip around each constellation point without touching other surrounding holes; glasspaper each clean.

◆ Finally, centre on those unturned portions between constellation and primary

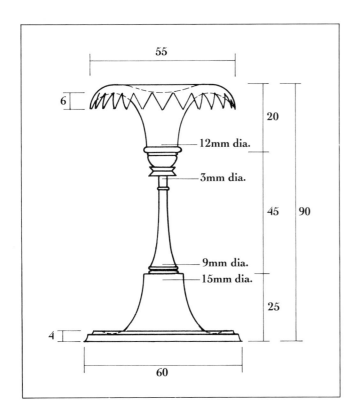

55

6

20

12mm dia.

3mm dia.

45   90

9mm dia.
15mm dia.

25

4

60

Fig 26.23 The stand.

Fig 26.24 Details on the stem turned with a fine skew chisel.

within the other, full of loose sawdust, and the turner will be full of pleasure.

points, and turn these parts away. Any minor 'pips' which remain may be removed with a carving gouge.

◆   The complete Chinese ball may now be removed and the plugs pulled out one by one. Four loose spheres will be captured one

Making the stand

◆   The stand is made of three parts: a central spindle, a top and a base; Fig 26.23 gives the dimensions.
◆   The central spindle is first turned

*Fig 26.25
Turning
the base.*

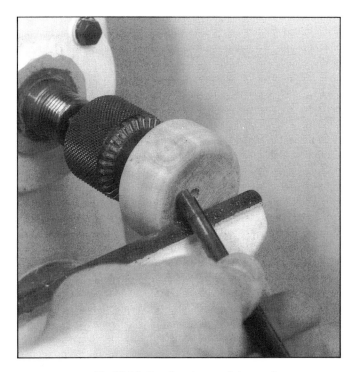

Fig 26.26 *Turning the top of the stand.*

Fig 26.27 *The underside of the top being turned.*

between centres from a 12mm (½in) square by 54mm (2⅛in) long piece of boxwood (*see* Fig 26.24).

◆ A 9mm (⅜in) long by 6mm (¼in) diameter spigot is turned at either end.

◆ Remove this piece from the centres. The driving dog at the headstock is replaced by a Jacobs drill chuck, which is used to hold the turned spigot at one end of the spindle, the other end being supported by the revolving centre.

◆ The spindle may be turned to the desired decorative details.

◆ The base is turned from a 12mm (½in) thick piece of boxwood.

◆ A 54mm (2⅛in) circle is cut from the piece, and a 6mm (¼in) hole is drilled at its centre.

◆ A small dowel of wood is held in the Jacobs chuck, and the exposed part is turned to a tight 6mm (¼in) diameter spigot.

◆ The drilled cut circle can be pushed on to this turned spigot, and the revolving centre brought up to support the end.

◆ The exposed (tailstock) face is turned flat and true; this will be the base.

◆ The piece is reversed in the lathe, and then the top side and edge are turned. The

top side is turned decoratively (*see* Fig 26.25). Remove the base from the lathe.

◆ The top is made from a 25mm (1in) thick piece of boxwood.

◆ A 54mm (2⅛in) circle is cut from this, and a 6mm (¼in) hole drilled at its centre.

◆ The drilled cut circle is pushed on to the spigot held in the Jacobs chuck, and the revolving centre is brought up for support.

◆ The top surface is turned and the edge 'rolled' over (*see* Fig 26.26).

◆ The piece is reversed in the lathe and the underside is turned (*see* Fig 26.27).

◆ The 'frilly' edge can be marked out and cut once the top has been fully turned and finished.

◆ To divide the outer edge, wrap a strip of paper around it, marking the points where they meet.

◆ Remove from the work and divide that distance into 16 equal parts, using a measure.

◆ Return the strip to the edge of the turned top and transfer those marks on to the wood (*see* Fig 26.28).

◆ Measure 6mm (¼in) upwards from the lower edge of the curved rim.

◆ Revolve the lathe and mark a line around.

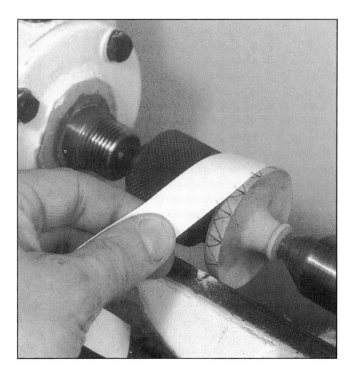

Fig 26.28 Marking out the divisions around the top.

Fig 26.29 Sawing the points along the edge of the top.

◆ Mark points on this top line, halfway between those 16 points below.

◆ Join up the points on the lower rim with those on the top line. This will produce 16 pointed teeth.

◆ Cut these lines, using a junior hacksaw or other fine saw (*see* Fig 26.29); first one angle all the way round, then the next.

◆ The waste wood should drop free. Clean up the V using needle files and a sharp craft knife, to produce the shape shown in Fig 26.30.

The top, middle and base can now be glued together and polished, and the Chinese balls will be displayed elegantly.

Fig 26.30 The top completed.

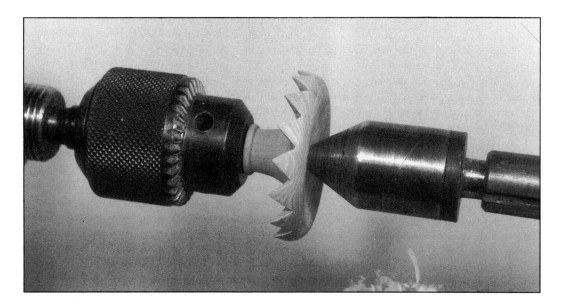

CHAPTER 27

INTERLOCKING SPHERES

T FIRST VIEWING, THESE INTER-LOCKING SPHERES DEFY LOGIC (*SEE FIG 27.1*). THE FEEL-ING FORMS THAT SOME TERRIBLE TRICKERY IS TAKING PLACE, BUT WHEN LOOKED AT AGAIN, IT CAN BE SEEN THAT BOTH PARTS ARE TURNED INSIDE AND OUT AND UNBROKEN.

I first saw a pair of interlocking spheres in a photograph of the work of François Barreau, an eighteenth-century turner; there was no explanation accompanying the photographs, just a description of his life and work. Of course I wanted to discover how these joined spheres were produced and to try turning some myself. After a long period searching through all the known books on old turnery techniques, I heard of a book which had recently been reprinted, *Manuel du Tourneur*, by Hamelin Bergeron. It contained engravings of interlocking spheres and the tools used in their manufacture, but the French text, when translated, left large and vital gaps in the method of production. I used to sit looking at those pages of engravings hoping for a sudden revelation, but it did not form.

Late one night, when I was just falling asleep, the problem came into my mind and the solution suddenly appeared with such clarity. It was the shape of the tools in those engravings which unlocked the problem.

A complete double hollow shell is turned; forget about the holes cut in the shell – there is just one, initially drilled through a profiled block of the two spheres pushed together. The inside is excavated so that the thin walls of the sphere's shells are turned

inside as they pass through one another. Once that is done, all the outer holes may be pierced and the section where they interlink may be cut, much as wooden chains are cut from one piece. In fact, this project may be viewed as a three-dimensional chain.

Once this understanding is reached, it becomes a relatively simple matter of

Fig 27.1 Interlocking spheres on a stand.

working out the details: the simple methods of holding the piece, the size and shape of the tools and the way in which the two shells can easily be separated.

Taken as a whole, this project may be a little daunting, but taken part by part, the work is quite straightforward. This project must be viewed as a long-term piece of work to be developed slowly.

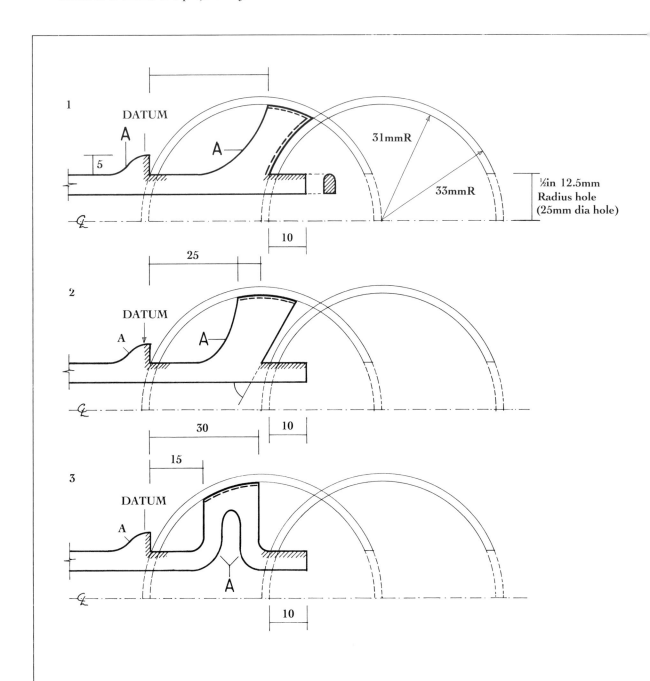

Fig 27.2 The six special tools and the area they cut.

Preparation

◆ Cut a 95mm (3¾in) long by 75mm (3in) square piece from a flawless piece of boxwood or similar fine hardwood. The length must be **exact** and square-ended.

◆ Prepare six special tools as shown in Fig 27.2 (a description of tool preparation is given in Chapter 3):

◆ Two special hole cutters, the one

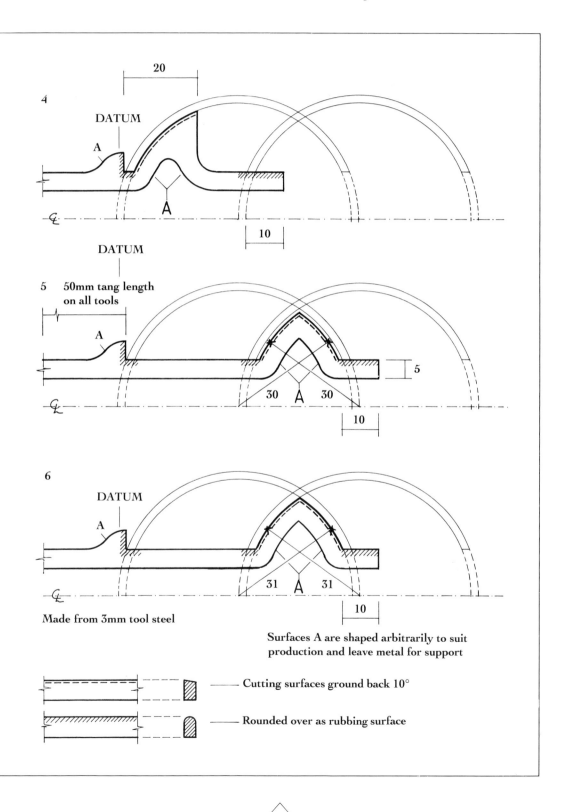

4

20

DATUM

A

A

DATUM

5 50mm tang length on all tools

A

30 A 30

5

10

6

DATUM

A

31 A 31

10

Made from 3mm tool steel

Surfaces A are shaped arbitrarily to suit production and leave metal for support

Cutting surfaces ground back 10°

Rounded over as rubbing surface

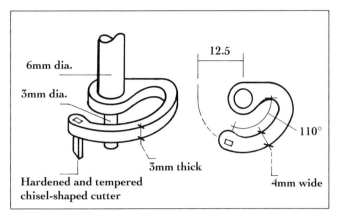

Fig 27.3 The hole-cutting tool: one cutting left-handed, the other right-handed.

left-handed, the other right-handed; *see* Fig 27.3, and again refer to Chapter 3.

◆ One angled round-nose tool, ground from an 18mm (¾in) wood chisel.

◆ A 25mm (1in) diameter sawtooth cutter.

◆ A simple mandrel will be required; a description is given in the text below.

◆ A cradle consisting of a wood disc attached to a faceplate and three long bolts supporting a second disc a short distance away. A full description is again given in the text below.

◆ A regular selection of woodturning tools.

◆ Lathe speed will vary from 1000 rpm down to close to 1 rpm. The lathe will sometimes be rotated by hand for vital final cuts.

◆ An important and valuable piece of preparation for this project is the development of a working relationship between the turner and an engineer.

Beginning the work

◆ Mark the diagonals on the end faces of the 95mm (3¾in) long by 75mm (3in) square piece in pencil, and set it accurately and centrally between centres.

◆ Turn as close as possible to 75mm (3in) diameter.

◆ Fit the 25mm (1in) sawtooth cutter into a drill chuck.

◆ Replace the revolving centre with the drill chuck, supporting the end of the workpiece with the centre of the sawtooth cutter.

◆ Turn the lathe on and work the cutter

into the wood, cleaning out the drill hole regularly to avoid overheating.

As the drill nears the full depth of the work, it must be stopped before reaching the driving dog centre. Withdraw it from the work, remove the workpiece from the lathe, and complete the drilled hole with the drill placed in a pillar drill. Centre the drill on the centre point left by the driving dog.

◆ This cylinder with a central hole may now be held on a simple mandrel so that the external profile may be turned concentrically.

Making the mandrel

◆ Threaded bar may be purchased from hardware stores or can be simply made, if you have the understanding and tools. I used a 9mm (⅜in) threaded bar 200mm (8in) long, and purchased two 18mm (¾in) washers and four nuts which fitted the threaded portion.

◆ One end of the bar should have a 25mm (1in) length turned down, just removing the thread.

◆ A small centrally drilled hole at the other end is needed for the revolving centre to fit snugly.

◆ Turn up three pieces of wood, two 25mm (1in) long, and one 12mm (½in) long. These all need to be 30mm (1¼in) diameter, with a hole through the centre which will just slide over the threaded area of the bar. Each piece needs to be exactly square-ended.

◆ Buy two rubber doorstops about 25mm (1in) long and the same diameter, or a little larger. Drill these out centrally to fit over the threaded area of the bar. (Drilling rubber is awkward.) Rubber bungs used in winemaking will work just as well.

◆ Fit two nuts about 25mm (1in) away from the end with the thread turned off. Tighten one nut against the other, and they will lock in place.

◆ Fit a washer next, and then one 25mm (1in) long by 30mm (1¼in) diameter prepared piece of wood.

◆ Slide on a rubber doorstop and a 12mm (½in) length of prepared wood.

◆ Finally slide on the next rubber doorstop followed by the second 25mm (1in) length of wood, the washer and the two nuts.

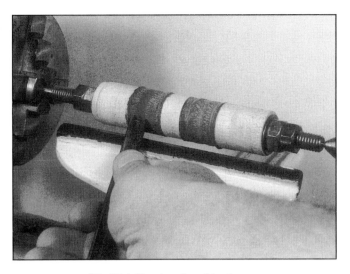

Fig 27.4 Turning the rubber bungs.

◆ Tighten the nuts sufficiently to hold the pieces together on the mandrel, which will now begin to look like a shish kebab (*see* Fig 27.4).

◆ Hold the unturned end in a three- or four-jaw chuck, supporting the other end on the revolving centre held in the tailstock.

◆ Begin turning the mandrel. Turn the wood just a hair's breadth under 25mm (1in) diameter, and the doorstops as well as you can.

◆ Turning rubber doorstops is an experience: persistence is the only requirement, as rubber bends away from the tool, no matter how sharp. Hold the tool in place for long enough, and the rubber will

eventually strike the cutting edge.

◆ I have just discovered that if you put the rubber in the freezer or ice compartment beforehand, it will harden enough to make the turning much more easy.

◆ To use the mandrel, slide the pre-drilled block on to it and then hold it between the chuck and revolving centre. Tighten the nut at the tailstock end, and the rubber doorstops (now inside the drilled hole) will be crushed, forcing them to expand. These doorstops then firmly grip the work. Tighten the outer nut against the inner, and the two nuts will lock together. The outer profile of the block may now be turned.

◆ Cut a template from card to match the profile of the two spheres linked together (*see* Fig 27.5).

◆ Turn the outside of the block down to exactly 66m (2⅝in) diameter.

◆ Turn the outside to match the profile of the card template exactly (*see* Figs 27.6 and 27.7).

◆ While the turned block is held on the mandrel, the primary and secondary (constellation) holes may be marked and preliminary drilling may take place.

◆ Measure 17mm (⅝in) from the extreme edge of the work closest to the headstock towards the tailstock. Mark a line around the work by holding a pencil exactly at that point whilst the lathe is turning.

◆ Place a pencil compass set to 35mm (1⅜in) anywhere on that line, and walk the compass around that line, thus producing

Fig 27.5 Template for checking the profile of the turned block.

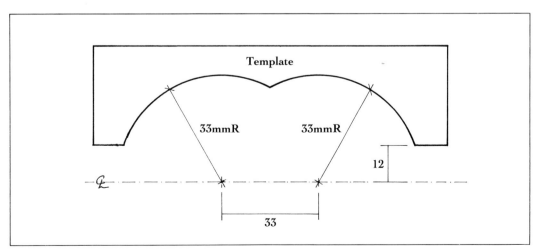

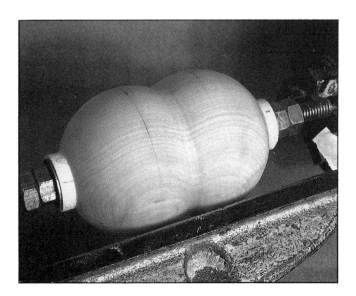

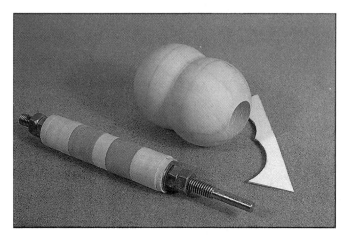

Fig 27.6 The turned block held on the mandrel.

Fig 27.7 The template, the mandrel and the turned block.

five primary points.

◆ Strike an arc towards the tailstock from one primary point; the compass setting remains at 35mm (1³⁄₁₆in). Repeat the motion at the next primary point. The two arcs will cross, and this will be a further primary point, this time very close to the line where the two spheres join. This procedure is repeated at all five original primary points, which will produce 10 primary points on one sphere end (*see* Fig 27.8).

◆ Repeat this process, but work from the extreme end closest to the tailstock and work towards the headstock. It is important that the first primary point !ocated at the tailstock end is horizontally in line with one of the previously marked primary points **which are closest to the joint line of the two spheres**. This will cause the primary points of both spheres near the joint line to be offset from

Fig 27.8 The markings for the primary points.

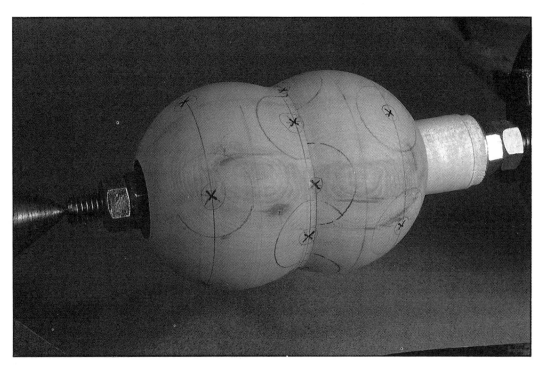

Fig 27.9 The cradle.

one another.

◆ Set a pencil compass to 12.5mm (½in) radius and draw a circle about each of the primary points. At the joint line only part circles will be able to be drawn: these circles define the holes to be cut later.

Setting out the constellation points

◆ There will be 10 constellation points around each circle, and they will be common to other circles. The following sizes are a guide only, so be prepared to adjust if necessary, as the curvature of individually turned spheres may vary slightly.

◆ Draw around each main circle, using the same centre, a larger but fainter circle at 16.5mm (²¹⁄₃₂in) radius.

◆ Reset the compass to 20mm (¹³⁄₁₆in) radius, setting the point on the position where the circles intersect the first line drawn around the block. Walk the compass around the circle. This will give five points, which will be equidistant between two adjoining primary centres. The top and bottom drilled holes are included.

◆ A further five points are marked each at a position equidistant from three primary points; the top and bottom drilled holes are included.

◆ Accurately drill a 3mm (⅛in) diameter hole exactly 3mm (⅛in) deep at each of these constellation points and the primary points. These holes are not only permanent marking, but will also act as depth guides when turning out the internal shape.

◆ The profiled piece may now be removed from the mandrel; undo the nuts and slide it off.

◆ To excavate the inside of this profiled block, it needs to be supported in a simple cradle (*see* Fig 27.9).

Making the cradle

◆ Purchase three 6mm (¼in) diameter bolts (with nuts and washers) 120mm (4¾in) long.

◆ Cut two pieces 110mm (4⅜in) diameter from a good hardwood (I chose elm). The first piece is 45mm (1¾in) thick and is screwed centrally on a faceplate.

◆ In the centre of this piece a 25mm (1in) diameter spigot 20mm (¾in) long is turned by turning away the surrounding area. Turn a hollow around this spigot, so that when the profiled block is pushed on to it the block will sit comfortably, its curved end partially supported within that hollow. The spigot locates the block, causing it to run on centre.

Fig 27.10 Cross section through the cage holding the turned sphere block.

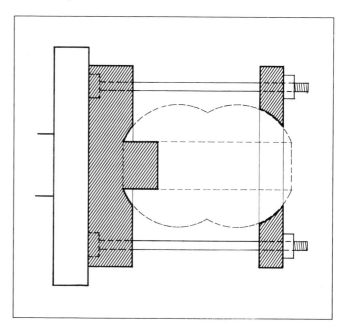

◆ The second 110mm (4⅜in) diameter piece is 20mm (¾in) thick. Place a compass set to 45mm (1¾in) radius at it centre and draw a circle. Place the compass at any point upon this circle, walking it around to produce six points. Select three equidistant points (missing out the ones between), and drill and countersink to accept screws at these points.

◆ Drill a 25mm (1in) diameter hole at the centre of this disc; this hole may now be slipped over the central spigot of the piece attached to the faceplate, making sure that the countersunk screw holes are facing outwards. The disc may now be screwed down on to the piece fixed to the faceplate.

◆ Turn into the top disc only a 50mm (2in) diameter hole through the 20mm (¾in) depth of the wood.

◆ Mark a datum point on the edge of the two discs so that they can be realigned.

◆ Remove each screw in turn and drill out to 6mm (¼in) diameter through to the faceplate, keeping the discs fully aligned through **all** the drilling.

◆ Mark a datum on the faceplate and the wood attached, and remove the piece from the faceplate.

◆ Counterbore the underside of the piece removed from the faceplate at the 6mm (¼in) diameter holes to accept the head of the long 6mm (¼in) bolt.

◆ Slide each bolt in place, then screw the piece back on to the faceplate, relocating it exactly.

◆ The internal shaping of the top hole now needs to be made. Find some plastic tube spacers – old felt-tip pen tubes, large Biro tubes – anything, as long as they are the same length. Slide one on to each of the bolts, and then slip the top piece of wood in place, tightening down the nuts. Turn the internal shape to accept the end of the profiled piece; use a card template to help achieve the exact shaping.

◆ To ensure extra grip, fix small pieces of glasspaper on the inside edge of this shape piece, using double-sided tape.

◆ The cradle is now complete, so fit the profiled piece in position (*see* Fig 27.10).

◆ It will help if each of the positions where a nut is located is numbered, so that when adjustments need to be made, this may be done sequentially.

◆ Adjust the cradle so that the profiled piece runs true and on centre.

◆ Tighten the nuts so that the top collar presses down on to the profiled piece, holding it in place. Rotate the work by hand to make sure that nothing catches before switching on the lathe. The work should now run quite closely on centre if care has been taken with the preparation, but one nut overtightened can cause the piece to run out of true. Touch a pencil lightly against the top exposed edge of the rotating work, and then switch off the lathe. The nut or nuts closest to the marked pencil line need to be loosened, and the nut or nuts furthest away need to be tightened to pull the work on centre. Continue to readjust until the work runs on centre. Occasionally the whole collar may need loosening, and the piece should be pulled across on centre and the nuts retightened.

◆ Paint the nuts white to make them more visible when the work is rotating; also trim off any excess metal screw thread protruding from the nut.

◆ The toolrest can now be brought across the face of the work and adjusted so that the specially shaped tools and the angled round-nose tool cut at centre height.

◆ Reduce the lathe speed to 350 rpm.

Turning inside the block

◆ The angled round-nose tool can be used to remove the majority of the waste wood, with a mark 25mm (1in) from its cutting edge made upon its shank. This tool must not be allowed to cut deeper than the mark, or it may cut into important internal parts.

◆ When a satisfactory amount of waste has been removed with the round-nose tool, the lathe speed is brought down to 250 rpm, and the first of the special tools is carefully inserted (*see* Fig 27.11), and very light and gentle cuts are made. Fig 27.12 shows a sectional drawing of this tool's cut.

It will be noticed that with all these special profile tools there is a rubbing point at the front which will rest upon the central unturned portion, and a depth stop closer to the handle. The combination of these factors should prevent the tool cutting beyond its prescribed depth.

Fig 27.11 *The inside of the block may be hollowed.*

◆ As the tool reaches its depth, the drilled holes should begin to show signs of wood dust dropping through.

◆ Move these tools in line with the internal curvature as much as possible.

◆ When the profile tool is close to full cutting contact along its length, the lathe speed should be reduced further, to around 200 rpm.

As these profile tools will be cutting over a wide surface area, the final cuts must be very light and delicate when they reach the full extent of their cut. Patience is required.

Any accumulated wood shavings can be

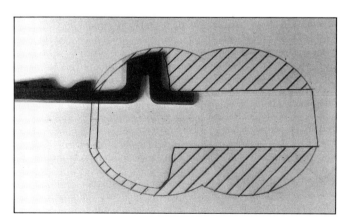

Fig 27.12 *One of the special tools shown in a sectional drawing.*

Fig 27.13 *The special tool removes a little more before the piece is reversed in the cradle.*

removed by placing a drinking straw into the hollow and blowing, remembering to **close the eyes** first.

◆ Once the first profile tool has cut its precise shaping, again use the angled round-nose tool or any other round-nose tool to remove waste in the area that the second profile tool will cut (*see* Fig 27.13).

◆ Work the tool in with light and gentle cuts as before, watching the drilled holes for signs that the correct depth has been reached.

◆ When tool 2 has finished its work, bring tool 3 into action, again using the drilled holes as guides to the correct depth of cut being reached.

◆ Tool 4 requires far more care than the previous three; when it is close to completing its cut, a very large area is in contact with the work and may cause the tool to be gripped and dragged in. It may be necessary to rotate the lathe with one hand, with the tool gripped in the other, to enable that final awkward internal corner to be safely cut.

These tools cannot always be directly placed in the position required: they may need to be slid along the curvature of the previous cut to bring them into exact position. Be cautious when the tool enters and is withdrawn from the main entrance hole. It may be necessary to rotate the lathe by hand for the final cuts made for each tool; if unsure or in doubt, rotate the lathe by hand.

◆ Having completed the excavation of one side of the shell, the piece may be removed

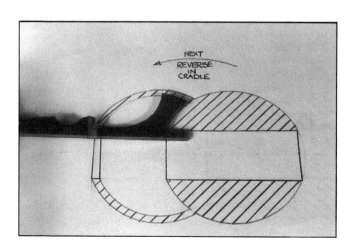

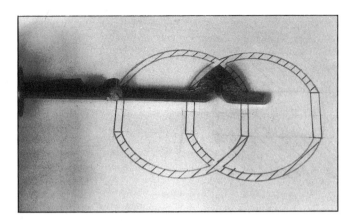

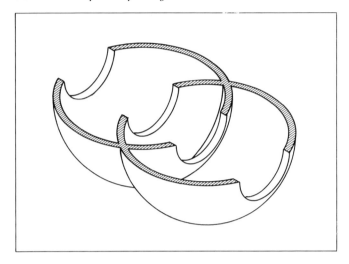

Fig 27.14 The central portion can now be turned out.

Fig 27.15 A section showing the hollow interior of the turned shell prior to piercing.

from the cradle and reversed. Lock it back firmly in position, and centre exactly as before.

◆ Excavate the newly presented side as described above.

◆ The central portion may now be cleanly cut, using tool 5 and then tool 6. The distance that these cut from the front edge of the shell is controlled by the front rubbing edge along the shank of these tools. The depth to which they cut is controlled by the frontal rubbing edges and the rubbing edge just behind the cutting area (*see* Fig 27.14).

◆ Work cautiously with these tools, as it is now the thin internal walls of the continuation of the spherical shells that are being cut.

◆ When tools 5 and 6 have been satisfactorily worked, the turning of the shell will be complete (*see* Figs 27.15 and 27.16). It may be removed from the cradle and set aside in a safe place.

Separating the spheres

The first holes to cut open are those closest

Fig 27.16 Looking through the hollow shell.

Fig 27.17 Making the first cuts at the holes.

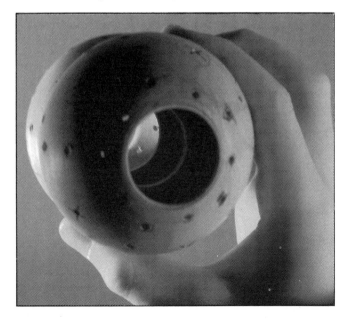

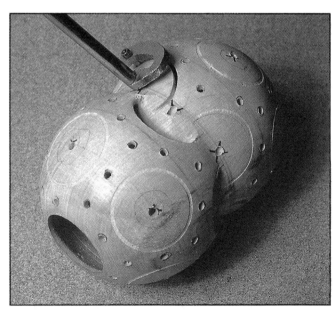

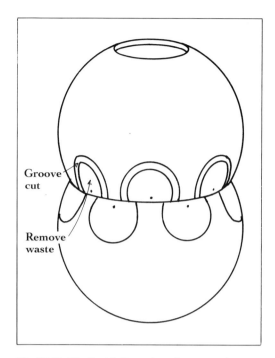

Fig 27.18 *The double lines show the area to be cut by the cutting tool.*

Fig 27.19 *Removing waste wood with a hand-held electric drill and burr.*

to the joint line of the two spheres, so at each of those points in turn:

Stage 1
◆ Push the central pivot of the special circular cutting tool into the centre drilled hole. Rotate it to cut through the shell to its largest arc (*see* Fig 27.17). Use left- and right-hand cutters to cut the largest sections possible, as shown in Fig 27.18.

Stage 2
◆ Cut half of the central circular disc away to reveal the inside: dental burrs in a small hand-held electric drill work well, but a series of small holes across the opening can easily be drilled, and will act as a guide and help for a final saw cut (*see* Fig 27.19).

Clean the area smoothly so that the curve of the one sphere runs naturally into the curved surface cut internally. Be very careful not to cut away the central pivot hole; if necessary, leave an island surrounding this hole. The central pivot hole will be needed to continue the cut under and behind the shell.

Fig 27.20 *An eye-shaped hole opened up at each side of each hole. The back of the hole is fully cut.*

Stage 3
◆ Clean out the void (eye-shaped space ⬭) between the circular cuts in both spheres (*see* Fig 27.20); again use dental burrs, drills, saws, files, or any tool with which you are happy (*see* Fig 27.21).

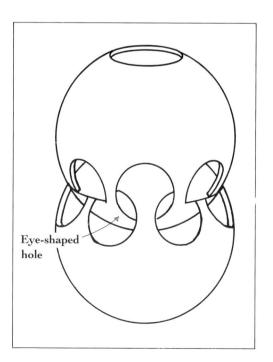

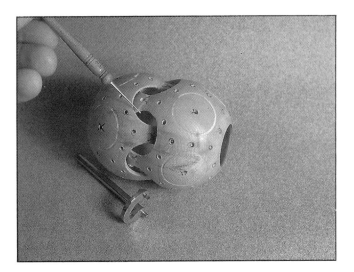

Fig 27.21 Removing the eye-shaped section and breaking through the shell.

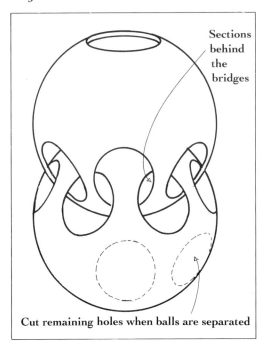

Fig 27.22 Clean away the sections behind the bridges.

Sections behind the bridges

Cut remaining holes when balls are separated

Stage 4
◆ Use the circular cutters to cut underneath the one shell to begin to release them from one another.

Stage 5
◆ At the back of each section between the circular cuts are small webs which still hold the two spheres together (*see* Fig 27.22); I cut through these parts using a dental burr held in a small hand-held electric drill. A more efficient method (which I unfortunately discovered later) is to cut the circular holes at all the other primary points; this will give a clear view and access to those areas, which may then be cut free. Use dental burrs, a fine pad saw or a junior hacksaw blade held in a handle, with the one cutting end free. Once cut, the area may be cleaned to flow into the under curved surface, using needle and riffler files (*see* Fig 27.23).

Stage 6
◆ Having cut all the primary holes using the circular cutters, as shown in Figs 27.24 and 27.25, the most worrying part begins – drilling the constellation holes. With all the time invested in the work so far, it would be unfortunate to cause damage at this stage. A 4mm (³⁄₁₆in) hole is drilled through those positions at the thinnest part on the bridge between two holes, and a 6mm (¼in) hole is drilled at those points equally spaced

between three primary holes.

All these holes now need cleaning with files and rifflers so that they are truly round. A general clean-up can be given to the whole piece (see Fig 27.26).

It may well happen that a few awkward moments may arise. Stop and think. Make adjustments to tools, and work steadily and

Fig 27.23 Undercutting behind the 'bridge'.

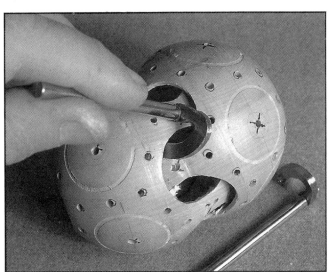

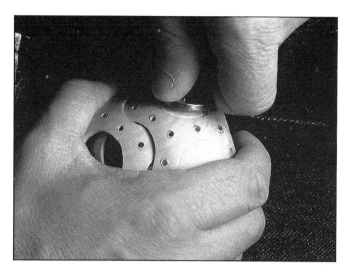

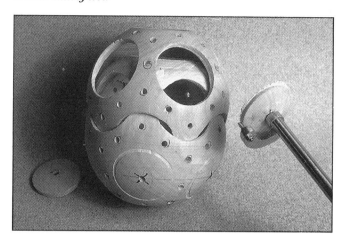

Fig 27.24 *Cutting the holes.*

Fig 27.25 *The remaining holes are opened with the circular cutting tool.*

slowly. Slight variations may occur and cause a difficulty at one stage or a problem at another: if that last web behind the bridging piece just cannot be reached, go slowly, and try to think of ways to reach the area. Open up the primary holes above, if they have not been opened already. Work and worry the part little by little, and gently ease through the area with fine saw blade or needle files. If frustration sets in it is far better to leave the problem intact for the next fresh day; problems often have magical methods of solving themselves overnight.

It is quite remarkable the effect that finishing this piece has upon the general confidence of a woodturner: having turned the outer profile accurately, having sweated and worried over those deep internal cuts inside the delicate shell, having cut the spheres apart and cleaned them up, turnery pieces which once seemed most difficult now appear less of a trouble.

Making the stand

The stand is produced in a manner similar to that described in making the stand for the Chinese ball (*see* Chapter 26). The central top support is slightly different, enabling the top sphere to be lifted, but solving that will be child's play after what you have just been through. It will be almost like a little relaxing turnery.

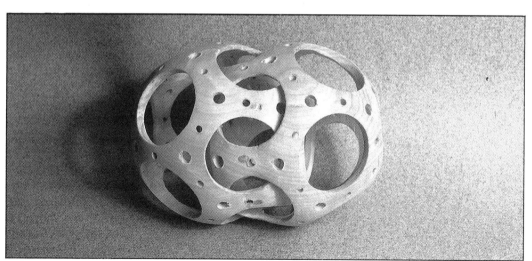

Fig 27.26 *The partially finished spheres ready to be cleaned up.*

Useful Addresses

The Society of Ornamental Turners
Hon. Secretary, Philip J Holden
17 Chichester Drive East
Saltdean
Brighton
East Sussex BN2 8LD

Metals and Materials

A J Reeves & Co. (Birmingham)
Holly Lane
Marston Green
Birmingham B37 7AW

Engineer

Hill's M & P Engineering Services
3 Stotfold Road
Hitchin
Herts SG4 0QN

Bibliography

John Jacob Holtzapffel,
Hand or Simple Turning, Vol. 4,
Dover Publications

John Jacob Holtzapffel,
Turning and Mechanical Manipulation, Vol. 2,
(out of print)

Hamelin Bergeron,
Manuel du Tourneur,
Inter-livres

Ornamental Turning Work of J C H Saueracker,
Society of Ornamental Turners

*L'Encyclopedie Diderot et D'Alembert, L'Art du
Tourneur,*
Inter-livres

Metric Conversion

Inches to Millimetres and Centimetres
MM – millimetres   CM – centimetres

Inches	MM	CM	Inches	CM	Inches	CM
⅛	3	0.3	9	22.9	30	76.2
¼	6	0.6	10	25.4	31	78.7
⅜	10	1.0	11	27.9	32	81.3
½	13	1.3	12	30.5	33	83.8
⅝	16	1.6	13	33.0	34	86.4
¾	19	1.9	14	35.6	35	88.9
⅞	22	2.2	15	38.1	36	91.4
1	25	2.5	16	40.6	37	94.0
1¼	32	3.2	17	43.2	38	96.5
1½	38	3.8	18	45.7	39	99.1
1¾	44	4.4	19	48.3	40	101.6
2	51	5.1	20	50.8	41	104.1
2½	64	6.4	21	53.3	42	106.7
3	76	7.6	22	55.9	43	109.2
3½	89	8.9	23	58.4	44	111.8
4	102	10.2	24	61.0	45	114.3
4½	114	11.4	25	63.5	46	116.8
5	127	12.7	26	66.0	47	119.4
6	152	15.2	27	68.6	48	121.9
7	178	17.8	28	71.1	49	124.5
8	203	20.3	29	73.7	50	127.0

Index

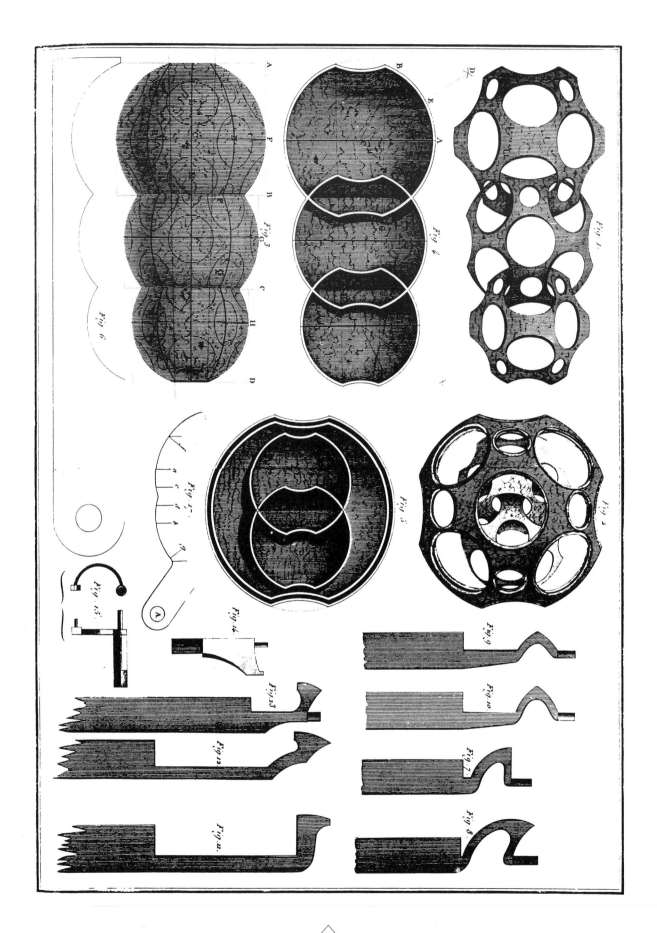

TITLES AVAILABLE FROM
GMC Publications

BOOKS

WOODWORKING

40 More Woodworking Plans & Projects	*GMC Publications*	Making Shaker Furniture	*Barry Jackson*
Bird Boxes and Feeders for the Garden	*Dave Mackenzie*	Pine Furniture Projects for the Home	*Dave Mackenzie*
Complete Woodfinishing	*Ian Hosker*	Routing for Beginners	*Anthony Bailey*
Electric Woodwork	*Jeremy Broun*	Sharpening Pocket Reference Book	*Jim Kingshott*
Furniture & Cabinetmaking Projects	*GMC Publications*	Sharpening: The Complete Guide	*Jim Kingshott*
Furniture Projects	*Rod Wales*	Space-Saving Furniture Projects	*Dave Mackenzie*
Furniture Restoration (Practical Crafts)	*Kevin Jan Bonner*	Stickmaking: A Complete Course	*Andrew Jones & Clive George*
Furniture Restoration and Repair for Beginners	*Kevin Jan Bonner*	Test Reports: *The Router* and	
Green Woodwork	*Mike Abbott*	*Furniture & Cabinetmaking*	*GMC Publications*
The Incredible Router	*Jeremy Broun*	Veneering: A Complete Course	*Ian Hosker*
Making & Modifying Woodworking Tools	*Jim Kingshott*	Woodfinishing Handbook (Practical Crafts)	*Ian Hosker*
Making Chairs and Tables	*GMC Publications*	Woodworking Plans and Projects	*GMC Publications*
Making Fine Furniture	*Tom Darby*	The Workshop	*Jim Kingshott*
Making Little Boxes from Wood	*John Bennett*		

WOODTURNING

Adventures in Woodturning	*David Springett*	Practical Tips for Woodturners	*GMC Publications*
Bert Marsh: Woodturner	*Bert Marsh*	Spindle Turning	*GMC Publications*
Bill Jones' Notes from the Turning Shop	*Bill Jones*	Turning Miniatures in Wood	*John Sainsbury*
Bill Jones' Further Notes from the Turning Shop	*Bill Jones*	Turning Wooden Toys	*Terry Lawrence*
Colouring Techniques for Woodturners	*Jan Sanders*	Understanding Woodturning	*Ann & Bob Phillips*
The Craftsman Woodturner	*Peter Child*	Useful Techniques for Woodturners	*GMC Publications*
Decorative Techniques for Woodturners	*Hilary Bowen*	Useful Woodturning Projects	*GMC Publications*
Essential Tips for Woodturners	*GMC Publications*	Woodturning: Bowls, Platters, Hollow Forms, Vases,	
Faceplate Turning	*GMC Publications*	Vessels, Bottles, Flasks, Tankards, Plates	*GMC Publications*
Fun at the Lathe	*R.C. Bell*	Woodturning: A Foundation Course	*Keith Rowley*
Illustrated Woodturning Techniques	*John Hunnex*	Woodturning: A Source Book of Shapes	*John Hunnex*
Intermediate Woodturning Projects	*GMC Publications*	Woodturning Jewellery	*Hilary Bowen*
Keith Rowley's Woodturning Projects	*Keith Rowley*	Woodturning Masterclass	*Tony Boase*
Make Money from Woodturning	*Ann & Bob Phillips*	Woodturning Techniques	*GMC Publications*
Multi-Centre Woodturning	*Ray Hopper*	*Woodturning* Tools & Equipment Test Reports	*GMC Publications*
Pleasure and Profit from Woodturning	*Reg Sherwin*	Woodturning Wizardry	*David Springett*
Practical Tips for Turners & Carvers	*GMC Publications*		

WOODCARVING

The Art of the Woodcarver	*GMC Publications*	Understanding Woodcarving	*GMC Publications*
Carving Birds & Beasts	*GMC Publications*	Understanding Woodcarving in the Round	*GMC Publications*
Carving on Turning	*Chris Pye*	Useful Techniques for Woodcarvers	*GMC Publications*
Carving Realistic Birds	*David Tippey*	Wildfowl Carving – Volume 1	*Jim Pearce*
Decorative Woodcarving	*Jeremy Williams*	Wildfowl Carving – Volume 2	*Jim Pearce*
Essential Tips for Woodcarvers	*GMC Publications*	The Woodcarvers	*GMC Publications*
Essential Woodcarving Techniques	*Dick Onians*	Woodcarving: A Complete Course	*Ron Butterfield*
Lettercarving in Wood: A Practical Course	*Chris Pye*	Woodcarving: A Foundation Course	*Zoë Gertner*
Power Tools for Woodcarving	*David Tippey*	Woodcarving for Beginners	*GMC Publications*
Practical Tips for Turners & Carvers	*GMC Publications*	*Woodcarving* Tools & Equipment Test Reports	*GMC Publications*
Relief Carving in Wood: A Practical Introduction	*Chris Pye*	Woodcarving Tools, Materials & Equipment	*Chris Pye*

UPHOLSTERY

Seat Weaving (Practical Crafts)	*Ricky Holdstock*	Upholstery Restoration	*David James*
Upholsterer's Pocket Reference Book	*David James*	Upholstery Techniques & Projects	*David James*
Upholstery: A Complete Course	*David James*		

TOYMAKING

Designing & Making Wooden Toys	*Terry Kelly*	Restoring Rocking Horses	*Clive Green & Anthony Dew*
Fun to Make Wooden Toys & Games	*Jeff & Jennie Loader*	Scrollsaw Toy Projects	*Ivor Carlyle*
Making Board, Peg & Dice Games	*Jeff & Jennie Loader*	Wooden Toy Projects	*GMC Publications*
Making Wooden Toys & Games	*Jeff & Jennie Loader*		

DOLLS' HOUSES AND MINIATURES

Architecture for Dolls' Houses	*Joyce Percival*	Making Miniature Oriental Rugs & Carpets	*Meik & Ian McNaughton*
Beginners' Guide to the Dolls' House Hobby	*Jean Nisbett*	Making Period Dolls' House Accessories	*Andrea Barham*
The Complete Dolls' House Book	*Jean Nisbett*	Making Period Dolls' House Furniture	*Derek & Sheila Rowbottom*
Dolls' House Accessories, Fixtures and Fittings	*Andrea Barham*	Making Tudor Dolls' Houses	*Derek Rowbottom*
Dolls' House Bathrooms: Lots of Little Loos	*Patricia King*	Making Unusual Miniatures	*Graham Spalding*
Dolls' House Fireplaces and Stoves	*Patricia King*	Making Victorian Dolls' House Furniture	*Patricia King*
Easy to Make Dolls' House Accessories	*Andrea Barham*	Miniature Bobbin Lace	*Roz Snowden*
Make Your Own Dolls' House Furniture	*Maurice Harper*	Miniature Embroidery for the Victorian Dolls' House	*Pamela Warner*
Making Dolls' House Furniture	*Patricia King*	Miniature Needlepoint Carpets	*Janet Granger*
Making Georgian Dolls' Houses	*Derek Rowbottom*	The Secrets of the Dolls' House Makers	*Jean Nisbett*
Making Miniature Gardens	*Freida Gray*		

CRAFTS

American Patchwork Designs in Needlepoint	*Melanie Tacon*	An Introduction to Crewel Embroidery	*Mave Glenny*
A Beginners' Guide to Rubber Stamping	*Brenda Hunt*	Making Character Bears	*Valerie Tyler*
Celtic Knotwork Designs	*Sheila Sturrock*	Making Greetings Cards for Beginners	*Pat Sutherland*
Collage from Seeds, Leaves and Flowers	*Joan Carver*	Making Hand-Sewn Boxes: Techniques and Projects	*Jackie Woolsey*
Complete Pyrography	*Stephen Poole*	Making Knitwear Fit	*Pat Ashforth & Steve Plummer*
Creating Knitwear Designs	*Pat Ashforth & Steve Plummer*	Needlepoint: A Foundation Course	*Sandra Hardy*
Creative Embroidery Techniques		Pyrography Designs	*Norma Gregory*
Using Colour Through Gold	*Daphne J. Ashby & Jackie Woolsey*	Pyrography Handbook (Practical Crafts)	*Stephen Poole*
Cross Stitch Kitchen Projects	*Janet Granger*	Tassel Making for Beginners	*Enid Taylor*
Cross Stitch on Colour	*Sheena Rogers*	Tatting Collage	*Lindsay Rogers*
Designing and Making Cards	*Glennis Gilruth*	Temari: A Traditional Japanese Embroidery Technique	*Margaret Ludlow*
Embroidery Tips & Hints	*Harold Hayes*	Theatre Models in Paper and Card	*Robert Burgess*

THE HOME

Home Ownership: Buying and Maintaining	*Nicholas Snelling*	Security for the Householder: Fitting Locks and Other Devices	*E. Phillips*

VIDEOS

Drop-in and Pinstuffed Seats	*David James*	Twists and Advanced Turning	*Dennis White*
Stuffover Upholstery	*David James*	Sharpening the Professional Way	*Jim Kingshott*
Elliptical Turning	*David Springett*	Sharpening Turning & Carving Tools	*Jim Kingshott*
Woodturning Wizardry	*David Springett*	Bowl Turning	*John Jordan*
Turning Between Centres: The Basics	*Dennis White*	Hollow Turning	*John Jordan*
Turning Bowls	*Dennis White*	Woodturning: A Foundation Course	*Keith Rowley*
Boxes, Goblets and Screw Threads	*Dennis White*	Carving a Figure: The Female Form	*Ray Gonzalez*
Novelties and Projects	*Dennis White*	The Router: A Beginner's Guide	*Alan Goodsell*
Classic Profiles	*Dennis White*	The Scroll Saw: A Beginner's Guide	*John Burke*

MAGAZINES

WOODTURNING ◆ WOODCARVING ◆ FURNITURE & CABINETMAKING

THE DOLLS' HOUSE MAGAZINE ◆ CREATIVE CRAFTS FOR THE HOME

THE ROUTER ◆ THE SCROLLSAW ◆ BUSINESSMATTERS

◆

The above represents a full list of all titles currently published or scheduled to be published.
All are available direct from the Publishers or through bookshops, newsagents and specialist retailers.
To place an order, or to obtain a complete catalogue, contact:

GMC Publications,
Castle Place, 166 High Street, Lewes, East Sussex BN7 1XU, United Kingdom
Tel: 01273 488005 Fax: 01273 478606

Orders by credit card are accepted

Singapore ball and cube in sphere

*Spiked star in cube and spiked
star in sphere*

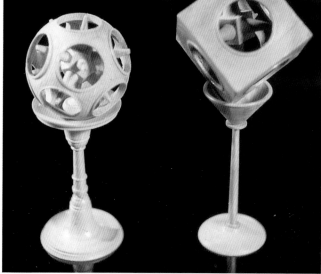

Chinese balls

Chinese balls

*Lidded box in sphere, interlocking spheres
and plug cut sphere*